ACCIDENTAL REBEL

PAT FALVEY

Beyond Endurance Publishing

First published in 2018 by Beyond Endurance Publishing, Co Kerry, Ireland

w: www.patfalvey.com

e: info@patfalvey.com

© Beyond Endurance Publishing 2018

ISBN: 978-0-9927125-5-6

Editorial and publishing services by Red Hen Publishing www.redhenpublishing.ie

Typesetting and design by Bright Idea, Killarney www.brightidea.ie

Printed and bound in Spain.

To Marie, Brian, Patrick, Lydia, Jack and Lily

CONTENTS

INTRODUCTION

FOR most of my life, I've been rebel. It isn't an attitude I consciously adopted but, as far back as I can remember, I have pushed against the limitations put on me – by family, by society and by myself.

From my earliest days, I felt like an outsider. Having moved in with my grandmother at the age of six, I entered the world of older people and – very significantly – the world of work and making money – and didn't inhabit the world of young people in the way that my siblings and others my age did. For the first twenty years of my life, my closet ally and friend was Nan, who, whether she knew it or not, sowed within me the seeds of rebellion that shaped who I have become.

Born in Cork city's northside, the poor relation to the more salubrious southside, I was always going to follow the Falvey men into the world of bricklaying where generations of them had plied their trade. The educational system expected people like me to leave school early and that presumption, coupled with my learning difficulties, ensured that I had left school and was working full time by the age of fifteen.

While I joined the family trade, I was in no way content to keep my head down and, as a brickie, I had big dreams, bigger than those of my father, or so I thought, and this didn't make for an easy time between us during my teenage years. A crisis moment in our family life in my mid-teens crystallised my first major life goal: I would become a millionaire by the time I was twenty-one. This was not only to satisfy my desire to move beyond the business and social confines of my family, but because I believed that financial security was the only way of ensuring our family was safe from attack.

As the 1980s dawned, I achieved beyond my wildest dreams as I kicked every box anyone tried to put me into down the road with a ruthlessness that quickly became my trademark. I firmly believed that I had the Midas touch and was untouchable myself. But the rebellious streak that allowed me break free of one set of expectations was also leading me down business cul-de-sacs where my lack of experience and unwillingness to listen to those who had trod the way before me left me fully exposed.

As the decade progressed, a brutal recession ravaged Irish businesses and families, and we were not immune. A perfect storm saw the Falvey Group of businesses undermined to the point where the bank came knocking on our front door, threatening to take the roof from over our heads. This was my lowest point; I looked into the abyss and wanted to stay there as the walls around me grew taller and darker by the day.

Just before I broke, I was saved - by family, a handful of friends and, in an unexpected way, by the very bank that had withdrawn its support months earlier. A chastened version of me emerged. I was now grateful to keep my head down, work hard and salvage what I could from the detritus of the preceding years. But I couldn't continue in this way, as my instinct to push against the limits of what I was told I could do kicked in.

Having learned some hard lessons, I wanted to spread my wings again and rebuild my business but I had become unsure of both myself and the world. Then fate intervened in an unexpected way when a man I barely knew, Val Deane, came into my office and persuaded me – very much against my will – to join him on a mountain hike in County Kerry.

On my second ever climb, I stood on the summit of Carrauntoohil, Ireland's highest mountain, and stated that I was going to climb Mount Everest. Mad. Ridiculous. Rebellious. It was all of that but the passion that my two first climbs had unleashed in me fired me up, not alone into a life of adventure but also into rebuilding my property business in Cork.

Seven years after stating my new climbing goal, I was standing on the highest point on the planet. During those years of apprenticeship, I pushed against a fraternity that didn't like my non-conformist approach or my 'I can and I will' attitude. Nothing and nobody was going to deflect me from my dreams. The risks were high but when I learned that one in every four climbers who attempted Everest died, I chose to focus on the fact that three would survive and that I would do everything I could to ensure that I was one of those. That resulted in a focus on training and preparation that was near obsessive.

Throughout my thirties and forties, I spent what amounted to years in the Himalaya, immersing myself in mountaineering, learning about the world from the climbers I met, and soaking up the different cultures and traditions of the locals I loved to spend time with. I found my natural classroom in gravelly, colourful Base Camps where I learned about geography, history, politics, religion and, most especially, about the power and magic of stories.

At the same time, I was keeping my business going in Cork and trying to keep my family life intact but it was a balancing act that I could never get right. When I admitted to my wife that I could never again be the man she had married, that adventuring was in my blood and I didn't want to stop, something had to give. My family had been paying a high price for my lifestyle for over ten years, always worried that the next expedition would be the one where my luck ran out and I, just like almost thirty friends and colleagues, would remain in an icy grave on the other side of the world. We decided it would be better if I moved out.

When I turned fifty, I began to listen more closely to what others were saying but the lure of the adventure playground proved too enticing for me to give up just yet. This was the decade when, instead of slowing down, I turned my attention to the South and North Poles, captivated by the expeditions of the heroes of Antarctic and Arctic exploration. Their names and stories enthralled me and inspired me to make my own contribution to Ireland's polar history.

At an age when most of my contemporaries were retiring from their trades and professions, I started the first of three attempts to reach the increasingly elusive North Pole, located in a part of the world where the effects of climate change have had a huge impact on the very nature of the Pole and how people get there.

As my fifties passed, it was inevitable that I couldn't continue living life at the breakneck speed and intensity that had been my tempo for over two decades, and when I really looked around me I saw how lucky I was to have a family that were still hanging in there, despite my long absences and habit of putting my own projects first. Before it was too late, I realised that I still had time to make amends; something for which I will always be grateful. The road was sometimes rocky but the goal was so valuable – the most important thing in the world, really - that I knew I would never give up, just as my family had never given up on me.

Now in my sixties, I remain a rebel. It seems to come naturally at this stage, although these days I try to be more discerning about what I rebel against. I remain determined to prove the truth of the motto that 'Life begins every day', and to that end I have set up the Forever Young Club for people between the ages of fifty and ninety who are determined to explore the adventure of life every day that they are alive.

I will never stop dreaming and taking action, and this is the lesson I try to share with all those who travel with me on adventure trips around the world. It thrills me to see people in every decade of life stepping outside the box and beyond their comfort zones into the full adventure of their lives. In their company, I am no longer an outsider; with them, I revel in being surrounded by fellow accidental rebels.

PROLOGUE

'STOP!' I yelled. 'I need help. I can't move!' As I knelt in agony on the ice, my shouts were lost in the blinding nothingness of Antarctica. For thousands of kilometres there were only three other human beings who could possibly hear me, but they were already too far ahead. I knew they wouldn't stop or look back until our next food break, due in an hour's time. By then, if I didn't get up off the ground and follow them, they would be almost 3km ahead of me. But every time I tried to walk, I fell. The pain shooting from my right buttock, down my leg and out through my toes was like nothing I'd ever experienced in nearly thirty years of expeditions. The pain of bone grinding on bone every time I made the slightest movement left me in no doubt that I had pulled a disc in my lower back.

It felt like a particularly cruel twist of fate. After thirty-eight days of weathering Antarctic storms and sub-zero temperatures, hauling our sleds across some of the most inhospitable terrain in the world and fighting through katabatic winds in whiteout conditions, this morning's weather had tantalised us with something we hadn't seen since we'd started our trek to the South Pole: the promise of a clear day and easier pulling as we finally reached the Antarctic plateau. I knew we could easily cover over 25km in these conditions but now, instead, fear was starting to paralyse my mind just as pain was paralysing my body. I tried to keep my focus on the one place I knew I might find relief: the medical kit in Clare's sled which held the painkillers and anti-inflammatories that I was in desperate need of.

Using my sled and skis as levers, I got to a standing position, but each time I tried to move I fell again. For almost thirty interminable minutes I kept up this pathetic dance, accompanied by intense pain and growing desperation. The team were still within sight but I knew that, unless they heard my calls for help, there was no reason for them to stop. Then, out of the blue, I saw Clare – who was leading the group – stopping to check her bearings. I shouted as loud as I could and Jon heard me. He looked back and they all waited as I made my tortured way in their direction. When I finally reached them, I fell to the ground and curled up in a ball of agony.

Jon suggested that I try to stretch but I was unable to do anything of my own volition. He then instructed Clare and Shaun to take hold of my legs while he took both my arms in his hands and all three of them pulled as hard as they could in an effort to unlock my muscles. When they finished pulling, Clare injected my bare buttock with an anti-inflammatory. There was a slight easing of the pain but the team could see I was in dire straits and decided to divide my gear between them. I got to my feet with difficulty and, anxious to keep moving, I struggled on for another twenty minutes before collapsing again. My team-mates caught my limbs and pulled me in all directions in the vain hope that it would ease the pain.

As soon as we set off again, I was in excruciating pain; after half an hour I could go no further. I was absolutely shattered, sweating and shaking even though the temperature was about $-25°$ C. We had covered less than 5km on a day when conditions were finally in our favour. I knew that my accident, caused by nothing more complicated than an awkward turn on my skis as I put my camera back in its bag after doing some filming, was a disaster for the entire team.

I lay on the ground as Clare, Jon and Shaun silently erected the tents. After crawling inside, I failed to find relief, whether sitting up or lying down. As I watched Clare get the stove going and prepare our meal, I cried. There was nothing I could do to help and the implications of the situation were becoming clear. Negative thoughts filled my mind: after all the years of training and the huge financial investment, our expedition was over; I was trapped in a tent on the freezing cold continent of Antarctica, badly injured and with no hope of getting the medical attention I needed; I could die if I didn't move or get airlifted out of there. I couldn't see beyond the bleakness. When you are strong you believe you have the ability to beat any storm, but when you are weak it is different and my body's vulnerability made me doubt that I could survive.

The options were stark: moving at our usual speed, we were about twenty days off the Pole with enough emergency supplies for five extra days. But my pain was so bad I couldn't move at all, so those five days didn't look like they would be of much use. We discussed calling in a rescue. This would mean the end of the expedition, not just for me but for all of us because of a complex insurance contract which stipulated that if I was taken off the ice the full team had to be evacuated or incur a $250,000 cost for a second plane pick-up when their expedition was done. The others didn't want to come off the ice and, despite my pain, I didn't want to be the reason they had to.

Once the stark realisation hit home that the entire expedition was in jeopardy, we knew we had to find alternative options. They were thin on the ground and not very appealing. We clutched at the so-called positives, agreeing that I was at the height of my pain and that, with medication and the others carrying my gear, we could attempt to continue towards the Pole. Even if we didn't get that far, we would get as far as we could.

I knew that there was going to be no cure for me on the ice and, no matter how long we lasted, I was going to be in pain for the rest of this expedition. The prospect of moving at all was harrowing but, once the decision was taken, I felt a sense of relief. What I needed to do was get the pain down to a point – maybe six or seven out of ten – where I would be able to continue and eventually carry my own gear again.

By the next morning, the pain had eased a bit and, with most of my gear in the others' sleds, I attached my harness to my almost-empty sled and started walking. But our plan ran into difficulty almost immediately. Pain kept me on my knees and, after a short time, the others had to take my sled, with each of them pulling it in turn along with their own one. Despite the torment I was in and our slow progress, I knew it was vital to keep moving, from both a mental and a physical point of view.

The monotony of the route was stifling, with nothing other than a map to let us know how far we had travelled during yet another day of pain and slog. As I pushed forward, locked in my bubble of misery, I started to ask why, at fifty-one years of age, with decades of pushing my body to its limits under my belt, I was here, in terrible pain, trying to reach a point in Antarctica almost 400km and another twenty days of physical and mental torture away.

I thought of the many successes and failures I'd had in my life: by my mid-twenties I had fulfilled my boyhood dream of becoming a millionaire before facing financial ruin during the economic recession of the 1980s; I'd looked into the abyss of despair and had come close to falling into its deathly grasp; I'd been to the top of Mount Everest and had completed the Seven Summits twice; I'd lost and – eventually, after years of trying – re-found my place within my family. I thought of my son Patrick, who had come to me shortly before I'd left for Antarctica. 'Dad,' he said, 'why are you doing this? Don't you realise how much your family has had to sacrifice over all the years of your expeditions? Do you know what you have missed out on?'

I began to wonder if the sacrifice all those expeditions demanded was worth the reward. I thought of the people I'd known, both friends and colleagues, who had died on expedition. I realised that they were dreamers, just like me. I didn't want to die in Antarctica but I was shaken and began to fear that I could end up like them. Then I thought of my grandmother, a small fiery woman who often said to me, 'If you think you can, you will and if you think you can't, you won't'. Now, more than ever, I needed her inspiration to keep me going. I needed to feel her spirit walking beside me.

I knew I had to focus on that dot on the map that indicated the South Pole and to keep moving towards it, no matter what. And so I continued. I wondered how I, a bricklayer from Cork's north city, had arrived at this place. My past life felt like a dream, as if it was someone else's story. I couldn't understand how I had climbed some of the world's highest mountains or had taken on the challenge of the Poles. But then I remembered: I had done it step by step, day by day, just as I was doing now as our small team edged its way towards the southernmost point on the planet.

PART ONE
GROWING UP IN NORRIELAND

MY GRANDMOTHER, THE INFAMOUS MARY B.

I went to live with my grandmother, Mary B., when I was six years of age in what was my first major adventure from home. My mother decided that I should move in with Nan as all her children had left home and Mum did not want her living on her own. I adored my grandmother and she loved me back in equal measure, so I jumped at the opportunity. That turned into seven years of what would become the most influential and formative period in my life. Nan lived on Orrery Road in Cork city's sprawling northside in a vast cityscape of over 4,000 social houses. Our district was designated disadvantaged and these homes had been built in the previous decades to alleviate the severe overcrowding in Cork's densely packed tenements. After a report on living conditions in the city had described its slums as a source of danger to the community, the city planners put their sights on the northside for many of its social housing developments.

The houses were built in military-style terrace blocks of six to twelve buildings to maximise land usage. They were small, two-storey, three-bed builds with pocket-size front gardens railed off by plain metal bars and a swinging iron gate. This was a part of the city, known derogatorily as 'Norrieland', where there were few social, cultural or educational facilities and where there was a strong sense of neglect compared to the more affluent southside. The only amenities we had – three churches, four schools, a seminary for priests and a parochial community hall – were all run by the Catholic Church.

Mary B., who couldn't read or write, was a tough, no-nonsense woman whose husband had abandoned her after the Second World War when he didn't return home from England. He left her with six children to rear and never sent any money to provide for them, something she never forgave him for. She remained very bitter and refused to go to his funeral. As a single parent, she had a hard life and struggled to make ends meet but she was a resilient woman and honed her skills as a carter going around the houses in our community collecting old clothes that people didn't want. She gathered her stock in a pram and then sold it to people at cattle marts and country markets. With a fast-growing population on the northside, there were a lot of doors to knock on and behind those doors were a lot of people who had gotten jobs at the Ford and Dunlop factories. This meant they had a few bob extra to spend and didn't need their old clothes.

Even though I was only six, Nan treated me as if I was a young adult and immediately put me to work as her helper. She was soon confident that I could do the rounds on my own and I was promoted from helper to apprentice. Cold-calling at houses was not easy. When I walked up to a door, knocked on it and asked 'Any old clothes?', I was afraid of the response I'd get and had to conquer my fear every single time. Lots of people turned me away; some insulted and tried to demean me but others were generous, delighted that I was taking away stuff they no longer wanted. 'A dumb priest never got a parish,' Nan used say. 'If you don't ask, you won't get.' I persisted and it paid off – I collected thousands of items of clothing, ranging from the nearly new to the very old. When I had a full load, I'd strap it tightly with rope to my pram and run down the steep, hilly streets to the city centre.

Nan had a small storage unit in a stone building at the Coal Quay, an area near the river where she and her family had a long history of street trading. This was the place where generations of Cork's poor came to buy cheap clothes, food and other goods. When I arrived with my load, Nan would always give me a big hug. 'You're my bar of gold and I love you to bits,' she'd say. Once I'd emptied the pram, she would segregate what I'd collected into bundles of what was wearable and unwearable. She cut the latter into rags before putting them in bags to sell as cleaning cloths to nearby factories and garages; nothing went to waste. With her sleeves rolled up, Nan stocked her merchandise high, ready for selling on the next market day. She insisted on paying me for my work and when she did well, she'd pay me a bonus. On top of that, she always gave me the pick of what we collected; I don't think I owned any new clothes until I returned to my parents' house at the age of twelve.

Even though she was illiterate, Nan had great common sense and saw opportunity everywhere. When she realised that I was an eager learner, she came up with the idea that I could sell broken timber as kindling at the same houses we collected the clothes from. My father was a builder so I got all the waste timber for nothing. When the government offered free turf to old-age pensioners, I used the pram to deliver the fuel to the elderly and was paid for that too. Although Nan allowed me to keep some pocket money, she made me save the bulk of my earnings. Having savings was very important to her; it was security for a rainy day and she'd had many rainy days while rearing her family on her own.

When I was just six years old, she marched me to our local bank to open my first bank account. The clerk gave me a bank book with my name on it and I made my first lodgement of ten shillings. To help me save, he gave me a piggy bank – a pink-glazed ceramic container in the shape of a pig – nicknamed Miss Piggy by Nan. It was completely sealed except for a slit on its back into which you put coins and paper money. All my money was swallowed into its belly and the only way I could get it out was to go to the bank, where the clerk had a key to open the locked door under its stomach.

Every time she paid me, Nan stood over me while I inserted the money into Miss Piggy. The ritual was always the same: I would put the money through the slit and she would then put the piggy bank on a shelf in a tiny, treasure-filled room under the stairs. It was here she kept all the stuff she had collected over several decades and I loved to explore this dark Aladdin's Cave. Armed with a flashlight, I'd enter this secret space of small jars and boxes that were filled to the brim with an endless variety of odds and ends. The air smelled of corroded steel from all the nails and screws that filled the many jars. I'd close the door and seal myself in this wonderful world before beginning the adventure of exploring all the exotic booty.

I often took down my piggy bank and tried to extract some of the money I had put in its belly. Then I'd take my bank book off the shelf and stare at the numbers written on the pages. The book smelled of linseed and I loved inhaling its scent as much as I loved seeing the numbers that indicated my growing savings. Nan used to play a game to see which one of us could guess exactly how much was in the piggy bank before we took it to the bank to be opened. She always won so I suspected she had a key. Her training worked and by the time I was twelve I had £750 in savings and was probably the wealthiest kid in the area.

If you think you can, you will

One day, when I was about eleven and was pushing my pram full of clothes to Nan's store on the Coal Quay, some American tourists, who were taking photos of life in Cork's poor inner city, approached me. 'You seem like such a happy kid,' one of them said, 'can I take your photo?' 'Of course,' I replied, 'I don't mind.' I'd just spotted an opportunity to make some money. Cheekily, I put my hand out and got paid for my first modelling job. A big smile and one click later, I had some extra coins in my pocket; it was the easiest money I'd ever earned. 'These kids are so happy,' the man remarked to his friend as he patted me on the head, 'aren't they better off poor compared to our American kids?' I was confused and wondered if it was me he was talking about.

When I got back to Orrery Road, Nan was standing in the small front garden. 'Are we better off poor?' I said. 'Why do you ask that?' she replied. I told her what the American man had said. I was standing on a bar of the gate, swinging backwards and forwards when Nan, standing at 4'11" and as round as she was tall, caught me by the ear, gave me a clatter across the back of the head and dragged me into the house. She only let go of me when we were in the front room. Over the two-seater settee were four pictures that hung in nearly every Irish household at the time. 'Look at them,' she ordered. 'See him there? That's the Sacred Heart.' She had great faith in him and in the Catholic Church. Dragging me up to the next picture, she said: 'That's the Pope, and he's the leader of our Church. And that man there, do you see him? He's Éamon de Valera, the president of our country. And that other man there,' she said, pointing at the fourth picture, 'that's John F. Kennedy, a man whose family came from Ireland. He was once the most powerful man in the world.' She loved JFK, just like most Irish people. 'I want you to remember this,' she said. 'You're as brainy and as powerful as any one of those and don't let anyone tell my grandson that we're better off poor.' I wasn't going to argue with her.

Throughout her life, Nan repeated to me her mantra that you can do anything you want to do and be anything you want to be as long as you believe in yourself. 'If you think you can, you will, and if you think you can't, you won't. So always think you can.' Those words were burnished in my mind and I never forgot them.

THE FALVEY CLAN

I barely knew my grandparents on my father's side. My grandmother, Julie, died two days after I, her first grandchild, was born and my grandfather died a few years later. They were dirt poor and had lived a very hard life. As was the norm in Catholic Ireland at the time, they had a large family and Tim, my father, was one of eleven children – ten brothers and one sister – who survived birth. His mother suffered three miscarriages, while two of his surviving brothers died in early childhood, one from scarlet fever and the other from pneumonia, something that caused great grief and hurt to my grandmother.

My grandfather, Paddy, who was a noted mason, was also a noted drinker and nicknamed 'Blacker Falvey' due to his ability to drink Guinness. He spent all his spare time in the pub, which ensured he didn't have enough money to care for his large family. This meant my father and his brothers were forced to go out to work at a very young age to help put food on the family table. At twelve, Dad worked barefoot on the farms around Cork city, picking turnip and beet. At thirteen, he left school and took up the family trade as a mason.

Dad was ambitious. From the moment he started working, he wanted something more than just to make a bare living. He wasn't going to settle for what was traditionally offered to people of his background and decided early on that he was going to do whatever he could to ensure he didn't live in poverty and deprivation. His big dream was to become a builder and to own his own house.

He saw that the only way to make that a reality was to work as hard as possible and become his own boss. By the time he was twenty, he had become a subcontractor to the larger local construction companies as the demand for houses in Cork city grew. He quickly became an employer, giving work to eight masons – including some of his brothers – and helping to build the social housing in our area.

Mum and Dad

My parents first met on a building site where Dad was working which was only ten minutes from where my mother, Bina O'Callaghan, lived. In her spare time, Mum would go and watch the construction workers building the houses. Dad took a fancy to this beautiful girl who turned up daily and, after two weeks, he asked her on a date. They went out with each other for three years before getting married in August 1956. During that time, my mother continued to live in Orrery Road, looking after her siblings when Nan was out selling while my father worked day and night to save enough money for a home for himself and his fiancée. When a site became available on Baker's Road, where they'd first met, he bought it and built a bungalow there in 1955.

Aged twenty and twenty-two respectively, my mother and father moved into their new home, right in the middle of the area where they'd grown up. It was where their neighbours and friends lived and where they hoped to make a good life for themselves and their family. There was never a question of building in any other part of the city; the Falveys were proud Norries and the northside was home. More importantly, Baker's Road was only ten minutes' walk from Nan's house and Mum wanted to be near her mother. I was born in June 1957 and my five siblings – brothers Richard, Paul and Barry and sisters Majella and Abina – all arrived in that order over the next sixteen years.

In stark contrast to the thousands of government houses surrounding it, our home was one of only three privately owned houses in the area, and it seemed to me from my youngest years that we were somehow special. This feeling was intensified by the fact that we had a car, an Anglia, when there were hardly any others in Gurranabraher. The house and the car were important for my father as symbols of his hard work and its rewards, and were tangible proof that his dream of a better life for his family was coming true.

SCHOOL AND SPORTS: FAILING AND EXCELLING

When I was four years old, I was sent to the nearby Catholic North Presentation convent school in Blackpool before transferring to the all-boys North Monastery primary school at the age of six. Every morning, until I was older and got a bike, Dad would call to Orrery Road to pick me up for school. I'd have already attended 7.30am daily Mass with Nan, who had notions of me becoming a priest. After school, my brothers and I walked or got the Number 2 bus home to Baker's Road where I spent a few hours with the family before heading down to Nan's for the night. Homework was meant to be done as soon as we got in the door but, from my earliest schooldays, I wasn't a diligent student. I hated study and avoided it if at all possible. Mum tried to help me but she was rarely successful. She had left school early herself and Nan was totally illiterate. The teachers took it out on students when they turned up with unfinished homework and I was reprimanded most days. I resented this and so began a cycle of years of punishment and rebellion that continued until I left school.

I came from a family for whom formal education wasn't a priority. My parents' expectation wasn't that I would become a scientist or a teacher or anything white-collared. It was that I, as the eldest son, would become a mason like my father and grandfather before me. I accepted from the time I could walk that Falvey men were destined to become masons and people like us didn't think that education served any great purpose in our lives. That ethos, coupled with the fact that I was working and earning money from such a young age, meant that formal schooling was something I put very little value on. This attitude didn't sit well with the teachers and resulted in me getting slapped regularly. They really believed that by hitting me I would become more diligent at doing my homework. I couldn't understand why they didn't see that I was a smart kid who knew how to earn money.

The punishments hurt, but I learned very quickly how to bear them and never cried when I was hit. By the time I left primary school, I didn't know how to read or spell, and I had no interest either. I looked at my grandmother who could neither read nor write but who, to me, was a great businesswoman. I thought I could do fine without bothering too much with books.

Despite her lack of experience of, or interest in, formal education, Nan got it firmly into her head that I should attend secondary school at St Finbarr's College in Farranferris, another northside city area. The college was a seminary for students who were going on for the priesthood and Nan enrolled me without mentioning it to my mother. Her dream was that I'd become a bishop one day. However, my mother intervened and said there was no way I was going to Farranferris. On the surface, it seemed as if the two women were arguing over whether or not I might eventually become a priest, something my mother didn't want. But the argument was really because Mum felt she was losing control over me. I was never disobedient to Nan but I was starting to give cheek to my mother and she decided to take action. I was told that I was coming back to live at Baker's Road and would be going to secondary school locally at the North Monastery. It was clear that this matter was not up for discussion.

It was hard to get used to the regime back at my parents' house. In Orrery Road, there had been few rules and Nan thought I could do no wrong. This was probably because, knowing how fiery she could be, I rarely went against her. My brother Richard replaced me at Nan's and all my other siblings took their turn at Orrery Road over the following years. Back at home, I became rebellious and finding my place in the family in Baker's Road was tough. In a way, I had become the invisible oldest brother. There was a bond between Paul, Richard and Barry that I was somehow outside. Even though I got to know them better in the following years, I always felt that there was a distance between us that didn't disappear until we were adults.

A tough institution

Known locally as 'the Mon', the Christian Brothers-run North Monastery was a tough institution for boys. The Brothers had always been proud of their illustrious alumni, including former government leader and renowned hurler Jack Lynch. Before I ever crossed its threshold, however, there was no expectation that I would rank among that list. I still had no interest in formal learning and couldn't see the point in studying languages, mathematics, science or geography. My attitude was that I wanted to be a mason, not a know-it-all. Most of my teachers told me I was stupid and that I'd never make anything of myself. They constantly criticised me but I had a self-belief that was stronger than their criticism. As far as I was concerned, they just couldn't see my potential. Today I would be treated as a kid with dyslexia and attention deficit hyperactivity disorder and would be given extra help, but those were different times.

The antagonism between me and the teachers fuelled my resentment which, in turn, drove my bad behaviour and complete lack of interest in classroom learning. The only thing that saved me in the eyes of the teachers was my sporting prowess. The Christian Brothers, who were renowned for their fondness of corporal punishment, would never have tolerated my attitude except for the fact that I was a rising star in the school's hurling and football teams and in athletics. Winning at sports was always highly regarded at the Mon and I made quick progress as a runner at inter-schools, county, provincial and, eventually, all-Ireland level.

Hit and run

The northside, where there was little for young people to do, was increasingly getting a name as a rough area. To provide an outlet for young people and to keep them off the streets, my Dad and a few local men set up the first-ever athletics club on this side of the city. Our training ground was Colmcille Park, a few minutes' walk from Baker's Road. It was a bare green area with no markings and no track; we just ran around the perimeter when we met for training. In competitions, we were very much the underdogs, but our club had some of the best runners in the country. From pushing that pram around the hilly streets, at twelve I was a hell of a fit kid and had a great trainer in Brian de Staic. My specialities were cross-country running and the 440 yards sprint and, in the course of a few years, I won over 100 medals with Northern Athletics. The fact that I was good at something that was getting public acknowledgement, especially as I was failing at the academic end of things, delighted both my parents and Nan.

Many northsiders, however, generally saw athletics as a sissy sport and there were always gangs mooching around, trying to intimidate club members. We were jeered and taunted by local bullies who didn't like that we were daring to be different. Some of the club members gave up athletics because of the bullying, but I loved the sport and continued with it until I was seventeen. Once, during a training session, Tom McKiernan, one of my close running companions, was attacked by a gang with a knife and slashed across the face. At the court case following this incident, I was summoned as a witness. One of the gang got a jail sentence which resulted in me becoming a target for them.

Around the same time, there had been a lightning moment in my life when I met and started going out with Marie Horgan, the girl who would become my wife. Her family lived in Churchfield, a stone's throw from Colmcille Park, and one night, shortly after the court case, I came out of Horgan's and was walking up the street when I saw four gang members emerge from the darkness. They took up positions at either end of the terrace; they wanted revenge and I was trapped. I turned right and they closed in; then I turned towards the other exit and they closed in there too. Within seconds, I was surrounded and, stupidly, I took them on. It was a losing battle that went on for a few minutes until Jimmy Dunlea, a friend of mine and a neighbour of Marie's, came to my assistance and they scattered, leaving me badly beaten. I didn't want the Horgans to know what had happened, so I stumbled home. My father brought me to hospital but, instead of being sympathetic, he nearly killed me for trying to take on four hoodlums. 'If this ever happens again, son,' he said, 'hit and run.'

After recovering from a punctured lung, I went back to training in the park. One night when we were done, I was making my way home to Baker's Road when I spotted three of the four who had attacked me in Churchfield. I knew they were waiting for me again. One of them was wielding a hurley but I wasn't going to turn back. As I got nearer, the guy lifted the hurley and hit me across the face. Although I was reeling from the blow, my father's advice rang in my ears: *hit and run*. I grabbed the stick from his hand and stood back: now I had the weapon. With all my strength, I hit him across the head and he fell to the ground, unconscious. 'Come on, ye bastards!' I roared at the others. They started shouting that I had killed their friend. At that point I looked, horrified, at the lifeless body. I heard someone shout to call the guards and get an ambulance.

Immobilised with fear and thinking I had killed someone, I stood there, frozen, with the weapon still in my hand. When the ambulance finally arrived, the paramedic revived the guy and he was taken to hospital. I was very relieved that he wasn't dead. I felt no pride in resorting to such violence, but after that incident I was never bothered or bullied by street gangs again and gained a reputation locally as being someone not to mess with.

A kid with attitude

My sporting success and the fact that I was working outside of school time made me think that I knew a lot more than I did. I had a stroppy attitude towards the teachers and gave them lip regularly. Once, when I was thirteen years old and saw a teacher assault a student, I told him he should take on someone his own size. I was a bit taller than him, so he hit me and I hit him back. I assumed I'd be expelled but, for some reason, the teacher never reported the incident. Then, in my second year at the Mon, I landed myself in a situation that had a far-reaching effect on my attitude. A new teacher, Brother Wright, was teaching us biology and science. One day we went to Nohoval village near Kinsale on a field trip to collect tadpoles from the river. The plan was that we'd watch them grow in a tank in the classroom and learn about the lifecycle of frogs.

A few days later, I was sitting in my usual place at the back of the room, falling asleep. Brother Wright threw a duster at me, hitting my head and engulfing me in a cloud of chalk dust. 'Falvey,' he shouted, 'this is a classroom, not a bedroom!' The class erupted into laughter. I was determined to get him back for embarrassing me and, shortly afterwards, when I was on my own in the room, I got a bottle of sulphuric acid and poured it into the tank, killing all the tadpoles. I regretted it immediately but it was too late; the damage was done and the tadpoles were dead. I knew the Brother would go off his head, but I didn't care. However, he called in Brother Keating, the principal, who said that if whoever killed the tadpoles didn't own up, the entire class would be punished. I stepped forward, knowing that the consequences were going to be dire.

As I followed the principal down the hall, I looked with dread at his black cassock and the leather strap swinging from his waist. When we reached his office, I waited for my punishment to begin. Standing in front of the principal, I was totally amazed when Brother Keating asked me if I liked school. The word 'No' was out of my mouth before I had time to think. 'Is there anything at all that you like about it?' he said. 'No,' I repeated. 'Do you like murdering God's innocent creatures?' he asked. 'No, I don't,' I answered, feeling very guilty about what I'd done. 'I'm sorry, Brother.' 'Well, there is no use in being sorry,' he said, 'I'm going to have to expel you and I'm going to have to tell your mother and father the reason why.' The minute he said that the big tough guy that I thought I was broke down crying. I knew my parents would wallop me for what I'd done and, worse still, they would be very disappointed in me.

What Brother Keating said next took me totally by surprise. 'I won't tell your parents and I'll give you one more chance but only if you tell yourself every single day that you like school.' *This guy must be a dope*, I thought. I immediately agreed to do what he asked. That, I assumed, was the end of it – but it wasn't. For the next six months, the principal made it his business to seek me out and ask how I was getting on. 'Great, Brother,' was my stock response. To my amazement, as the weeks passed, I started to like school better and, later in life, when I was facing the most extreme situations, I realised the value of what the Brother had taught me about affirmation. It was the first lesson I ever had in neuro-linguistic programming, something that was little known at the time. I stopped being so rebellious towards my teachers and learned that the messages we send to our brain have a huge bearing on how we experience life.

Over forty years later, I was in my house in Kerry when a tall man arrived at the front door. 'I'm looking for Pat Falvey,' he said. 'That's me,' I replied. "Do you remember me?' he asked. It was Brother Keating. I was taken aback that he had come looking for me. He told me he had been following my career over the years and wanted to thank me personally for speaking positively in public about my experience with him, particularly as, at that time, the Christian Brothers in general were getting a lot of bad press.

FATHER AND SON BATTLEFIELD

Although he wasn't the eldest son, my father was known as the 'don' of the family. He was the one the others admired and aspired to be like. Seeing this gave me ambition from my earliest years to follow in his footsteps. He had been growing his business consistently since getting married, and it was going from strength to strength. By my early teens, he employed forty men and was a popular boss with most of them. My initiation into the family trade had started when I was twelve and worked for my father during my holidays and on days off school. I'd stopped working with Nan by this stage and was firmly in the world of hard-working, hard-drinking men. My uncles Paddy and Donie, who were the fastest masons in Europe – or so they told me anyway – were legendary. They were renowned far and wide for the speed and accuracy with which they laid bricks and built stone walls. As their apprentice, I was impressed by their ability and determined to be as good as them as quickly as possible; competitiveness was always a trait among the Falvey men. They were hard taskmasters and, within two years, I was laying up to 1,000 bricks a day and getting £3 per 100 on contract work. It was a lot of money at the time, especially for a teenager.

Friday was pay day for the men and payment was always made in Paddy Taylor's pub on the Commons Road in Blackpool. The men were paid in cash and a good portion of what they earned was spent in the pub before they went home to their families. Dad often stayed on for a few pints; he liked to socialise and was known to be generous, buying rounds for all and sundry. But this practice was something that didn't go down too well with my mother. She had a family to rear and had witnessed Granda Falvey's drinking and definitely did not want Dad following in his footsteps.

Good times turn bad

When I was thirteen, Dad got a contract for the development of twenty-eight Georgian-style houses at Mount Oval in Rochestown, an upmarket suburb on Cork's southside. This was his first really big housing development and we were all very proud of him. It was a prestigious project that would take a couple of years to complete. Within a short space of time, however, the developers started to mess him around, regularly holding back 10 per cent of the monthly payments. Within two years, the amount owed to Dad was significant. He still believed that all was okay and that he'd get paid in the end. However, just as the project was about to be completed, the developers left Ireland and disappeared. Dad was now in serious trouble financially as his cashflow dried up. Within months, the business he had worked so hard to build was facing financial ruin as liquidation and bankruptcy loomed.

Like hungry wolves, creditors came with their demands. Even the men who had worked for my father for years were panicked and came looking for the money owed to them. For the first time in his life, Dad couldn't pay his bills on time. While not of his making, he became caught in a Catch-22 situation and no longer knew what to do. His mind became frazzled from the stress and he sought release from the mounting pressure in the time-honoured Irish manner by 'turning to the drink', as if booze was some great oracle to be consulted at times of extreme duress. Dad was not a hard drinker but now he was drinking more and coming home later. Whenever my mother confronted him, they'd argue. There were times he was so drunk I had to go to the pub to bring him home. I was very young and didn't understand why he was behaving as he was.

Then, one night, there was an incident that became a turning point in my life. Dad was out on one of his binges and I was in the house with Mum when there was a loud knock on the door. 'Holy mother of God, who's making that racket?' my mother said as she hurried into the hall. Standing there was a man I recognised. It was a labourer who worked for my father, drunk out of his mind.

'Is Tim at home?' he slurred. 'He hasn't come back yet,' Mum replied, knowing it would be much later that night before he made an appearance. 'I want my fucking money now,' the man demanded angrily. Not believing her that Dad wasn't there, he tried to force his way into the house. He pushed in the door, knocking my mother to the floor.

Even though I was only fourteen, I reacted with rage, catching the man by the throat and pushing him outside. Holding him up against the wall, I told him to get away from our house. 'If you ever again do that to my mother, I'll fucking kill you!' I roared. He got loose and ran off. When I went back inside, Mum was crying. I stood there, not knowing what to do to ease her pain. All I could think was where the hell my father was and why he wasn't there to deal with this situation.

After that night, I became increasingly hostile towards my father because I'd had to act as my mother's protector while he was – as I saw it – having a good time in the pub. He was a man that I had always admired and adored and he was my greatest mentor, but I just couldn't understand what was going on with him. I didn't realise the pain and the anguish he was suffering because of what was happening to his business. All I knew was that I had more money in the bank than he had, and I thought he was a fool who was leading our family into financial ruin.

Return from the abyss

In the summer of 1972, I was fifteen years of age, angry and determined to ensure our family was going to be okay, so I left school to work full time. I bought a car which Marie's father got for me and I secured insurance and a licence by faking my age. My mother believed Dad was just going through a bad patch and that we needed to try and keep everything running until he came back to his old self, so I went around to jobs he was contracted for and checked that they were running okay as he had lost interest. Despite everything, I still adored my father and wanted to prove myself to him. I would show him and everybody else that the Falveys weren't to be walked on.

I was a naïve and cocky teenager who started telling everyone I was going to be a millionaire even though I didn't really know what that meant or how I would do it. All I knew was that a million should be enough to ensure our family wouldn't ever be poor again. Most people laughed while others thought I was getting above my station. They told me not to be ridiculous. 'You're a mason,' they'd say, but their taunting didn't put me off my goal of becoming rich beyond anything I could imagine.

One night, a few months after I left school, we got a call from Paddy Taylor's pub. Dad was drunk and they wanted me to come down and bring him home. Mum was hopping mad. 'Put on your coat,' she told me, 'we are going to get your father.' Just like Nan, my mother was a fiery matriarch with a temper and I could see she was on a mission. She had never before come to the pub with me to collect Dad, and I cringed at the thought of how he would react to her showing up and what the reception would be from his so-called friends.

She didn't care what anyone thought as she marched into the dimly lit, smoke-filled bar, and Dad was too drunk to be embarrassed by our sudden appearance. Mum didn't hold back in her verbal attack and he put up very little resistance as we each took an arm and half-dragged, half-pulled him home. My mother loved my father to bits but she'd had enough. She threatened to throw him out if he didn't stop drinking and cop on. She told him that he was no longer the man she had married. Where, she challenged him, was the fighter, the dreamer, the man that loved his family? Miraculously, this was the catalyst for Dad to stop drinking. It was like he awakened from a stupor and saw the chaos that was happening all around him.

From the moment he sobered up, Dad was back in the fight. He refocused and faced the challenge of sorting out his business head on. If the developers thought they were smart, my father was now determined to outwit them. He called a meeting with Mum, his brothers, me and a few loyal employees. 'We are going to do something very unorthodox,' he said, 'and I need your help to make it work.' It was the first time in a long while that I'd seen a smile on his face. 'What do you want us to do?' Finbar, my uncle, asked. 'We are going to take occupation of two houses in Mount Oval,' Dad explained. One house was just finished with the sale agreed but not yet closed, and he still had the keys for final snagging. The other house was owned by one of the developers who had left the country and Dad had found out, despite it not being advertised, that this house was now up for sale.

The developer had sent a snag list to be completed and Dad's interpretation of the contract was that we still had a right to be on the site. The next Monday at 4pm, he and my uncle went to the developer's house. The housekeeper, who knew them well, let them in to start completing the snag list. She finished work at 5pm and Dad assured her they'd lock up when they were finished. As soon as she left, he changed the locks and took occupation of the house with Finbar while another uncle, Donie, and I moved into the unfurnished house.

When the housekeeper arrived the next morning, she was locked out. Dad asked her to inform the owner that we had taken occupation. Naturally, he went berserk. He called the guards to have us evicted and arrested. When they arrived, my father explained that he had no option but to take possession of the houses. 'You can't do that,' the guards said. 'We can and we have,' Dad replied. 'They can sue us if they want but we are not moving until they pay us what they owe.' The guards left and informed the developers they'd have to go to court to sort things out. Our solicitors were instructed to fight any move to have us evicted and to be ready for a court challenge. The developers were now in a position where they couldn't finalise the sale of either of the two houses. They told my father they were going to sue him. 'Sue away,' he replied. 'I don't care, I'm as good as broke anyway.'

We settled in for the long haul. Dad couldn't afford to keep his employees in occupation as there were still other jobs that had to be done and money to be earned, so it fell to family members – mainly Dad, the uncles and me – and a handful of the men to do that. Those who got to stay in the house owned by the developer had a comfortable set-up, but the unfinished house was not furnished and we had to sleep on mattresses we brought in. We also had two old armchairs and we used camping gas to boil water.

Mum brought us food and Marie's father used to drive her to the house I was in so that we could see each other. I'd light a fire and some candles and we would listen to music on a record player I had brought in to help pass the time. It had to be operated by battery as the developers had cut the electricity supply to the occupied houses. A very strong bond developed between Marie and me during the eight weeks we were in occupation and I was always very grateful for the support she gave me and my family during this tense time.

We used to rotate who was in which house, so everyone got a few nights in the furnished house. I was there with Finbar one evening when we saw a minibus stopping at the end of the drive. Four tough-looking guys got out and walked in our direction. We realised pretty quickly that the developers had decided to take the law into their own hands and had hired a few hard men to sort us out. They looked intimidating as they approached the house carrying baseball bats. 'What are we going to do?' I said. 'Fuck them,' was my uncle's reply. He had a shotgun with him, ready for trouble, which was now coming up the steps. 'Get the hell out of here!' a voice on the far side of the door shouted. Finbar opened the door and pointed the shotgun; the men stood back in shock. Then he raised the shotgun and fired over their heads. As they ran down the drive he shouted after them. 'I'm telling ye now, don't come back.' We didn't see them again.

About five weeks later, my father was called to a meeting to agree a settlement. He was owed about £50,000 and the developers said they'd hand over a lump sum of £28,000 and pay the rest through arbitration. Dad guessed that once he got the £28,000 he'd never get another penny, but he wanted to pay his employees and his suppliers so he took the lump sum and accepted the write-down. He did get another – small – payment later, but was never paid the full amount.

The Mount Oval drama was finally over and I was left with the belief hardwired into my brain that I would never, ever let anyone walk over me. It was another two years before my father finally got his business back on an even keel and, from then on, he refocused on general contracting. As soon as things got back to normal, he did something that filled me with pride: he changed the name on his lorry from Tim Falvey to Tim Falvey & Sons Ltd. When I looked at those words, I felt they were an acknowledgement of my contribution to supporting the family during the Mount Oval dilemma. Coming through this most difficult time in our lives had shown me that our bond and commitment to each other was stronger than anything that might pull us apart.

Dreaming big

By the time I was sixteen years of age, I was given a position as a director in Tim Falvey & Sons, along with a 20 per cent stake in the company. I now had full responsibility for twenty men, all of them older than me though most assumed I was older than my age. Sometimes I had up to three jobs going at the one time and I was being paid general foreman rates as well as bonuses for profits I contributed to. But it was still a pittance in the face of my dream of becoming a millionaire. At seventeen, I was impatient and getting frustrated with my progress. Every day before I left home, I'd look in the mirror and say *I'm going to be a millionaire*, but things weren't happening nearly fast enough for me.

One day I went to my father and said I was doubting my ability to achieve my dream. 'I'm not sure if this is working out. Maybe I should go to college instead,' I said. 'What do you think?' 'You're doing well, son,' he replied. 'You are the biggest dreamer I have ever known and I believe in you.' He then gave me a piece of advice that I have used throughout my life. 'Dream and dream big, but always remember that following your dream is where the success lies. Let achieving it be the bonus.' I was surprised at Dad's absolute belief in me and it gave me a confidence boost.

I realised that to succeed I needed to expand my knowledge, so, three weeks later, I signed up to a two-year night course in construction and management studies at Cork Regional College. Unlike school, I loved my time in college, where I was learning skills in engineering, architecture, surveying, building technology and management that I knew I could use.

FINDING LOVE

While I was still looking for my big business break, I had already found love. There was so much to admire about Marie. She was beautiful, refined and very quiet; the opposite to me in so many ways. When we finished work each day, Marie and I would sit in her parents' kitchen and talk endlessly. I didn't realise it then, but she was like my own private psychotherapist; I'd talk, she'd listen and I'd re-evaluate. What really amazed me about her was that she allowed me to be myself; she didn't try to change me when I told her of my dreams of vast wealth and of the mansion I was going to build for us. Having grown up with a frugal background, these weren't things she necessarily wanted but she was still willing to listen and to support me. At the same time, she would quickly take me down a peg or two when I started giving out about my parents, telling me to show them the respect they deserved. From our earliest time together, this wonderful person was a stabilising influence in my life and her parents became like another mother and father to me.

Shortly before I turned eighteen, Marie and I got engaged. That June, my mother organised a big party at home for my birthday. It wasn't the norm in those days to put your age on the cake and there were no banners hanging up in the house with 'eighteen' written on them. The extended Falvey and Horgan families were in attendance and it was turning into a great night when one of the relatives commented that I was very young to be engaged. Marie looked as if her world had stopped.

When we'd started going out together we hadn't ever talked about our ages. I had finished school, was working full time and had loads of money, and many people made the assumption that I was older than my actual age. Marie thought that I was about two years older than her but the truth was that I was, in fact, two years younger than she was. She was horrified to discover that she was going out with a younger man and wanted to break off the engagement there and then. I was terrified at the thought of losing her. I told her that no matter what age I was – something I could do nothing about anyhow – I loved her and wanted to marry her. It was several weeks before I could convince her to stay engaged, but she finally relented and we set a date for our wedding.

Marriage

We knew we wanted to live locally on the northside and be near our families. We also wanted to build our own house, but the available sites were too expensive. Instead, we bought off the plans for a private development of three-bedroom terraced houses in Barnavara, Mayfield. About two months before we got married, we got the keys to the house, which wasn't too far from where our parents lived. It was basic and simple, with bare floors and painted magnolia throughout. The only thing in the kitchen was a sink but we paid the builder an extra £180 to install a Murray kitchen, just like the one my parents had in Baker's Road. We bought a carpet and a couch for the sitting room while the dining room was furnished with a table and four chairs that we got as a present. We splashed out on a bed, two lockers and lamps for our bedroom; there was no question of buying more than we could afford but we still had the feeling that this was our palace.

We saved all we could and kept our socialising to a minimum. Neither of us had much interest in going to pubs, and I had taken a dislike to them since my father's lost years. We did, however, really enjoy the cinema and went as often as we could. There was something else we did that was unusual for people of our age and background: every Friday night, we went to the Fastnet Restaurant at Jury's Hotel near the city centre. It was mainly older businesspeople who frequented the place and we were definitely in a minority, both as teenagers and as northsiders, when we dined there. Most of the other Norries present were staff and we had a great rapport with them. These nights out were, I felt, our reward at the end of hard, working weeks. As well as that, being in such salubrious surroundings made me feel successful. We could see all the movers and shakers from Cork's business world mingling at the bar, and after dinner we'd join them. It proved to be very useful networking and I made a lot of business contacts on these occasions.

Marie and I got married in the church in Gurranabraher on 11 June 1977, nine days after my twentieth birthday. It was the first wedding I was ever at and we were both incredibly happy on the day; it was as if we were in a sunlit place where everything was possible and nothing could go wrong. We flew out to Salou in Spain the next day. Neither of us had ever been abroad before and we were in awe at how exotic everything was, from eating dinner at night instead of the middle of the day to hanging out by a pool. By the end of the two weeks, we had spent all our money and were ready to return home to start married life.

OPPORTUNITY KNOCKS

I was impatient for the right business opportunity and soon found it. I had learned a lot about the profit to be made from new developments during the building of our house in Mayfield. I saw that for every three houses the builder completed, the value of one was clear profit in his pocket. Cork's population was growing at a rate of 2,000 per annum and this, allied with an increase in affluence thanks to strong employment in local factories, resulted in the construction of 700 houses annually in the city up until the end of the 1970s. It wasn't just better pay that was driving this boom; young people were changing and now wanted more for themselves. In the past, people who grew up in social houses had moved into similar housing when they got married, but now they wanted to buy their own private homes. I saw an opening and set about planning my move away from general construction into housing development.

I started researching the market and, shortly afterwards, I met up with a few men who became pivotal in my business life. Kerryman Joe Carey and Frank Sheahan from north Cork had both just returned from Canada and set up a real estate company in Cork city. Although they were closer in age to my father than to me, their outlook and dreams reflected my own and we clicked. They were selling sites for a developer called Owen O'Callaghan and when Joe introduced me to him, there was a chemistry between Owen and me also. All three men seemed to like my passion for progress and success. I quickly did a deal with Owen to purchase four sites for £12,000 and negotiated a licence for twenty-eight more which I could pay for as the houses were sold. This was an unusual way to do business and Owen later told me that the only reason he did the licensing agreement was because I reminded him of what he was like when he'd started out. This renowned businessman not only gave me the break I so desperately wanted but also became a lifelong mentor to me.

I saw this as my chance to start making my dream of becoming a millionaire come true. I took £1,000 out of the savings I'd put aside for our new home and paid it down as security to purchase the sites. I knew I was on to a winner; now all I had to do was convince my father to back me. He had credit with all the suppliers and he had collateral – the family home on Baker's Road. We sat down and I explained that I needed £12,000 to kick-start the project and buy four sites. We talked about the plan in detail and I was delighted that he took me seriously. I showed him my business plan for the project, predicting profits of £150,000 within twelve months. He said to count him in. From where I was standing, everything looked perfect. Our next step was to contact the bank manager, Mr O'Driscoll. When we met with him, I explained everything before leaving the business plan with him.

Within the week, O'Driscoll contacted my father and said the bank wouldn't support us. I was working on a site when Dad told me the news. 'He can't refuse it,' I shouted. 'Who does he think he is? This is gilt-edged. Is the man mad?' I wouldn't accept the refusal and decided to go to the bank, there and then, in my wellington boots, to challenge this man. I asked to see him and was told to wait. For two and a half hours, I sat there, determined not to move until I had spoken to him. Finally, his secretary appeared and informed me that Mr O'Driscoll was ready to see me. I was confident I could persuade him to change his mind.

'How can I help you?' he enquired condescendingly when I sat down. 'We applied for a loan and you refused us,' I said. 'Yes, I did,' he replied smugly. 'I don't think it's commercial and, anyway, I think you are too young.' 'But the business plan and the cashflows are there,' I said. He cut me off. 'I've made my decision.' 'Can't you change it?' I pleaded. 'This is my golden chance.' 'No,' he answered before promptly asking me to leave. As he held the door open, I stood face to face with him. 'You know what?' I said. 'You're a fucking idiot.' He looked at me and said, 'I want you off this property'. I was escorted off the premises with no idea what to do next.

The manager was determined to have revenge for my lack of respect, and he extracted this by reducing my father's overdraft by half. Dad was really thrown by this. 'What the hell did you say to him?' he asked. 'They are just after halving my overdraft. I don't know how I am going to survive.' I hadn't told him about my visit to the bank but now I had to and suddenly I didn't feel so smart. 'Son, will I ever teach you?' he asked in despair. 'You have to learn to be a bit more diplomatic.' All I could do was apologise. Practical as ever, Dad's response was, 'We'll just have to get over it'.

New man, new attitude

We went back to our accountant and told him the news. He was shocked that my father's overdraft had been reduced as a punishment for my behaviour, especially as Dad had been with the same bank for over twenty years. The accountant then admitted that he'd always considered the bank manager to be a bit of a prick. Although it didn't solve our problems, it was good to hear this. 'There's a new guy at another bank who has a reputation for being progressive,' he said. 'Let's talk to him.'

We set up a meeting and I was given strict orders to keep my mouth shut. The bank manager asked the questions and my father and our accountant gave the answers. The manager liked what he saw on paper but said that he needed security for the £12,000 loan and the overdraft in the form of the deeds to the house at Baker's Road. Dad agreed and the deal was sealed. Within two hours we were out the door and I was on the phone to Joe Carey to tell him the news: we were in business. I couldn't wait to start and quickly set up Falvey Housing Development Ltd.

The development – Ravenscourt – was located in Donnybrook in Upper Douglas, which was just outside the city at the time. The contracts were signed and I purchased the first four sites and secured the option on the other twenty-eight. Our sale agreement with the client was that we would get a £1,000 deposit. On signing the contract we would get £4,000; on completion of the ground floor we got £4,500 and by the time we got to roof level we were paid 80 per cent of the total sale price. This meant that by the time we had 40 per cent of the total work done, there was just 20 per cent outstanding in payments. This put my cashflow in the black fairly quickly.

Carey Sheahan sold the first four houses within a day. They told me clients were lining up for the rest. I instructed them to keep selling, and within twelve weeks all thirty-two houses were sold. I didn't waste a minute before starting work, and within three months I had been paid £32,000 in deposits and £128,000 in contracts signed. I employed seven of Dad's brothers to do the masonry and they had all the houses to ground floor level within a few months. By the end of three months, I had surpassed all my budgets and had over £250,000 in the bank. Within six months, I replicated the licensing agreement with other developers for sixty-four sites in Ballincollig and another thirty-two in Maryborough Hill. All these sites also sold out within weeks.

By the end of the year, I had over 100 houses under construction and had £750,000 in credit in the bank. The rate at which it all happened was incredible, and to my liking. I was on my way, moving with the kind of speed that had helped me win medals in athletics. Although my father was a shareholder, I saw these developments primarily as my projects. Dad would come out to look over things and he'd let me know when he wasn't too happy with what I was doing, but I wasn't taking any of it on board; this was my time to make my mark. Aged twenty-one, my dream of becoming a millionaire was well on the way to becoming reality.

DREAMS COME TRUE

Our life quickly fell into a regular routine. I was gone every morning by 7.15am; I'd pick up the first round of men at half past and start work at 8am. I finished about 7pm and would get home by 8pm. I also worked every Saturday until 1pm. Marie was still working as a secretary but she finished earlier than me and would have dinner ready for me each night. We socialised with our parents and Marie's sisters, visiting each other's homes and going for a drive on Sundays. Starting a family as soon as possible was something we both very much wanted, and our first son was born in March 1979. I was pouring the foundations at Ravenscourt when I got a call to say that Marie had gone into hospital. I wanted to go to her but I couldn't leave the site because there were only three men there and five loads of concrete were being delivered. I worked as fast as I could, taking only a few seconds to hose down my boots before driving like a lunatic to the hospital. The baby hadn't arrived by the time I got there and as I paced the corridor outside the labour ward, I saw there were knobs of concrete still on my boots.

It was a very special moment when Marie and I sat on the bed, looking adoringly at our son. I loved the idea of being a father; it became another driver for me to work even harder to make sure my family had everything they needed. Within a few months of Brian's arrival, Marie gave up work to be a full-time mother and housewife. We were a perfect team; I was working day and night earning money for the family while Marie took full control of the house and looking after our son.

We continued going to the Fastnet on Friday nights. It was our date night and gave us the opportunity to catch up on each other's lives and discuss future plans. I was full of talk about building the home I'd dreamed about since I was a young teenager. From Marie's perspective, we had everything we needed – a lovely home, a new baby, our families close by, plenty of money coming in; we loved each other and didn't need to prove anything to anyone else. She'd tell me we were fine where we were and that we had plenty of time, but I had no intention of slowing down.

Beechwood

While we were happy in our home in Mayfield, I only ever saw it as a temporary arrangement. Although I couldn't articulate it in so many words at the time, I wanted to ensure my family would never be vulnerable to attack and saw financial security as the strongest line of defence. The big house would be the physical declaration that mine was a family that was protected and cared for. I had said I would build a mansion for my family and things were now in place for me to start making that dream a reality. While I was working on the Ravenscourt development, we started looking around our local area for a site. We still wanted to stay on the northside of the city and eventually bought some land in Kerry Pike, a picturesque village just 4km from where our parents lived.

From the time we had occupied Mount Oval, I knew that the house I would build would be based on those houses, only bigger and grander. I had kept the development brochure and would regularly look at it, imagining how I could improve on the design. I had learned draughtsmanship at technical college and drew up plans for the home we would call Beechwood years before I even knew I would ever be able to afford to build it. The final design, signed off by an engineer, was for a 3,500sq ft house with a 650sq ft annex.

The ground floor consisted of a large kitchen-cum-dining room, utility room, lounge and sitting room. There was also an en suite bedroom downstairs beside a sauna room, something which – by Irish standards at the time – was an unusual inclusion. Upstairs were four spacious bedrooms including an en suite off the main bedroom and one separate bathroom which boasted a bidet; the height of sophistication, or so I thought. The en suite was opulent, with a double bath, a shower, toilet and bidet. In fact, the house had two bidets, which were a source of great hilarity when Nan came to visit; she could never figure out what to do with them and thought they were for washing her feet. The two-storey annex was ready for conversion into a living area for my grandmother or my parents when they were older but its immediate use was as a double garage downstairs and office space upstairs. A glass door led to a patio where we had a hammock and a barbecue for outdoor living.

Once the plans were submitted, we spent all our spare time going around shops, studying everything to see which tiles and carpets we would buy. This time round, everything was going to be in place before we moved in and everything was going to be brand new. No corners would be cut; I was building this house for life. It took nine months to complete and by the summer of 1980, on my twenty-third birthday, Beechwood was ready for us to move in. Seven years after the sit-in at Mount Oval when, as a sixteen-year-old, I'd looked at those Georgian-style houses and decided that one day I'd build a similar one, that dream had come true.

The smell of success

Everything in the house, from the furnishing to the wood and woollen carpets, smelled of success to me. I had a sense of having finally arrived at a place where I had long imagined myself being. I felt we were a dream couple with our young son in our dream house where everything gleamed and looked good. 'You always said you'd do it and you did it, fair dues to you,' Nan said. My parents and parents-in-law were delighted for us. It was a historic moment for both families and we had a big moving-in party where the champagne flowed. With Beechwood, I was making a statement to myself about who I was and where I was going. The house had to be matched by the car and, like my father before me, I opted for the Mercedes brand. How you dressed, the car you drove and the house you lived in all made statements about how successful you were, and I wanted to make sure my statement was loud and clear.

My parents called regularly, as did Nan, who was a much-loved visitor to Beechwood. We had a very nice lifestyle and every year we went abroad for two weeks in August – the traditional builders' holidays. Marie's parents used to come with us and we travelled to different countries in Europe, touring extensively

46

around whatever region we were in. I loved spending time with the family even though I found it hard to switch off from work.

Two or three times a year, Marie and I hosted big parties for business colleagues and friends. We would have up to 100 guests with caterers in to prepare and serve the food and drinks. These were lavish affairs; I was always a great networker and saw these parties as an important part of that strategy. We had some great nights, but the get-togethers that I still enjoyed most were the parties in my parents' house in Baker's Road, where friends and long-term employees gathered for an informal session and a great singsong that could go on into the early hours.

Nan had a saying, 'New house, new baby', and Marie and I were thrilled when Patrick, our second son, was born in 1983. I had a very traditional approach to fatherhood and saw my main duty as that of provider, while Marie was the homemaker and the parent who raised the boys. I saw myself as very much following in my own father's footsteps: we had always known that, when he was working long hours, he was doing it for the family. A few years after we moved into Beechwood, my parents moved from the family home in Baker's Road to just 1km down the road from us, where Dad built their dream home.

THE SKY BECOMES THE LIMIT

My father and I formed Falvey Group and from 1980 my business life took off on an incredible upward trajectory. By the age of twenty-three, I had achieved far beyond my boyhood dream – I had the big house, the big cars and more money than I had ever dreamed of. I had an amazing wife who loved and supported me and two young sons, but still I wasn't happy: I wanted more. My goals changed and my new driving force was to create the biggest construction and property management company in Ireland by the time I was forty. Then I would retire from the business world and live off the wealth I had created.

My new dream was big, but I had huge energy and this attracted some amazing people to key positions in the organisation who drove and implemented those ideas. Within the group we soon created subsidiary companies, all bearing the Falvey name: Tim Falvey & Sons (general construction); Falvey Housing Development Ltd (private housing estates); Falvey Homes (private one-off houses); and Falvey Industrial for building factories.

I was looking for partnership funding for projects I wanted to get off the ground and had given the banks permission to seek out investors. At the end of 1983, I was invited by one of the investment banks that I was dealing with to a meeting in Dublin. A client of theirs from London wanted to expand into

Ireland through acquisition. The invitation intrigued me, so I agreed to attend, flattered to think that Falvey Group was considered to be in this league. Up until then, most of our meetings had taken place in branch offices in Cork and I really felt that we were now hitting the big time.

The meeting took place in a state-of-the-art boardroom with a table set for dinner as if we were dining in a five-star restaurant. There were two waiters serving the seven people present, which included three from the London-based property investment company, three from the investment bank and me. We were served Châteauneuf-du-Pape, the wine that Marie and I always drank when we went to the Fastnet Restaurant. This, I thought, was the way to do business. When we raised our glasses, I silently said cheers to my wife for always having believed in me. As I looked around the table, I thought of all the people who had tried to put me down and who'd told me I was an idiot and a clown who would never get anywhere. I thought of the teachers who'd told my parents that I would never make anything of myself and wondered what they would think if they could see me now.

The conversation soon turned to the reason we were there. The English developers wanted to expand into Ireland and thought Falvey Group would be a good match for their portfolio. Even though I wasn't interested in selling per se, I wanted to find out more about the process and the value they would put on our company. The bank had given them our accounts from the previous three years and, based on that information, the developers said they were willing to open negotiations at £2,500,000. I responded that I needed to discuss the offer with my father as he was my business partner. When I got back to Cork, Dad asked me what I thought and I said if we held on for another few years, Falvey Group could be worth £10,000,000. My father agreed and I rang the investment bank and told them we wouldn't be selling.

The Midas touch

By the end of 1984, I had invested heavily in about seven businesses outside the Falvey Group, including pirate radio stations, cyanide inking, screen printing and publications. Both my father and our financial director advised against getting involved in businesses we knew nothing about and about which I didn't have the wherewithal to make an informed evaluation, but that didn't stop me from going ahead in the hope that I would hit the jackpot. I trusted myself and didn't ask anybody's advice. We had a multi-million pound turnover and I believed I had the Midas touch without ever actually knowing who Midas was. At the height of our expansion, we were building over 200 houses annually and were employing about 250 people, between direct and indirect labour. Everything was happening very fast and we had more money than I could ever have imagined; I felt that nothing could go wrong.

We were now based in a large headquarters in Blarney Street on Cork's northside. Dad and I shared employees across projects but I also had my own core team who worked for me all the time. My uncles went between Dad and me and all three of my brothers were now working with him in Tim Falvey & Sons. I still didn't have what could be called a normal fraternal relationship with them; I was seen as the boss and wore that hat happily, even with family. What kept us close, however, was that we finished every conversation with the words 'I love you'. Mum had always emphasised the importance of family unity to us and, from our youngest days, she had drummed into us that, no matter what, family came first and we had to be there for each other. 'I love you' – said automatically and without much thought – cemented a subconscious connection that helped smooth over the many arguments we had.

THE GALLOPING MAJOR

I was the type of person people either loved or hated: I was confident, ruthless and very good with ideas. I soon earned the nicknames 'Galloping Major' and 'JR', the latter after a famous character in the American television show *Dallas*. I had zero mercy for those who stood in my way and I didn't tolerate anyone or anything that interfered with my ambition. It was strictly business for me; we had a job to do and I wanted it done well and on time. My public profile as a businessman in Cork and the Munster region started to grow. Magazines and papers did regular features on me and the Falvey Group, and I was never short of a word or a story for the press. I was very comfortable when it came to self-promotion; talking to the papers and on radio was a doddle for me and I was soon looking for more impactful ways of bringing the Falvey brand to a wider audience.

I was always intrigued by the ads that played before the feature film began at the cinema. I'd see American salesmen speaking directly to the audience, introducing themselves personally and talking about how their product would enhance your life. These guys became my role models. I realised that people would buy more readily if they could identify with the salesperson, so I set about ensuring that everyone knew who I was and what I was selling. I started doing ads in the cinema, on radio and on television; basically, I was everywhere. I wrote the words and jingles myself and did the voiceovers too. My approach worked

51

and the Falvey brand quickly became a household name. My own dreams had come true and now I was well on the way to selling the dream of owning their own homes to all who heard me.

Self-doubt

I loved success; it fired me up and energised me. However, as the group expanded and our contracts became more complex, I found it difficult to read some of the documents. I didn't want to read them fully either; I wasn't interested in the finer details so I hired the best legal and financial people money could buy to deal with that end of the business. I knew how to make money but I didn't want to get caught up in the nitty-gritty of officialdom. As far as I was concerned, I had ideas, they made money and that was it. The balance sheets looked good and that was enough for me.

I was learning, though, that the business world was a strange place. Everyone, as nice as they were, was a shark in a small pool. But that didn't bother me unduly; my confidence was high and buoyed by the cash that was flowing into our company.

In spite of my success, however, I did have moments of self-doubt. I felt there was an inadequacy in me and it used to piss me off to feel that way. I was now mixing with the upper crust of Cork's business world and I noticed how strong my accent was. I couldn't read or write properly and, as I expanded beyond the familiar Falvey stronghold into the wider business world, I often felt uncomfortable. People were friendly to me but I felt that they saw me as a rough cog, a bit of a likeable rogue, and I had doubts about whether they really respected me or my ability.

A TSUNAMI GATHERS

In 1984, although mortgage interest rates rose to 18 per cent and business interest rates went as high as 38 per cent, I continued buying up land and sites and our borrowings continued to rise. We had loads of cashflow which I used to bankroll my investments. The economic winds of change were blowing all over the country but, at twenty-seven, I thought we could weather any storm. Like many others, I didn't see the economic tsunami that was about to engulf Ireland.

The seeds of this disaster were sown by the Fianna Fáil government in the 1977 budget which abolished car tax and approved borrowings to fund spending. Throughout the first half of the 1980s, successive governments continued to borrow massively and the tax rate spiralled as high as 60 per cent. Added to this was an overvalued currency which wasn't devalued and regulated until 1986. Economic problems outside Ireland also impacted on a fragile economy, with a net result of massive unemployment and huge emigration throughout the 1980s. In Cork, within a matter of months, both the Ford and Dunlop factories closed with the loss of almost 1,700 jobs. It was devastating, not just for the city but for the entire southern region. For buyers and sellers in the area's housing business, it was a cruel blow.

My father's construction business was hit as interest rates rose and property prices remained the same. As a group, we bankrolled each other for a period of time but then my borrowings started to take his company down. Dad was eventually able to stabilise his business because he had no big borrowings and general construction was carried out on a more controlled basis than development work. He also had the experience of having come through a few recessions in previous decades and had learned to roll with the punches.

It began to become more and more obvious that I didn't have the experience to manage such a big company. But even though I was starting to get over-stressed, I rarely listened to my father, preferring to shout him down, often just for the sake of winning the argument. Blinded by my own arrogance and flying in the face of everything that was happening, I persisted in expansion mode. I bought more land and propped up my investments using company cashflow in the belief that the bank would continue to give me money. I also kept on all my employees, which was another drain on company finances.

I was a genius when it came to working a margin, but even I couldn't work a margin on a 38 per cent interest rate when it should have been 12 per cent. No matter how good you are, if the economy goes against you, it is a battle. Yet, there were still some businesspeople making money and holding on to it. These were the ones who hadn't been too greedy and who hadn't overtraded. Unfortunately I wasn't one of that group.

Trouble looms

I realised my problems were serious when I had 300 sites – which should have equalled eighteen months of stock – that I couldn't sell. I still believed that I could trade my way back to financial stability, but then I got a call from my bank requesting that I come in for a business review. They told me I needed to reduce my overheads and get my overdraft down. Then they appointed accounting firm Touche Ross to go through the finances of the entire Falvey Group. The accountants said that if I took a number of steps, they believed I could trade my way out of trouble and the company could be brought back to viability. The bank promised to support the Touche Ross recommendations for a survival plan if we gave personal guarantees. In effect, they demanded the deeds of Beechwood as security.

I couldn't believe that we were going to have to sign over the deeds to our home, but I knew we had to do it and convinced Marie to sign the guarantee. I told her it was just a blip and that, with time and a bit of luck, everything would soon be back on track. She had some savings and insisted that I take this money to help with the group's cashflow problems. We had to collect all outstanding debts, so I had a meeting with my office team and we came up with a plan of action. Everyone pulled out all the stops and over a two-week period we collected £300,000. I lodged every penny we collected in that frenzied time. As soon as I did, the bank cut my overdraft of £400,000 to £100,000, which put the company into an immediate cashflow spin. A banker, I realised, is a person who gives you an umbrella when the weather is fine and takes it back when it begins to rain, and the lucky break I'd been hoping for didn't materialise.

Things started to get really tough; I had more property and sites than I could ever have dreamed of owning and now they were like a noose around my neck. Nobody could buy or rent and I was cornered. I couldn't make repayments and the bank wasted no time in writing threatening letters to Marie; they knew well where to direct their arrows when calling in our personal guarantees. They also called in my father's guarantees and put my parents under pressure. I'd had a dream of creating a life where my family would always be protected from any kind of danger and now, through my own actions and lack of experience, I felt I had made all of us vulnerable.

We had two young children and, as far as Marie was concerned, our home was at risk. I explained that we were not in immediate danger as there was a process that would take time, but I couldn't calm her fears. All she knew was that the bank was after us, we had no cash to give them and they were threatening to take our home. Her belief was that the bailiffs were coming and we'd soon be out on the street. We had endless arguments about what to do to get out of a situation where everything we had worked for and held dear was in danger.

Marie was the one who, after all the fighting and crying, tried to be realistic. She said that if we lost our home we could rent or apply for a government social house. For me, that signified a failure I couldn't cope with. Beechwood was always more than just bricks and mortar for me: it was a goal I'd reached at the end of a journey that had started one night when I was fourteen and my parents' home and my mother's personal safety had been breached. It was my fortress and I couldn't let it go, although I had no idea how I was going to hold onto it.

Nightmare territory

Throughout the weeks and months of 1985 and 1986, I was in and out of the bank constantly, trying to find a solution to a problem that was growing by the day. The bankers were loading interest on top of my borrowings and the sum owed was mounting. The interest rate in Ireland was now at 39 per cent as opposed to 6 per cent in other European countries, and there was no way my business could survive that. I was in a head-wrecking space and the relentless stress impacted on my ability to operate efficiently. Then the bank called me in again and told me they were stopping all funding to Falvey Group. Very simply, they said, there was no money left to keep the wagons rolling and I would have to wind down the sites and let employees go.

At that meeting I broke down and cried, feeling I'd let everyone down. If I had stuck to my core business I might have survived but, against good advice, I had taken my eye off the ball and was now bringing the entire group down. I felt like a complete failure and my inner critic had a field day: *I should have stopped earlier. I shouldn't have taken Marie's savings to help me bankroll the company. I should have told the bank to fuck off.* I thought I should have seen the early warning signs of the recession, but nobody saw them, or took any notice if they did.

I could see nothing but the wall around me getting higher by the day. In December 1985, Christmas loomed like a nightmare. I was trying to hold everything together and hadn't told my workers about the dire straits we were in. The only people who knew the full extent of the company's financial crisis were Marie, the bank and one or two close staff members. As far as the majority of my employees were concerned, we were still working, still getting in the money. They didn't know that I had little or nothing left to pay them with.

From as far back as I could remember, my father's policy had always been to pay the men first and yourself last. As a boss, I had always abided by this practice, but this year I found there was hardly enough money to pay them, much less myself. As the festive season drew closer, they were expecting not only their pay but their usual bonus as well. I couldn't give it to them, but my pride prevented me from explaining why and they thought I was just being a stingy bastard. They didn't know I was struggling to pay creditors and subcontractors and that any money we were making was being swallowed up in repayments to the bank.

That Christmas holiday was bleak. When we went to my parents' house on Christmas Day, all I could say was 'I am a failure'. My parents' response was, 'You know we're here for you, we are your family'. For me, their words were meaningless. I was in a black hole and could no longer see my way out of it. I felt helpless in every single way. Less than a week earlier, on 19 December, Nan – my beloved grandmother and lifelong mentor – had died at the age of eighty-one. She was in the local hospice when she passed away, but I was under so much pressure, trying to gather some cash for my family and workers, that I hadn't fully engaged with the fact that her life was ebbing away. I was fire fighting, and the loss of the woman who had been such an influential force in my life didn't seem to register. I felt I had failed her; she had taught me so much and had been so proud of my success. I had kept my financial problems from her during her final year but, even though she had died, I didn't want to think about her while I was in a place of shame and hopelessness.

Hiding in the boardroom

Throughout 1986, we were still building estates and had one-off builds going on as well, but any money we made was being swallowed up by the bank. I was from a business family where paying creditors, paying the men at the end of the week and honouring your commitments was very important. As far as I was concerned, I was now losing that family honour. I couldn't pay my debts; I couldn't pay my mortgage, my insurance or even afford to put petrol in the car. I spent most of my time frantically looking at margins, re-pricing and creating new spreadsheets to see how we could increase those margins. I was a busy fool, endlessly redoing figures.

In the office, I locked myself into the boardroom where I could hide away from all the people I felt I had failed. These were the people who had never doubted me and who had supported me through all my grand dreams and schemes. Now, due to my arrogance and lack of experience, it was all about to come crashing down around us. I stayed out as late as I could and only went home in time to go to bed. I couldn't stop staring at the figures, hoping that I could magically make them add up. I didn't want to believe that all that I had worked so hard for was slipping irretrievably away.

DARKNESS DESCENDS

My dominant feeling was one of being trapped. The world was still moving around me but my mind was caught in a place of crucifying turmoil. Memories from my teens, when my own father had lost his way in a haze of depression, came rushing back and it seemed as if I was reliving that period of his life. I now understood the pain and anguish that he had gone through when his business was falling apart and worried about what my two young sons would think of me now that I was facing what felt like certain failure. Unbelievably, I still thought I was outwardly holding it together, but I wasn't. Family and close staff members could see that there was something wrong with me. However, no one – not even Marie – knew the extent of how down I was feeling. I didn't talk to anyone about my feelings; in 1980s Ireland, the last thing you could admit was that you were depressed because of the stigma that would be heaped on you and your family.

Thoughts of suicide came to me a few times but I always tried to snap myself out of that mindset. My conscious mind told me that I shouldn't be thinking like that so I tried to push all dark thoughts away. I was supposed to be this strong character, the Galloping Major. *How could I not deal with this?* I couldn't understand how someone of my outgoing, positive disposition could even think of ending their own life. I'd thought that people with depression were nuts and here I was now, sinking under the weight of my own black dog. I retreated into myself and when I started getting palpitations and panic attacks, I thought I was having a heart attack. I was hospitalised twice with the same complaint which was diagnosed as hypertension. Then I was prescribed anti-depressants. The pressure was immense; each day I was trying to put on a coping face that said everything was okay. I felt if I showed weakness to the outside world that the house of cards I was trying to prop up would come down even more quickly.

The blackest night

We always paid salaries and bills at the end of the month and when it came to pay day in September 1986, there was nowhere near enough in the bank account to meet our obligations. That night, after work, I left the offices in Blarney Street, got into my car and headed out of the city. Sometimes, when I wanted to clear my head, I found it therapeutic just to drive. I travelled out the Dublin road in a trance. About 20km outside the city, I turned the car and headed back towards Cork. I'd felt low before but never anything like I was feeling now.

As I drove down by Silversprings, I was shaking. *What am I going to do? I'll never get back from this; it's fucking over.* It was about 8pm when I reached the city. There was very little traffic around as I drove up through Tivoli. I came around by Barry's timber yard on Water Street and drove towards the open wharf on Horgan's Quay. I was clipping it fairly fast and, coming around the corner, I remember thinking *this is it, I am going to drive into the river.* I put the boot down and within seconds I was doing about 60mph. I was surrounded by nothingness as I drove straight for the wharf. Suddenly, the image of my two sons' faces appeared before me. I jammed on the brakes and their screeching filled the air. The car swung to a halt and I stumbled out, shaken. I was within inches of the end of the quay. I could see the high tide as I looked across the river to the Ford factory. There was nobody around as I got into the car and drove back to the office. I drank a bottle of whiskey and cried.

Honest talking

When I got home, Marie and I argued because I was late and drunk. I couldn't hide my despair from her and broke down, telling her what had happened earlier. 'I need your help,' I said, 'I don't know what's happening to me.' My wife, as ever, was my rock. 'Don't worry,' she said, 'we'll survive.' Her love and understanding were my salvation and gave me the space I hadn't been able to give myself.

A few days later, I went to my parents and told them how bad I was feeling. They were shocked that I'd attempted to take my own life but their response was one of love and support. 'We'll work this out together,' Mum said, 'you're not a quitter.' She then gave me a copy of a poem whose words became etched in my mind:

> *When things go wrong, as they sometimes will,*
> *When the road you're trudging seems all uphill,*
> *When the funds are low and the debts are high,*
> *And you want to smile, but you have to sigh,*
> *When care is pressing you down a bit –*
> *Rest if you must, but don't you quit.*

I confided in some close friends whose understanding helped me see that my situation wasn't the end of the world. The sense of relief that I got by opening up about my problems was huge. It helped me realise that I was not alone and that I needed to get my head straight and take positive action. So I did something I'd been putting off for too long: I rang the bank and asked for a meeting.

FACING REALITY

Everyone who needed to be present was there: the bank representatives, our lawyers and accountants, my father and me. I laid myself bare and explained that, because of what was happening to my business, I was suffering from depression and needed their help. I think they were taken aback that the mouthy, cockily confident young man they knew me to be was gone and in front of them sat someone who felt he had lost control of everything. They assured me that we could work together but they were unsparing in telling me what I had been hiding from for a long time: the dream was over and I was as good as broke. They said if I agreed to the sale by auction of the 300 sites I owed they would not liquidate the company. Additionally, they would roll the interest until the sites were sold. They demanded that I close or sell off all companies and shares that I had an interest in outside of our core business as these were a drain on resources. I had to commit to concentrating on completing the houses that I was currently building and which did not need extra borrowing.

There were no other options put on the table. If I didn't agree to what was being proposed, the bank would sell off the group's land and sites and I would have no power to stop them. Liquidation was my greatest fear as this would have affected every single one of our companies and would have meant the end of Tim Falvey & Sons, my father's business. On the other hand, if I agreed to what was being proposed, we could avoid liquidation and Dad's business would be safe. I had feared this moment for a long time, but I couldn't see any other way out. When I finally said 'I accept the proposal', I broke down and sobbed uncontrollably, devastated. I had lost most of what I had built up over the past decade and, from now on, I would be – essentially – working for the bank.

But the banks weren't the only people I owed money to; there were also our employees and creditors. My father had taught me to always look after the people I was dealing with on a daily basis and without whom I'd never have been able to build a business in the first place, so, after the meeting with the bank, I went to everyone I owed money to and explained that while I couldn't pay them in cash, I wanted to give them something in lieu. I traded off everything that was disposable – dumpers, diggers, scaffolding, mixers; any moveable asset I had, I gave to them.

My new reality was grim. Paying back what I owed was my only goal. I no longer had any confidence or self-belief that I could become successful in business again. Previously, I could see opportunity everywhere, but now I saw only obstacles and dangers. While I was no longer in the grip of dark depression, my mindset was one of negativity and fear. I was burnt out and constantly exhausted, but I had to keep going.

One autumn day, Valerie, one of the office staff, was chatting to me about her father, Val Deane. He had been a client of ours when he'd bought one of our houses. I found it hard to concentrate on what she was saying, but pretended to listen as Valerie talked about her father's interest in hillwalking. She said it might be nice if I joined him on one of his treks. 'Fine,' I said in an offhand way, 'tell him to call in whenever he's passing.' I promptly forgot the entire conversation and went back to my spreadsheets. A few days later Val showed up. As he chatted pleasantly I wondered how he could not know that my whole world was falling apart and that his daughter's job was in danger. He was going on about mountains and fresh air and nature and I thought he'd never leave. When he invited me to go hillwalking with him in Kerry, I agreed just to get rid of him. At home I complained to Marie. 'It might do you some good,' she said. I didn't think so; I was a workaholic, not a walkaholic. Sunday arrived and I reluctantly and resentfully made my way to the Cork Opera House for 9am.

I never knew if Val's attempt to get me out on the hills was accidental or not; Valerie never said anything to me about it afterwards and I didn't ask. What I do know, however, is that journey to Kerry changed my life in ways I could never have imagined.

PART TWO
FROM MANGERTON TO EVEREST

LIGHTNING STRIKES

I parked my car and joined the group outside the Opera House. Val had a big welcome for me and introduced the others, who were mainly members of Cork Mountaineering Club. They were all older than me by several years. If I'd had doubts before about what I was doing here, they were intensified now. Going for a long hike with a group of middle-aged people was the last thing I wanted to do. *How the hell did I land myself in this situation?*, I wondered. The car shares were arranged and Val and I got in with three others. We all chipped in a few quid for the petrol. I was silently relieved that I'd parked my Mercedes a short distance away; there was hardly anything in the tank and I didn't have the cash to fill it up. If I'd been asked to drive there was no way I'd have been able to buy enough fuel for the journey, even with my fellow travellers' contributions. We started moving and as we drove out of the city, the good humour of those in the car began to grate on my nerves.

Approaching the County Bounds, I looked sulkily at the 'Welcome to County Kerry' sign. Val and the others were talking about what a beautiful day it was. My thoughts at that moment couldn't have been more at odds with his. *What am I doing inside this small car, going somewhere I don't want to be, listening to these strangers talking about what a beautiful day it is?* As we got nearer to our destination, the talk became even more animated. Val pointed out the window at a double peak in the near distance. 'Pat, look over there,' he said. 'They are the Paps of Danú, the Mother of the Gods of Ireland.' He went on to tell the story of how the name came about. I silently reprimanded myself for taking the day off to listen to what seemed to me to be a load of irrelevant bullshit and to hike up a mountain I had no interest in.

I was relieved to get out of the car when we arrived at the base of the mountain and just wanted to get the hike over as quickly as possible. I took a half-hearted look at Mangerton, standing at 839m, and immediately dismissed it. *Anyone can climb that*, I thought. We set off and the group spread out in single file as we made our way upwards. At least now I had more physical space and my mind went straight back to all the problems I needed to sort. But within minutes I was winded.

I was stunned: here I was, surrounded by people who seemed to be much older than me but who were stepping out with ease and good humour, chatting and laughing while I was struggling for breath. There was no way I was going to make it to the top. I didn't want to do this bloody hike and now I was afraid that I would fail and be a laughing stock. Another failure was the last thing I needed. I was well outside my comfort zone but my natural instinct to compete kicked in. I started to focus on what I was doing; I studied the ground to see where to put my feet and tried to find a pace that I could walk at. *Take a step. Breathe. Take another step. Breathe.*

Then something strange happened: the sound of the others' chatting receded and, more remarkably, so did the all-consuming thoughts about my financial nightmare. The effort of walking uphill was demanding my full attention. Very quickly, my mind became tranquil as the physical exertion of walking up Mangerton focused my busy brain and forced me to be present to what I was doing.

When the group stopped for lunch, I could have cried with relief. I sat down and, for the first time since we'd set off, I looked around me. It was a beautiful, clear day and I could see the Lakes of Killarney stretching away in the distance to the west of us. A scent caught my attention; it was yellow gorse. I'd never smelt it before and loved its sticky, sweet smell. I was wrecked but I was starting to enjoy myself. We were soon back on the move and my head went down again. I was focused on every step but I was starting to get a kick out of the challenge. When we got to the top, I was elated. For the first time in what felt like a long, long time I was successful at something and it felt good.

The others were pointing out the peaks visible from the top of Mangerton. I spotted one rising higher than all the rest. 'What's that one called?' I asked. 'Carrauntoohil,' Val answered, 'Ireland's highest mountain. We're climbing there next week.' These people, who, only hours earlier, I'd thought of as old fogies, had transformed before my eyes into heroes.

As we descended, I was completely buzzed. There was an energy running through me that I hadn't felt in a long time. I was hooked and wanted more than anything to climb again next week, to get out of my frazzled mind and into that tranquil, focused place that climbing Mangerton had brought me to. Before we got back to the cars, I asked Val if I could join them the following Sunday. He agreed and I was delighted. At the same time, I couldn't fully comprehend what had happened on this mountain to bring about such a sea-change in my mindset. Crossing the County Bounds on the journey home, I saw the sign that now said 'Welcome to County Cork'. The minute I read those words my heart sank and I started thinking about the banks, my business failure, my personal troubles. I was going to have to go to work in the morning and start dealing with all that crap again. The hours I'd spent in Kerry had been like being in Shangri-La and I didn't want to leave.

Life changes

A part of the magic stayed with me and I felt different that week; something inside me had changed though I couldn't pinpoint exactly what it was. Marie could see how enthusiastic I was when I told her about Mangerton and the plan to climb Carrauntoohil. She was relieved that I was feeling better. I started gathering as much information as I could on Ireland's highest mountain, something I would have considered a complete waste of time only a week earlier. I bought an Ordnance Survey map and *Walks and Climbs in Kerry* by Seán Ó Súilleabháin. I found everything about the challenge of climbing Carrauntoohil compelling; I read rescue reports and reports of those who had died on the mountain. I lost three nights' sleep but it wasn't because the bank was holding a gun to my head; instead, it was because I was excited and fearful about the climb ahead. I had a real sense that this was a dangerous mountain; that week, it was my 'Everest'.

Sunday finally arrived and five of us headed to Kerry. Along with me, there was Bill McGregor, Bernie Moran, Ella Dineen and Val. This time, when we came to the County Bounds and I saw the 'Welcome to County Kerry' sign, I was excited. I finally got it; I now understood what my companions had been so excited about the previous week. *It was a beautiful day, the colours of the mountains were beautiful, the Paps of Danú were sitting there in all their glory. We were about to have an adventure and I was ready for the climb.*

We parked in Cronin's Yard and set off on the long walk into the Glen, the most popular trail for walkers and hikers. This climb was much tougher than the previous week; it was steeper, with more scrambling and dangerous sections. I had to focus on every step I was taking and then the same magic happened again – I stopped thinking about anything other than where I was putting my feet. Everything receded from my conscious mind as I moved higher and higher up Carrauntoohil.

Val stayed with me throughout the climb and, after four hours, the cross at the top came into view. Despite my exhaustion, I was reinvigorated when I saw that iconic structure, originally installed in 1950 by thirty local families from nearby Beaufort to mark Holy Year in the Catholic Church. Less than five minutes later, Val and I put our hands on the cross that marks Ireland's highest ground; we were at the summit. He congratulated me and I had tears in my eyes as I clenched my fist and punched the air. 'Yes! I've done it,' I shouted. As I was taking in the stunning views at 1,038m, I turned to my companion and, without even thinking, said, 'I'm going to climb Mount Everest'. Val laughed and I knew what he was thinking. I was in a state of euphoria; I knew nothing about mountaineering and yet, here I was, stating that I was going to climb the world's highest mountain. I felt excited but at the same time a calmness came over me; my grandmother's spirit was with me and her voice was saying, 'If you think you can, you will'.

On the journey back to Cork, my mind was buzzing with my new goal: *I was going to climb Mount Everest.* At fifteen, I had said I was going to become a millionaire without knowing how I would achieve that. Now, at twenty-nine and with no climbing experience, I had a new goal. It wasn't just the challenge of such a big goal that attracted me; I had experienced something magnetic on those two Kerry mountains that I had only known previously when I was competing with Northern Athletics: a still mind. Whether by nature or nurture, I had a mind that was like a perpetually moving gyroscope, rotating in any direction it chose. Ever since I was a young fella, flying up and down the hilly streets of

Cork's northside, collecting and selling, I was always moving, doing, planning, achieving. Now I was planning again and my mind was already spinning, but there was a difference: in order to achieve my new goal, my mind would be forced into stillness each time I climbed. That stillness was my new drug.

Mountain magic

After that first trip up Carrauntoohil, I started climbing every single weekend. When I went to Kerry, my heart would lift at the sight of the 'Welcome to County Kerry' sign. It became symbolic; it seemed to say *you're here to climb, you're here to find peace of mind, you're here to succeed, you're here to get ready to climb Mount Everest.* Over the next few months, I climbed Carrauntoohil many times on my own. I loved to bivvy at the summit under the cross. Sitting under a starlit sky, I felt free there to think clearly. Climbing energised me and I started to become competitive again. Every week I would come up with new challenges to beat my own record on the mountain. I would climb it faster, or by harder and more dangerous routes. My competition was with myself and I was winning when I climbed. This feeling helped me to regain my mojo; my negative mindset gradually disappeared and was replaced by a more positive outlook. I stopped taking the anti-depressants that my doctor had prescribed. Now, instead of taking a pill, I went climbing.

I realised that fear, whether real or imagined, was not something to hide or run away from but something which had to be faced, and succeeding on the hills gave me the confidence I needed to help me make a number of crucial decisions I'd been avoiding. The clarity I got when climbing allowed me to reappraise my situation honestly and realistically. I had reached rock bottom but I didn't want to stay there. What was left of my boyhood dream was a family who loved me, my trade as a mason, and a handful of friends and employees who'd stuck by me for reasons I didn't understand but that I was very grateful for. These were the blocks with which I would build the foundation for my new life. I accepted that my pinstripe suit was gone and that I was starting from scratch again. But I knew it wouldn't always be this way; I knew that I would find a way to plan big business goals again and I was excited as I faced the journey ahead.

THE FIGHTBACK

As the fog of depression cleared, I began to see that the plan I'd agreed to with the bank was potentially very dangerous. Worst of all, I saw that, because Marie and I had given personal guarantees, we were exposed to losing Beechwood, our family home. If the bank went ahead with its proposed auction of my assets, I feared that vultures would swoop in and everything would be sold at less than its true value. Even though I now had a good relationship with the bankers, I understood that all they wanted was to turn my property into cash; getting its full value wasn't a priority for them. The problem for me was that if they sold at a price that was less than my debt, I would still owe them money without having any means of paying it back, and it was inevitable they would then come after Beechwood. They had screwed me over once before by cutting my overdraft when I wasn't expecting it even though, months earlier, they had promised to support me. That had started my spiral into depression and I was determined not to go down that road again.

My brain was spinning, trying to see a way out of this danger. Marie was the one who had always feared that the bailiffs would throw us out of our home, but now it was me who had waking nightmares about losing the roof over our heads. My fears were so real that one evening I decided I needed to warn my wife about the impending threat. Telling her that we were in real danger of losing our family home was one of the toughest things I'd ever had to do. Our eight-year-old son overheard his mother crying and asked what was happening. I told him that we might have to move house. 'Why?' he asked through his tears. I had no answer. I thought back to when I was fourteen years old and my father's business was on the edge and how I'd felt then. Although I had played a big role in my own downfall and felt like a fool, I knew in my heart and soul there was no way I would let Beechwood go.

Eureka moment

One night, on a bivvy on Carrauntoohil, I came up with an idea that I thought was the perfect solution to a growing problem in the housing market. The core of the issue was a shortage of affordable housing for young people in Cork city. At 10 per cent, the deposit was too high for most young couples trying to get on the property ladder. Even with both parties working, there was no way they could save the amount demanded by the banks and building societies to secure a mortgage. Sitting under the cross on Ireland's highest mountain, I devised what I considered an ingenious plan to solve this problem. The first thing I needed to do was to stop the bank from selling my landbank as these sites were part of my solution. I also realised that, as long as they couldn't put a precise value on my assets, the bank couldn't come after us because the courts wouldn't accept an estimated figure on my debt. Beechwood would be secure for another while and, if my plan worked, I intended ensuring it remained our home.

I took my first steps shortly before the bank's proposed auction of my assets, at the end of 1987. I personally called to all the local developers and builders that I thought might be interested in the sale. I opened my heart to them, explaining that I was afraid that I was about to lose my family home. If any of them bought my property, I said, the bank would be able to put an exact figure on my assets. Then, assuming the proceeds from the auction were less than what I owed, they could come after the guarantees and we could be evicted from our house. They seemed sympathetic but the day of the auction was nerve-wracking as Marie and I waited to see how our future would pan out. Amazingly, nobody bid on the land. When I thanked every potential bidder for having my back, they told me the reason they didn't bid was that they knew it could just as easily have been them in my position.

The first part of my plan had worked and I now had some breathing space.

70

The next step was to get access to my landbank from the bank. I wanted them to agree to release my sites under licence to individual buyers that I would sell houses to. Such an agreement would mean that the bank would remain the owner of the site and would have a direct contract with the buyer who wanted a new home. The contract for building the house would be with me at Falvey Housing. This approach would mean that no building could take place until the bank had been paid the price of the site. As far as I could see, it was a risk-free proposal for them; they hadn't been able to sell my landbank at auction but I was now offering them a way of turning that earth into cash. I drew up a business plan which showed that, within four years, the bank would be paid back all the money I owed, with interest.

Securing the licence to develop the sites was one thing; solving the deposit shortfall for potential buyers was another, and this is where the ingeniousness of my plan was really going to come into play. I would set up a finance agency, Home Loan Finance (HLF), under the Moneylenders Act to enable buyers who were purchasing a property from Falvey Housing to acquire a bridging loan so they could pay their deposit and secure a mortgage from the bank. To ensure that the loan was secure, I would get a personal guarantee from the clients' parents and weekly repayments to HLF would start at a rate of £20 per £1,000 borrowed on the loan.

At that time, the gross profit from the average house was £9,000 and the maximum I would lend was £3,000. HLF would issue a cheque payable to the client while Falvey Properties would write a letter of sale for the client to give to the bank to prove they had paid the full 10 per cent deposit to the estate agent, which was Falvey Properties. Our estate agency would then be assigned the cheque written by HLF, which we would tear up while lodging whatever cash the client paid. In this way, we would be lending non-existent money to clients, but Falvey Housing, which would be contracted to build the house, would apply the deposit and bridging loan from the overall house price. The fact that the money didn't actually exist wasn't a problem as far as I was concerned because I would be both creditor and debtor. Basically, I would be using the potential profit from each house sale as a source of funding for future sales.

The financier, estate agent and builder were, effectively, the same person – me. It was a high-risk plan but I really believed it could work. I discussed it with my father and also asked advice from Owen O'Callaghan. They both thought the idea was a bit off-the-wall but they believed that, if I could get the bank to agree to my proposal, it could work. I then spoke to my solicitors who also agreed that the plan, though unusual, was feasible and legal. They set about sorting out the legal end of things and putting Home Loan Finance in place. As soon as that was done and we had a licence to lend money, I was ready to bring my proposal to the bank. I decided, however, not to go into any details about how I was going to ensure buyers would secure their deposits as I guessed my approach would probably be a bit too creative for them.

Licence to build

I rang the regional bank manager who was in charge of the Falvey Group account. He was the same manager who had loaned me £12,000 in 1977 when I did my first licensing agreement with Owen O'Callaghan. He had taken a chance on me then and I was hoping he'd do the same this time round. I told him I had a business proposal that I thought would be beneficial to the bank and we arranged to meet. When we were face to face, I was really nervous as my future business success depended on this man agreeing with me. I outlined my idea but the manager didn't think the plan could be enacted legally. I then produced a contract from my solicitor showing him otherwise. I explained that we would have two contracts for clients to sign – one for the site and the other for the building of their new home. The former would be with the bank, which would receive direct payment, while the latter was with Falvey Housing, which would be paid only for the actual build.

Initially I wanted the bank to set aside twenty sites from the Falvey portfolio which I would undertake to sell within three months. For every site sold, the bank would be paid between £4,500 and £6,000, depending on the house type, as soon as the contract was signed. If I was successful with the first twenty sites, I wanted the bank to grant me a licence for a further fifty sites from our portfolio which I proposed to sell within a year. I couldn't read the manager's face as I spoke, but I continued anyway; there was no point in stopping now. If I sold fifty sites, I said that I wanted the bank to undertake to set aside a further 100 for me to sell within another twelve-month time span. Then, if I met all these sales deadlines, I wanted the bank to agree to release the balance of my 300 sites to me.

My business plan showed that we could sell houses in the £30,000 to £45,000 bracket on a phased basis with a 30 per cent gross profit on sales. If the plan worked, we would be sitting on potential sales of £11,000,000 (€72,000,000 at today's value). I wouldn't have to worry about paying interest as I had built that into the repayments of the site cost. I could see the manager was impressed by the figures. He asked a lot of questions and challenged me on each element of the proposal. I was expecting this and was able to defend every aspect of the plan. If I didn't meet the targets within the time schedules set out, I said that the bank could sell my landbank on the open market and I wouldn't obstruct them this time round.

The manager knew the lengths to which I'd gone to safeguard my property when the bank had tried to sell it before. Now I was saying that I would no longer object to an auction if I failed so he knew I was very, very serious. As soon as I finished speaking, he said he would be happy in theory to give me the green light but had to consult with head office first. He was willing to take a chance on me again and I was immensely grateful. He added that, although he knew I would do my best, he didn't think I'd be able to pull it off. I hadn't told him about Home Loan Finance and kept that more unorthodox part of the plan to myself.

Within a few weeks, the bank and I had signed an agreement. The ink was barely dry when I began an advertising campaign in the local papers and on radio, publicising not only the houses for sale but also the financing options we were offering. Within eight weeks, we had sold twenty sites and had started building. All my old creditors and suppliers stood by me and were happy to do business with us again. By the end of six months, I had loaned £150,000 to young couples and was receiving £3,000 a week in repayments on the loans. Risky as it was, the venture worked and, within a few years, I'd sold all 300 sites from our original portfolio and had started buying up more land and property again. I was back in full business mode though I had no intention of forgetting the hard lessons I'd learned over the previous years. I had three full-time staff in the office and subcontracted all the building work out. Everything now was calculated and planned meticulously, with no overruns and no borrowings.

Over the next few years, with the support of my family and a great team that believed in me and had stuck with me through all the bad times, I paid off the bank, got rid of our personal guarantees, secured our family home and avoided financial ruin. We built up a solid building, auctioneering and financial services business. The Galloping Major was gone and left behind was me, a hard-working Norrie who had nearly lost everything but who was getting back on track and dreaming big dreams again.

CLIMBING TOWARDS A NEW LIFE

I was the new kid on the block in Cork Mountaineering, the youngest member of the oldest mountaineering club in the county. My apprenticeship began under Val Deane, Con O'Leary, Bill McGregor, Ella Dineen and Máire Ní Mhurchú, all hugely experienced mountaineers. I was in awe of their knowledge and passion for mountaineering and was hungry to learn everything they knew. In them I found great mentors who encouraged my enthusiasm and gave it direction. Con was well into his sixties when I joined the club and I was mesmerised by his talk of climbs in the Alps, Scotland and Wales. Val and Bill showed me how to use a compass and a map; prior to that, I'd never even noticed where the sun rose and set. I also started to learn rock climbing skills with John Thompson and Pat Long.

By December 1986, I had climbed with the club in the Comeraghs, the Galtees and the Knockmealdowns. I got to know my home county of Cork, hiking and climbing in places I'd never been before. I learned other important lessons from Cork Mountaineering Club too; being with them taught me that life was not all about the creation of wealth and that you didn't have to stay in a five-star hotel and spend a lot of money to have fun. Before I joined the club, I hadn't slept in a room with six or eight people, all snoring and farting, since I'd been at Irish college. I took to the people and the climbing lifestyle like a duck to water.

I was growing in confidence all the time and was soon back to my old self – the person who thought he could do anything. I often climbed Carrauntoohil on my own and on one occasion, when the weather was really bad with snow covering the mountain and cloud enfolding it right down to its base, I suddenly realised how alone I was as I climbed up the Devil's Ladder. Although I hadn't brought a map or compass with me, I still continued upwards until I reached the summit. I thought I knew this mountain well, but getting back down was a nightmare. I had used cairns as markers on the way up but couldn't find them on the way down as the wind-blown snow concealed them and I lost my way in whiteout conditions. I eventually found the top of the Devil's Ladder and made my way down safely. As soon as I was out of danger, all I wanted to do was tell everyone about my great adventure.

When I told Val about my experience, he got really mad with me and warned against such folly. He said that I was becoming brash about my ability without yet having the necessary skills to deal with the many dangers the mountains throw up. He told me about Tiglin National Adventure Centre in Co Wicklow and I immediately signed up for the mountain leadership (ML) course there. On my first training weekend I was blown away to meet Paddy O'Leary, the centre director, and to hear talk of the big names in the Irish mountaineering world – people such as Calvin Torrans, Claire Sheridan and Joss Lynam. I was like a child learning about the world for the first time, soaking up everything I could about how to be in the mountains. I honed my skills very fast and, within a year, I was leading climbs with Cork Mountaineering.

My training, which took me to every corner of Ireland, also gave me the opportunity to meet people of a similar mindset who were training to be self-sufficient and who loved adventure. I told everyone I was going to climb Mount Everest and I think Paddy and some of my other instructors found my attitude hard to take; there I was, a mouthy unknown from Cork, talking about climbing Everest when I was still, in the eyes of many, so inexperienced. Nonetheless, after completion of the final assessment, I felt confident that I'd gotten everything from the course that I needed to be self-sufficient in the mountains: I was ready to spread my wings.

Hunger for knowledge

I began going to Scotland where I met and climbed with some great technical mountaineers. There I learned about moving on snow and ice as well as all about efficient crampon and ice axe use and how to survive in harsh conditions. I did alpine courses and continued my apprenticeship in France, Italy and Switzerland under the International Federation of Mountain Guides Associations to gain further skills. I never did their guiding certificate course because my interest was not in guiding in the Alps. I was always very clear that my climbing interests and intentions lay in the Himalaya. To be proficient on the world's highest mountains, I wanted to learn everything, from alpine skills and camp craft to avalanche recognition, crevasse rescue, how to travel on glaciers, efficient rope skills and the best rescue techniques. I needed to gain expertise in all these areas so that I could climb on peaks where the risks were high and self-leadership was vital for survival.

During these early years, I was constantly coming into contact with outstanding climbers from all around the world, most of whom didn't have official qualifications. Their driving passion was the same as mine – a pure love of adventure and climbing. I always learned best when in the field and would never apply myself to something just because someone said I should do it when I couldn't see the reason why. Despite my attitude, Paddy O'Leary at Tiglin acknowledged my passion for the mountains and my determination to go to the Himalaya. He told me that I needed to get more experience in mountain rescue and gave me the name of Con Moriarty, training officer with Kerry Mountain Rescue and one of the most charismatic and naturally talented climbers in the country.

THE MOUNTAIN MAN

Towards the end of 1988, I went to Killarney in Co Kerry to meet Con Moriarty in his outdoor and adventure shop. The Mountain Man, as he was known, was a wild-looking fellow in his early twenties who reminded me of a young Grizzly Adams with his great 6'5" height, long hair and beard. He had a twinkle in his eye and a dazzling smile, and we took an instant liking to each other. I told him I needed to get mountain rescue experience and wanted to join Kerry Mountain Rescue (KMR). I also told him of my goal of climbing Everest and all about the training courses and mountaineering I'd done. Con told me about his dreams and experiences on the mountains; it was as if we were kindred spirits. After about an hour talking, he turned to me and said, 'Shut the fuck up, Falvey, and let's go climbing'. I thought this guy was crazy when he said 'I'll assess you now to see if you can join Kerry Mountain Rescue' as he caught me by the arm and marched me out of the shop. He put his *Sorry, closed to go climbing* sign on the door and rang a friend, Mike O'Shea, who was also a member of KMR, explaining to me that two people were needed to make an assessment.

After parking at Cronin's Yard, Con led the way up Collins' Gully on the northeast face of Carrauntoohil. When we stopped on the edge of Howling Ridge, he started asking me a load of questions about climbing, testing my knowledge. I answered as well as I could and then he asked me to lead the climb in Collins' Gully, a classic winter climb that was banked out in snow. It was one of the most memorable climbs I'd ever had, with two of the most fun-loving, piss-taking, passionate mountaineers I'd ever met. After descending, we went to the pub for a few celebratory drinks. I'd passed Con's impromptu test and he told me I was now an official member of Kerry Mountain Rescue. He then invited me to a training session the following Sunday, and so began my time with KMR.

The group was recognised as one of the top mountain rescue outfits in Ireland, mainly because of the experience of its members. Kerry had the highest and hardest hills to climb in the country and, consequently, also had a high number of rescues annually. There were some great climbers on the team when I joined, all of whom were open to teaching me all they knew, especially Con and Shea – as everyone called him – who had similar dreams to mine of one day going to Nepal and the Himalaya. With them, I felt I had connected with two soulmates.

As a member of KMR, I learned all about ropes, knots, pulley systems, protection, balancing belays, rope strength, breaking strains of crabs, and harnesses. I became very competent in rope and gear management and camp craft in all conditions. Con, as training officer, had a huge interest in the technical aspect of climbing and rescue. He was breaking new ground all the time and was very progressive. He was also controversial and not afraid of the consequences. One of his innovations was the placing of a hut on the northeast face of Carrauntoohil. He organised the whole thing with the help of volunteers, including me, who spent weeks fixing the building. The hut was made from an old plastic water tank which we faced with stone and topped with grass sods so that it blended with its natural surrounds. We furnished it with six bunk beds and even brought up a radio and a battery-operated television.

All the mountain rescue members thought the hut was a brilliant idea; it was somewhere we could position ourselves when we were out on rescues and we could also store provisions there. However, it wasn't viewed in the same light at the headquarters of the Mountaineering Council of Ireland (MCI). They went ballistic when they heard about the hut, stating that we had built the highest building in the country without planning permission and would have to dismantle it. MCI member Dermot Somers came to Killarney demanding a meeting with Con. He was very clear that, as far as the official organisation for mountaineering in the country was concerned, the hut had to go. The discussion became very heated, but Con wouldn't back down. Dermot left and the hut remained. It became something of a symbol of what we in Kerry felt the official climbing fraternity saw as our rebellious attitude.

The issue over the hut was my first inkling that there was a 'them and us' in Irish climbing. For generations, rules and regulations around mountaineering in Ireland had come from the Dublin and Wicklow region of the country, where some of the finest climbers were based. Now there was a rookie gang emerging in Kerry who appeared to be taking things into their own hands. This Kerry crowd, headed by Con Moriarty, was not complying with the rulebook. The MCI probably saw us as unorthodox rebels who needed to be reined in, while we saw them as being overly concerned with officialdom and resented what we felt was their interfering. We wanted to explore the limits of climbing in the country's highest peaks and didn't like a committee on the other side of the island telling us what we could or couldn't do. We had no intention of letting them, or anyone else, put restraints on us that we considered arbitrary and outdated.

A young mentor

Mountains and climbing were in Con's blood. He was born in the Gap of Dunloe in the heart of the MacGillycuddy's Reeks and, from when he could walk, he was out in the hills, absorbing the terrain and its stories like a sponge. The Reeks were his kingdom and, when he came of age, Con was determined to explore every corner of the wild and beautiful landscape of his home county. When I first met him, he was already breaking new routes in the region, including Ferdia, Cú Chulainn, Primroses and Howling Ridge. His eyes would light up when he talked about the climbing and history of his home area, its culture, mythologies and people. I had never met anyone like him before; his passion was almost tangible and certainly irresistible. Climbers from all over the world came to meet Con, drawn to him like a magnet.

From the beginning, he recognised my enthusiasm and encouraged it fully. With Con, I was climbing hard routes on the mountains, pushing myself to my limits and learning many skills from a guy who was several years younger than me but who had this amazing natural ability and passion. For the next three years, I was in Kerry as often as I was in Cork, climbing hard, mainly with Con and Shea. I also climbed regularly with Tim Hickey and Ciaran Corrigan, both members of KMR and who, like myself, were in thrall to the vast knowledge of the Mountain Man. They were a wild and talented gang who were also great fun. Through them and the wider KMR group I met up with many other climbers that I learned a huge amount from, including Tony Farrell, Tim Long, Ivan Counihan, Pat Grandfield, Adrian Devlin and Mike Barry.

All the time that I was climbing at home with Con and Shea, our overall goals were the same: we wanted to climb the big mountains in the Himalaya and the Alps. Con would rattle off the names of mountains that I knew nothing about but that we were going to climb together in exotic locations like Nepal, India and Pakistan, as well as peaks in France and Italy. His list included Mount Everest, K2, Annapurna – mountains that were all over 8,000m – as well as more technical climbs such as Shivling, Ama Dablam, the Eiger and the Matterhorn. He talked about great climbers that he had an in-depth knowledge of but whom I'd never heard of. He spoke of Mallory and Irvine, Shipton, Messner, Bonington, Doug Scott and Don Whillans. He gave me books and magazines to read about the great mountains and the people who climbed them. I learnt about their psychology and mindset and what it was that drove them to climb, to adventure and to explore these exotic places.

I saw Con as the master and myself as the apprentice. Coming from a tradition of tradesmen, I knew that the apprentice must respect the master and be willing to go on a journey of learning, training and discipline in order to become proficient and, eventually, to also become a master. Although Everest was still my main focus, Con opened my mind to the wider world of adventure beyond my dream of standing on the world's highest summit.

BASE CAMP KILLARNEY

Con's place was a really interesting spot to hang out. His two-bedroom apartment, situated over the Mountain Man shop, was an open house and on any given weekend there could be up to twelve bodies bunking down on the floor. There was an endless collection of eccentric, opinionated characters arriving and departing. They were dope-smoking, hard-drinking, quick-talking climbers who liked nothing more than to argue about the ethics of mountaineering. No one ever had a key for the apartment, including Con, and more often than not the only way in was through a window on the first floor. This posed a climbing challenge where someone would have to scale the wall using a hard very severe (HVS) climbing move incorporating a dynamic lunge to get from the ground up to the first floor, more often than not pissed as a skunk. Once inside, the person would come down and let all the others in.

Some of the biggest names in the world of climbing turned up and it was an honour for me to be in their presence and to hear of their adventures. I met the likes of Paul Pritchard, Andy Cave, Stephen Venables and Mick Fowler, along with Jimmy McKenzie and Jim Leonard from Ireland. I was in awe of them but when we climbed in the Reeks and socialised together, I began to see these heroes as real human beings and understood that I, too, could do what they were doing.

Rookies adventuring

Con, Shea and I used meet up as often as possible to train and go out on the hills. Rain, snow, blizzards or storms didn't bother us; in fact, the rougher the weather, the better. In the summertime, I'd leave Cork and arrive at a climbing crag in Dingle, Kenmare or Killarney at 6pm and we'd climb until midnight and then I'd drive back to Cork. When we did a new route we'd talk about it for weeks afterwards, analysing the moves, the feel, the fear, how we felt about the texture of the rock, the condition of the ice and how we could improve on our techniques.

In Kerry, we had a great mix of terrain right on our doorstep and even more options within driving distance. We did cragging as well as rock climbing on mountains and cliff faces and we really loved doing big mountain routes. A lot of these varied between crappy and good terrain and we often had to dig our hands in through boggy sods and dirt before gaining purchase going up vertical faces. Kerry offered endless shite terrain on steep routes and it was here that I learned many skills that later allowed me to feel very comfortable on the snowy flanks of the Himalaya.

Overall, in Ireland, there was very little snow and ice but when we got this weather, it felt like Santa had turned up with a sack full of presents. Our luck was in over the winters of 1989, 1990 and 1991 which offered up perfect ice and snow climbing conditions at home. We went out on Carrauntoohil and, because we knew the time was limited and the weather could change fast, we'd keep climbing until we'd done all the routes that we wanted to do under those conditions. When we got a day or two of good ice it was such a joy just to click in with an ice axe and know you were going to be safe. Irish ice was normally thin and brittle so to get good, solid ice was like manna from heaven. Climbers from other countries with more snow and ice often found it difficult to deal with tough terrain because they had trained on good rock and firm snow and ice and hadn't ever been challenged by the type of terrain we went out on in Ireland.

I loved being out in the elements, fascinated to see how I could survive in extreme conditions. What I found later is that, barring the cold, the conditions I encountered in other countries were never anything worse than those I had faced in Ireland.

83

A NEW CLIMBING GOAL

One day in January 1989, I was coming off Carrauntoohil, soaked to the skin and about to head home to Cork when I got a call on my mobile. It was Con asking me to meet him in Kate Kearney's Cottage, a local watering hole for climbers in the scenic Gap of Dunloe. He seemed very excited and when we met he gave me one of his big bear hugs and ordered two pints. Before saying a word, he devoured his pint in two quick slugs then shouted to the barman for another round. 'Falvey,' he said, 'we're going. I've got the permit.' I had no idea what he was talking about. 'Where are we going?' I asked. 'I got the permit for Ama Dablam,' he answered excitedly. I took a gulp of my pint. 'Are you serious?' I asked. 'Yes,' Con said. 'Will you join the team?' I couldn't believe it. 'Yes!' I shouted, 'count me in.' Less than three years earlier, I'd started my apprenticeship and here I was now, going to the Himalaya to climb what was considered to be one of the world's most beautiful and technical high-altitude mountains.

Over the next few weeks, Con put the full team together for the Irish Ama Dablam Expedition. Mike O'Shea, from Beaufort, was the youngest of the team. I'd been climbing nonstop with him and Con for three years and had never failed to be amazed at his rope work and technical climbing abilities. He had a winning demeanour and was the biggest joker you could ever meet. Mick Murphy, an outdoor education teacher from Cork, was an experienced adventurer on water and land and a very talented mountaineer. Tony Farrell, an electrician from Dublin, was an experienced mixed climber on ice and rock with a calm temperament and a great sense of humour. Skinny, quiet and reserved, Ciaran Corrigan was a very good rock climber. He was also a great singer and was as chilled out as it's possible to be. Our Base Camp manager, Tim Hickey from Killarney, was a hillwalker who worked with Con in the Mountain Man shop. Con, Shea, Ciaran, Tim and I had climbed together many times and were all members of Kerry Mountain Rescue. That we all knew each other and were friends was an important consideration for me. Mountains are dangerous places and no matter how proficient you are, you are always surrounded by risk; having highly trained friends with you could, I believed, only be a bonus.

During the next two years, we spent a huge amount of time training and climbing together in Kerry, Scotland, England and the Alps. This not only ensured we stayed fit but also gave us the opportunity to get to know each other better as a team. I was discovering that my innate skills were physical strength and a huge ability to endure, in terms of both stamina and physical hardship. As a result, the lads nicknamed me 'The Donkey'. I'd do three- to ten-day survival expeditions where I'd put on my backpack and head off, carrying loads of up to 30kg in order to build my strength and test my skills.

Obsession

As part of my training schedule, I would climb Carrauntoohil two and sometimes three times in one day. The first ascent would be a speed climb which took about two and a half hours. I'd no sooner be back in Cronin's Yard than I'd set off again on a second, slower climb, this time carrying a light pack. I'd return to base and then do it for a third and final time, sometimes spending up to fourteen hours a day training. Just to test my camp craft skills, I'd often put the tent up in the garden at home at Beechwood. I'd cook my meal in it and then sleep there for the night. At times, Marie and the kids thought I was losing the plot.

I was obsessive and found it hard to trust that I was good enough to do what I wanted to do. I was also doing a lot of reading, especially about the dangers of high-altitude climbing. However, when I finally got to the high mountains, it felt as if a lot of what I read, especially around perceived dangers, had been embellished. I had planned for the dangers I read about, even though, in the end, they weren't what I encountered. The only time the conditions and terrain were as challenging as I'd seen them described was on my polar expeditions when it was as physical, as cold and as debilitating as described in books.

I was becoming a fully-fledged mountaineer. I had started as a hillwalker, then I learned how to rock and ice climb, how to navigate and be self-sufficient in the mountains. It was only when I could do all of those things that I classified myself as a mountaineer. I was my own harshest critic when it came to my ability and I was always striving to be better. I became what we call a mixed climber in the mountaineering fraternity. For me, mountaineering was an amalgamation of ice and rock climbing, of camping and of moving across tough terrain in fine, wet or snowy weather, or in the height of a storm. It meant being able to navigate and make decisions, being able to look after yourself and your team in all conditions and situations and on all types of routes.

Funnily enough, my early experience in the building industry came in useful when I encountered narrow ridges on high mountains. In those times, before health and safety rules were advanced, we regularly built walls at thirty feet standing only on a nine-inch plank. As a result, I could easily find my balance and walk on narrow mountain ridges and climb steep faces without any fear of falling. My progression in a short space of time was fast, but my interest and commitment were huge.

THE EIGER 1991

Con's plans for Ama Dablam were well under way by 1990, with the expedition date set for February 1991. Although I had climbed in several European countries, I still had concerns about my abilities. I wanted to be an efficient team player but I was keenly aware that I was the last of the group to come to climbing. I didn't have much experience in high-altitude mountaineering and wanted to get an independent source to assess my technical ability and preparedness to climb Ama Dablam. I was advised to contact Pat Littlejohn, then a director of the renowned International School of Mountaineering, who was based in Switzerland. Pat was a world-class mountaineer and instructor with climbing experience all over the world, particularly in the Alps and the Himalaya.

I spoke to him and explained my concerns. He said that a good test for me would be to climb the Eiger in Switzerland, as its north face was about the same technical grade as Ama Dablam, although at a lower altitude. Pat was heading to an international ice meeting in Vallon di Cogne in northern Italy where many top ice climbers were assembling, and was planning to climb the Eiger after the meet. To my surprise, he invited me to join him on the trip. He said he'd take a look at my climbing at the ice meet and if he thought I was good enough, he'd consider letting me join him on the climb. I was flattered; this was a mountain I had been fascinated with because of its iconic place in mountaineering history and I said yes immediately.

I flew to Italy in January 1991 where I met up with Pat and his climbing partner Eddie Cooper, from Belfast. There were many other climbers at the training ground, including luminaries like Chris Bonington and Doug Scott who were very forthcoming with advice on climbing Everest. I was awed just to be in their presence. Pat, who was an expert on rock and ice, said I could join him and Eddie on their ice climbs in the training ground. I had honed my ice skills in Ireland and Scotland and was already getting up some fairly hard routes so Italy didn't take too much out of me. We did some amazing multi-pitch waterfall ice climbs which I hadn't done to any great extent previously. It was steep, bungled ice and I loved every minute of it.

After five days at the training ground, Pat said that he thought I was able for the Eiger and that I could join himself and Eddie on the climb. My confidence soared; this was a serious mountain, with its 1,800m north face considered to be one of the most challenging and dangerous ascents in the Alps. Since 1938, at least sixty-four climbers had died attempting the face, nicknamed 'Mordwand' (murderous wall) by German climbers.

Pat and Eddie's plan was to do the Lauper Route but when we arrived at the base, Pat decided that the face was not in condition. The ice was black and solid, almost like steel, and presented too much of a risk. This put the kibosh on Plan A. Disappointed, we descended to Lauterbrunnen village for the night to rest and reassess our situation. Pat decided to change our route to the south ridge of the Eiger, starting from the Mönch. Plan B was no less a challenge in winter conditions than Plan A, and would test my skills on dangerous ground.

Sitting in a cafe that same evening, we fell into conversation with other climbers who told us the chilling story of two French mountaineers who had died just days earlier after falling from the south ridge. The death of any climber is always unwelcome news and hearing about this tragedy created an uneasy feeling in our group, but nothing apart from the very worst the elements could throw at us was going to stop us pursuing our objective.

A close shave

I couldn't sleep that night, excited at the adventure that lay ahead. We set off the following morning, 29 January, and for several hours we trudged through unremarkable snow that felt more like a slog than anything else as we made our way to the Mönchjoch hut. At the climbers' shelter below Mönch's summit we rested before roping together to traverse to the South Col. Carrying heavy packs and with our heads down, we slowly made our way across a steep glacier field towards the ice-encrusted southern wall of the Mönch. We had traversed the glacier for almost a mile when we literally froze in our footsteps. A massive explosion was sending tremors down the ice slope. Somewhere above our heads, ice and snow had come loose from the mountain and we were now in direct danger of being hit by an avalanche. 'Get the fuck out of here and quickly!' Pat shouted. We retreated in deep snow to safety at the edge of the glacier, all the time fearing that the track we were cutting could trigger another avalanche. Luckily, the snowslide came to a stop somewhere above us.

We found what we thought was a safer path lower down where we could cross the glacier, but when we were just over halfway across, there was a second – louder – explosion that sent shockwaves down the slope and paralysed us with fright. 'Shit, whichever direction we take we run the risk of being hit if the avalanche comes down,' Pat said. 'Let's just go for it. At least if we can get onto the ridge we will be at the start of our climb.' Nobody disagreed. We played out as much rope as possible between ourselves so that if one of the team was swept away, the remaining two would have time to dig in and act as human anchors. That was the theory anyway. However, we knew deep inside that nothing could withstand the force of millions of tons of snow and ice careering down the side of the mountain.

Eventually, after what seemed like an interminable period of anxious, snail-like progress, we reached the rib of the snow-covered rock. This was the gateway to the main arête between the Mönch and the Eiger; we were safe. Then there was another explosion and the avalanche swept down on our tracks. *Fuck*, I thought, *that was a close shave*. 'I wouldn't like to do that again. Bloody dangerous,' Pat said calmly as he looked across the avalanche's main drag which we had somehow managed to cross without incident.

We took a welcome break to eat and replenish our energy before continuing on our ascent across the arête between the two saddles. This ridge was dangerously exposed with up to 1,000m fall-off on both sides. Just then one of Pat's crampons broke, which made continuing extremely dangerous, so, after about two hours' climbing, we decided to call it a day. We abseiled down a 50m pinnacle under which we set up our bivvy for the night, strapping our tiny single-skin tent to the rock. Before we settled down for some much-needed sleep, Pat told me this was the place where the two French climbers had fallen to their deaths. I didn't sleep much that night, anxious that we, too, could be blown off the mountain.

The next morning we were up with the sunrise. The sky was blue and there was a rising wind. Pat made his way with the security of one crampon only and after about five hours of interesting climbing, we arrived at the rock band below the summit. The wind was relentless at this stage and did its best to beat us down, but we persisted and eventually made it to the summit snow line and, finally, to the summit itself. It was bitterly cold and, while it was a relief to have reached the top of the mountain, I didn't have much time to savour the triumphant moment because, after a short break to refuel our bodies, we started the descent. As the winter day was short and Pat was slowed down due to having one crampon only, we had a further bivvy on the Eiger's western flank before descending safely the following morning at 11am.

After the lads departed I stayed on for another few days in Switzerland to gain extra altitude training. I made my way to Zermatt where my intention was to climb the Matterhorn. However, the weather conditions were not favourable and instead I climbed a 4,164m peak called Breithorn, one of the easiest of the 4,000m peaks.

I learned a lot from my experience with Pat and Eddie, who taught me so much about the practical and technical side of climbing. But it wasn't only that; I also learned a lot about the mindset and psychology needed to be a successful mountaineer from them. I learned that if conditions weren't right it was okay to change direction and to take another route; I learned that constant assessment is needed in an environment where change is happening all the time; that big goals are only achieved one section at a time; that asking for help and support is a good thing; that people are usually happy to help those in whom they see passion and eagerness to learn.

As I travelled back to Ireland, I realised that my five-year apprenticeship in mountaineering was now complete. I was confident and ready for the expedition to Nepal, happy that I had done everything possible to ensure I was a proficient and self-sufficient mountaineer.

AMA DABLAM 1991

When applying for our permit to climb Ama Dablam, Con dealt directly with the relevant authorities in Kathmandu. Traditionally, for Irish expeditions, such applications were made through the Mountaineering Council of Ireland. Word filtered back to us that the powers that be in the council were not happy that the rookies in Kerry were circumnavigating the procedures they had put in place. They had created rules and regulations to set and maintain standards in the mountains, including for Irish teams in the Himalaya. When Con bypassed them for the permit, it was as if we, as a team, were giving them the two fingers.

They knew that Con was an accomplished mountaineer, although they didn't like his attitude. They would also have known of the abilities of Shea and Mick Murphy. Tony Farrell, Ciaran Corrigan and I were more or less unknown quantities. Their worry was that here was an Irish team going to climb a high mountain where there might be an accident, or a fatality, that could bring Irish mountaineering into disrepute. But Con was no gambler; he knew his team and our abilities and he had every confidence that we could achieve our goal. We set off from Ireland ready to prove just that a few weeks after I returned from climbing the Eiger.

The Himalaya

'Out the left-hand side of the plane you can see Mount Everest,' the captain of the flight to Kathmandu announced over the intercom. Within seconds, nearly every passenger was scrambling towards the twelve-inch windows to try and get a glimpse of the world's most famous mountain. Con and I had window seats and held vantage viewing positions, obscured when the others piled in on top of us like a rugby scrum to try and get a first glimpse of the Himalaya, the greatest mountain range on the planet. We stared out the window, in awe at the sights unfolding before our eyes. 'Look, Falvey!' Con said excitedly, pointing at the different peaks. 'There's Mount Everest, Cho Oyu, Lhotse, Makalu, Ama Dablam!' I didn't know how he was able to name them all. I could only identify one: Mount Everest.

Immediately after we arrived in Nepal's capital city in February 1991, we made our way into Thamel, the area of the city made famous by artists and hippies who came there in the 1970s in search of enlightenment. By the 1990s, it was the main gathering spot for the growing number of climbers to the Himalaya and the staging post for expeditions and treks in Nepal and Tibet. The Hotel Thamel was our base for six days while we sought to clear our expedition equipment and food through customs. The officials' main interest was to extract as much money as possible from what they perceived to be wealthy climbers from the West. Several days later, and after paying out an extra $200, our gear was released. Then we had to check, double-check and treble-check everything. There was no room for miscalculations or mistakes; attention to detail was critical as any piece of essential equipment misplaced, forgotten or not working could mean disaster and cause our expedition to fail. Two years of planning and preparation had gone into this and now, for the final time, we had to ensure we had everything we needed for our eight-week trek into the mountains.

Mind-blowing Kathmandu

Exploring Kathmandu was like entering a magical, crazy otherworld. The city was an intriguing mix of cultures, traditions, smells, sounds and colours. On every narrow, ancient street there seemed to be an army of beggars, traders, hawkers, holy men, the blind, the crippled and – most startling of all – leopards, filling every available space. Everyone was trying to eke out a living, by running a small business, performing tricks or by begging. There were street urchins everywhere, many barely old enough to walk, imploring us for food and handouts. Sacred cows and rabid dogs, many of them grossly deformed, roamed freely through the crowded streets. They fed from the human waste that was dumped alongside the footpaths. In the sewerage-filled river, traders washed fruit and vegetables before selling them. I couldn't figure out how people weren't getting electrocuted by the electric wires that swung dangerously from each building, or knocked down by the endless bikes, rickshaws, motorbikes and cars that tore through the streets. I had never in my life seen such chaotic scenes. Despite having grown up in a disadvantaged area in Ireland, the poverty I saw all around me here made me realise how lucky, in fact, I had been.

Kathmandu, where every second day is a holy festival, was like an open-air museum with its ancient buildings, shrines and golden pagodas. There were nearly as many temples as houses and as many statues of Hindu and Buddhist deities as there were inhabitants. I visited some of the most important holy sites, including the Buddhist Swayambhunath Stupa, also known as the Monkey Temple. Situated on a hilltop above the city, it is a fascinating jumble of Buddhist and Hindu iconography. At Boudhanath Stupa, one of the most important places for pilgrimage and mediation for Nepalese and Tibetan Buddhists, I spoke to lamas and monks about their beliefs before taking the opportunity to meditate and pray with them to the gods of the mountain for a safe expedition for our team.

I also went to the famous Hindu Pashupatinath Temple in the eastern part of the city. Here I saw sights that were eye-popping, including bodies being burned as part of an ancient rite of final passage. Equally mesmerising was the sight of various holy men – the sadhus and babas – some with hair down to their feet and others with extraordinarily long moustaches and nails. Dick Baba stood out; he could lift concrete and granite blocks with his penis. Another baba clamped his member with red-hot irons. This apparent madness was to show people the supernatural powers given to them by the gods. I found it all both shocking and intoxicating.

En route to Mother's Necklace

After six days in Kathmandu, the expedition proper began. We had given ourselves eight weeks to complete it, which allowed for extra time for unforeseen events or bad weather. Ang Rita, our sirdar, organised a team of porters to load our gear onto the bus that was taking us from the capital to the town of Jiri, the trailhead where we would begin trekking. The eight-hour journey on narrow, winding roads was hair-raising. A few of us chose to sit on top of the bus rather than in it because we were convinced it was going to crash and we wanted to be ready to jump. Most climbers fly from Kathmandu to Lukla before starting the trek to their Base Camps but we decided to trek from Jiri – a journey of ten days – as we hadn't been at altitude before and Con felt that the longer walk in would help with our acclimatisation.

The trek gave us a great opportunity to see life in the rural areas of the Dolakha District in the Janakpur Zone. We walked through farmland and villages and met the local people, ate the local food and tried all the local brews, including butter tea and rakshi. In the months before the expedition began, Ang Rita, who was from Kharikhola – one of the villages on our route – had worked with us to organise a schools and medical aid project. A primary school in the Black Valley in Kerry had been twinned with a school in Kharikhola and we had brought along lots of items from the kids in Ireland to the school in Nepal. In thanks, the schoolchildren put on a concert in our honour. We also brought out some general medicines and gave them to the local hospitals. It was shocking to hear the average life expectancy in the area was only forty-five but tuberculosis was rife at the time. I'd noticed a lot of coughing in the badly ventilated tea houses we visited where the ceilings were black from the smoke of open fires.

In the temples we visited along the way we met local lamas and monks who promised to pray for us. In the early 1990s, Ama Dablam was climbed by only a small number of people and locals feared for those climbing what is locally known as Mother's Necklace. The peak was revered and there was a lot of concern about us even attempting it. I was fast picking up that something more than the sum of our skills was going to be needed if we were to have a safe expedition. It seemed that, for the locals, success had nothing to do with how well prepared we were. Rather, it had to do with whether or not the mountain gods would allow us to succeed.

Despite now being an agnostic, I hedged my bets and prayed to the Sacred Heart. I was physically ready for the climb, but spiritually I knew there was a lot I had done that could make the gods angry, whether I believed in them or not. I had psyched myself for the climb's steepness and technical challenges, but now I started to get worried that the gods of the mountain might strike me down. We did puja en route with the monks at Tengboche and Pangboche monasteries and again at Base Camp to appease the gods and to ask them to grant us a safe expedition.

Siege tactics

Ama Dablam, often called the Matterhorn of the Himalaya, is a stunning, pyramid-shaped mountain whose summit stands at 6,812m. Regarded as one of the world's most beautiful peaks, it is known for its steep, icy faces and challenging ridges. As we trekked along the route shared by those who were heading for Everest Base Camp, Mother's Necklace dominated the eastern skies. About three days out from our Base Camp, the road diverged and we found ourselves the only team en route to Ama Dablam. As we walked, Everest became visible at the end of the Khumbu Valley, its summit protruding above the ridge line of Nuptse and Lhotse, whose bulk prevented us from seeing the full magnitude of the world's highest mountain. That first sight sent a shiver of anticipation through me but, for now, my focus was on Ama Dablam. When the latter came into full view, its presence had a sobering effect. From a distance and through binoculars, it looked unclimbable, with its steep flanks and narrow summit. From just above Namche Bazaar, where we spent two nights, it was more spectacular looking than Everest. As we crossed the final grassy valley into Base Camp at 4,570m, we knew we had to start breaking the climb down in our minds or we'd be overwhelmed.

Of the four teams attempting the climb that season, we were the first to arrive. There were three trekkers with us whose presence helped cover some of our expedition costs. Husband and wife Pete and Rose Spellman, along with Mick Hennessy, were planning to climb Island Peak, the 6,189m trekking peak about 10km from Ama Dablam in Sagarmatha National Park. Shea and Tony Farrell led them while the rest of us set up at Base Camp and started stocking the camps en route up the mountain. They were gone for most of a week, during which we all had a good opportunity to acclimatise to the thin air. This was my first time at such altitude and I was one of the lucky ones because it didn't have any noticeable adverse effect on me. By the end of the week, we had Advance Base Camp (ABC) set up and were pushing upwards reasonably fast. It took two weeks in total to fix up to Camp 1 and stock it fully.

We were using a siege-tactics approach, going up and down the mountain, stocking the camps and putting fixed ropes on all the dangerous ground to help ease of access to the upper slopes and to facilitate a quick and safe descent. Our plan was to have three waves of two climbers so that if one group had to descend for any reason, the next two would follow through. This would be a real team effort and whether one or all six reached the summit, we saw it as success for the entire team. As the leader, Con decided how the teams would be split up. He and Shea would go first and fix ropes from Camp 1 to Camp 2 on the exposed southwest ridge on the Yellow Tower. The second wave would be Tony and me, with Mick and Ciaran making up the third wave.

Poisoned fruit

As soon as the camps were set up and our trekkers were about to leave, the weather, which had been very settled and clear until then, suddenly turned and snow began to fall heavily. The other three teams had arrived at this stage and the snowstorm, which grounded everyone, gave us a chance to get to know each other. This was the first of a total of seven storms, including a shocking thunder and lightning storm, that would hit us while on Ama Dablam. After a few days, the sky cleared and the trekkers left. Con and Shea set off early up the mountain. After several hours of climbing, they arrived at ABC and unpacked, planning to spend the night there before advancing to Camp 2 the next day. After dinner, they opened a tin of pineapples we'd bought in Kathmandu and devoured its contents. We had a strict food stock control system and the lads had a good laugh at the fact that they'd managed to steal a tin of fruit from the general pile. Several hours later, they were no longer laughing when they were both struck by severe food poisoning. Unknown to either man, the tinned fruit was contaminated and four years beyond its use-by date.

Tony and I were on the way up when we met Con and Shea making their way back down, looking like ghosts. We couldn't believe what had happened to them. Shea was so ill that he had to be evacuated to a local hospital in the village of Pheriche, a day's walk from Base Camp. He was having trouble speaking and was suffering from weakness, blurred vision, tiredness and vomiting. During the next two weeks, he lost over two stone and was diagnosed with botulism, a rare and potentially fatal illness. This meant that his expedition was over before it ever really started. Tim Hickey, our Base Camp manager, stayed with him until he felt better and they were both able to return to Base Camp. Con fared slightly better and stayed at Base Camp during his recovery, determined not to give up hope of being able to climb later on.

An elusive gully

We were now down to four climbers and the push was on to fix the ropes on the most technical sections of the mountain. Ciaran and Mick were the next team to move out onto the southwest ridge. The climbing there was dangerous, with lots of loose rock leading onto the exposed ridge that was dotted with rock towers, the most imposing of which was the massive Yellow Tower which had a 1,000m fall-off at either side. They made it to Camp 2 at 6,092m, fixing rope along the most challenging sections before returning to Base Camp that night. Next morning Tony and I set off from Camp 1 carrying heavy packs and enough rope to fix the remaining section of the mountain for a summit push. We set up our tent on top of the Yellow Tower and the following morning we left camp, ready to push through the most difficult section of the climb.

We arrived above Camp 2 from where we had to move across punishingly poor snow, ice and rock to gain the upper slopes. As we traversed, we came across a climber who appeared to be sitting calmly in the snow, looking out from the mountain. It was only when we drew closer that we realised the man was buried up to his waist and was dead. This shocking sight was a stark reminder of the risk involved in what we were doing. We said a silent prayer for him and his family and later found out that he was a Canadian climber who had perished in a fall while abseiling three years earlier.

We had heard reports from previous expeditions of a snow and ice gully above Camp 2 which we thought would be our doorway to the upper slopes, providing steep but solid climbing for 200m until we reached the highest section of the mountain. But no matter where we looked, we couldn't find the snow-

97

filled gully; all we could see was a huge face looming above us with a mixture of dangerous ice and rock above a gully devoid of snow. I was still searching for the elusive channel when I heard Tony shouting. 'Well, fuck me, Falvey, have a look above your head!' About 70m directly above us were a rope and a snow picket dangling in mid-air where the snow and ice should have been: we were in the gully which was now bare rock. As we looked up, a large boulder came crashing down, barely missing us. 'We wouldn't want to hang around here too long,' I remarked, throwing a nervous glance at the dead Canadian.

We heard the rumbling of more falling rock and knew it was far too dangerous to remain in the gully. We looked around, determined to find an alternative. There was a cliff to our left, topped by massive overhanging rocks. Tony spent the next two hours scaling the face until he reached the overhang. Not far above it, on mixed ground, he grasped onto a boulder that immediately came away from the mountain and dropped straight down. I was directly underneath and, as it hurtled towards me, I closed my eyes. *This is it*, I thought, *it's over*. Then I heard the rock hitting hard against the slope just above me and bouncing outwards before continuing its downward trajectory. I was relieved, though shaken, as I made my way up to Tony. We continued fixing ropes on the most dangerous sections of the upper slopes before returning to Camp 2 to rest for the night. In our small Gore-Tex tents, perched on a very exposed section of the mountain, we dreamed of reaching the summit, which we believed was now very achievable. The next day, however, brought a different reality. We had made a lot less headway with the ropes than we thought and there was much more work to do. Exhausted after several hours of fixing, we returned to our tents at Camp 2. Mick and Ciaran joined us, also ready for a summit attempt.

Storm-trapped

That night, a ferocious storm was unleashed, trapping us in our tents for the next three days. We ate, dozed, read, wrote and told jokes but mainly laid there, silently waiting for the weather window to open and release us from claustrophobic boredom. Finally, on the third morning, the sun rose above a tranquil horizon and Tony and I hurriedly pushed up the mountain towards our ultimate objective. Mick and Ciaran followed shortly behind. It was sheer joy to be climbing again after three days of confinement. Progress during the day was slow as we had some more rope fixing to do. We didn't make it to Camp 3 and, that night, exhausted, we decided to bivvy 60m below the camp site. With our ice axes, we cut a ledge approximately 2m by 1m, about the size of a coffin, and set up home for the night, strapped to the mountain face by ropes attached to our harnesses for fear we'd fall off our exposed shelf and down the 2,000m face. Sleep was elusive as we twisted and turned, unable to keep ourselves warm.

When dawn broke, I had to smash through a solid block of ice that had formed over the opening of my bag, sealing me in like an ice mummy. The day looked good for climbing but we quickly realised that the night of exposure and freezing conditions had resulted in our sleeping bags becoming saturated with water. There was no way of drying them and we knew that if we had to stay another night on the mountain, we'd most likely get frostbite or hypothermia. After seeing the dead climber, we didn't want to take any chances and decided that, as we had enough time to make another attempt, we'd go back to Base Camp and dry our gear before heading for the summit again.

Ciaran and Mick, who had bivvied less than 50m below us in a snow cave, had avoided the worst of the cold and wet and continued up past us and along the corniced, knife-edged Mushroom Ridge that leads to Camp 3. We wished them the best; they were now en route for a summit attempt. After a tough day's climbing, they bivvied for another night in the snow, intending to go for the summit the following day. The next morning, though, Ciaran wasn't well. He had started feeling ill the day before but assumed it would pass. However, when he woke up he was so sick he knew that he couldn't continue. Tony and I had just arrived back at Base Camp when Ciaran radioed Con. It appeared from his description that he had acute mountain sickness (AMS) and descending to lower altitude was the only cure.

At this point, we discovered that Mick was still heading for the summit. This meant that Ciaran was going to have to come down on his own over an exposed and dangerously narrow ridge. At least we knew he'd have the fixed ropes to keep him safe as long as he didn't accidentally come off them. We couldn't believe that Mick had left him to descend on his own. Ciaran wasn't making an issue of it; he was saying he was fine but anyone experiencing AMS is like someone with a hangover or a heavy flu, and clear thinking is not their forte.

Con was deeply concerned. His condition had improved since the food poisoning so he started making his way up the mountain to meet Ciaran.

Miraculously, by the time Con met him, Ciaran had gotten down safely as far as Camp 1, where he was being looked after by some American climbers. All the while, Mick was making tortuously slow progress. We could see him through binoculars from Base Camp, looking like a fly on a huge white tapestry as he made his way to the summit. He finally reached the top of Ama Dablam at 5.30pm that day, 4 April 1991. After checking that Ciaran was feeling better, Con continued upwards to meet Mick, who would now descending on his own. Shea, Tony and I went out from Base Camp and escorted Ciaran back to his tent, shocked by how ill he looked. His physical appearance bore no resemblance to how he'd looked thirty-six hours earlier when we had last met him.

Two days later, Mick Murphy limped into Base Camp with Con. There was a great sense of relief that all of the team were safe and champagne and wine bottles were uncorked as we toasted what was, in fact, the only success on the mountain that year. Our team also recorded an Irish record: this was the first time ever an Irish climber had reached the summit of a mountain in the Nepalese Himalaya. Our joy was tinged with disappointment, however, because we had always said that a mountain is not worth a toe or a finger and Mick had severe frostbite. It was so bad that we feared he might lose some of his toes. Ciaran was slowly improving but we weren't sure if he would recover fully. What was beyond doubt was that neither of them could walk out of Base Camp so we had to call in a rescue helicopter the day after Mick returned.

Then the seventh storm of our expedition blew in, and we were stranded for another week at the bottom of Ama Dablam. Eventually, the helicopter was able to land and airlifted both men to Kathmandu. The storm and the wait for evacuation meant that all weather windows were closed for us to make another summit attempt.

I'd had a lot of expectations around the Ama Dablam expedition. I wanted to see if I could deal with high mountains and altitude, and I found that I could. I also wanted to clear my thoughts on who I was becoming, who I had been and which version of me was the truest one. Since I'd swapped a dream of material riches for that of climbing Everest, I'd been like someone who was between two worlds, living two disconnected lives. I had become very adept at compartmentalising the various aspects of my life, but I knew I needed more integrity in how I was living.

I'd hoped that my time in the Himalaya would provide space for the decisions I needed to make and, in an unexpected way, it did. This expedition was my first major high-altitude climb as well as being my first time in a Third World country and the experience had a profound effect on my mindset. For some reason, meeting the Nepalese and Sherpa people had a profound effect on me, while the Buddhist monks had taught me a little of their philosophy and I wanted to learn more. As I walked out the Khumbu Valley, I turned one last time to look at Ama Dablam. As I gazed at the magnificent, glistening jewel, I knew that I would return to attempt to reach its summit. In the distance at the end of the Khumbu Valley, a white plume of cloud flew like a Buddhist prayer flag from the lofty peak of Mount Everest. Nothing, I knew, was going to keep me from the goal I'd set myself on top of Carrauntoohil.

EVEREST BECKONS

Having seen Everest, I became obsessed with joining a team that was going there as soon as I could. When word came through the grapevine that some Irish climbers had secured a permit to climb the world's highest mountain in the spring of 1993, I believed I could be a contender for the national team. I suspected, however, that my chances of being chosen were slim as I was not known to the fraternity. I was still willing to take a shot and, remembering my grandmother's words – *if you don't ask, you won't get* – I asked and was told that the selection had been finalised. I was disappointed, but I wasn't going to give up on my dream. Being part of the national team wasn't to be, but I knew that all I needed to do was keep faith and my dream would come true.

As luck would have it, while on a climbing weekend in Scotland a few months later, I met English climber Mark Miller in a bar in Glencoe. I had known him from meeting on previous climbs in Scotland over the years and we had become quite friendly. Mark had an enthusiastic personality and a love of big mountains and I immediately connected with his passion. We talked about our recent expeditions and Mark asked me what was next in my sights. I told him I wanted to climb Everest but was without a team. He told me that, coincidentally, he had just received a climbing permit for Everest for autumn 1993 through his new extreme adventure company, Out There Trekking (OTT), and that he was putting a group of top international climbers together. Mark would be organising the logistics for climbers who had the experience to self-lead on the mountain. He made it clear this would not be a guided expedition but one where the leader co-ordinated everything and supplied a 'backbone' of good climbers to help push the route. *This sounds like an exact fit for me*, I thought; I soaked up every word he said.

The following day we went climbing together and I expressed an interest in becoming part of the expedition. For me, the most important thing was that this would be a team of self-sufficient mountaineers and not a guided expedition. Mark said yes straight away. Outside of my climbing skills, he thought that my social skills would benefit the group. I had a strong, instinctive feeling that this was meant to be and returned home delighted that I was now on the road to making my Everest goal a reality.

Over the next few months, I kept up correspondence with Mark and Andy Broom, his partner in the adventure company, asking questions about the logistics of the expedition and the experience of the other team members. I was aware that I was going to be part of a team that I didn't know, climbing on one of the most dangerous mountains in the world. I knew this expedition would attract a lot of experienced, ego-driven climbers who didn't know me and who wouldn't give a shit if I got in trouble because I wasn't good enough. I understood that the rules of engagement weren't going to be the same as if I'd been with a team of people I'd be climbing with for years, and I had a responsibility to minimise the risks for myself.

I wanted to know the strategy that was being put in place regarding how people would get a chance at a summit attempt and Mark assured me that the climbers chosen would be those who adapted best to conditions on the mountain. They would be picked by consensus of the entire group; there was no question that they would necessarily be the most experienced climbers. I was happy with this approach, knowing that if I performed well, it would give me, as a less experienced high-altitude climber, a chance of going for the summit.

In Mark, who was thirty-one years of age, I had found a leader I could trust and whose company I enjoyed. Satisfied with the approach he and Andy were taking, I got on with my training. Then, on 26 September 1992, the unthinkable happened when Mark, along with seventy-one others, was tragically killed on a

Pakistan International Airlines plane that crashed into a mountain just before landing in Kathmandu. He had been on his way to an expedition to Makalu and to do a reconnaissance for our Everest expedition. Everyone who knew him was in shock; it was hard to think that such a young and talented friend had been cut down in the prime of his life.

The following month, Mark's business partner Andy contacted all the team members and informed us that the expedition would go ahead, in Mark's memory. I now more than ever wanted to summit Everest in honour of my dead friend. A new expedition leader had been appointed; I didn't know Jon Tinker, but when I looked up his credentials I was happy to continue with him as leader.

In December, Andy organised a boot camp in the Peak District in England. This would give team members a chance to meet Jon and would give Andy a chance to update us on the progress of the expedition. I asked him if I could bring my wife along, explaining that I wanted her to have a chance to meet up with the organisers and other team members. I felt it might ease some of her concerns if she met up with the team I would be part of. Andy agreed, and I was delighted that Marie joined me at the boot camp as I really wanted her to know that the team I was joining was professional and supportive of families, as well as the climbers themselves.

Eight members of the team turned up in Sheffield, with some bringing their partners. As we got to know Jon, it became clear that he had a very different personality to Mark; he was quiet and serious and didn't socialise easily. He also had a different leadership style and when it came to what he expected from team members, he didn't mince his words. He was direct and factual and laid down the rules of engagement for the expedition, and I liked that about him. We were informed that we had to sign a disclaimer that we accepted the risks and that, if we died, no team member would be held responsible. When fully exposed to the reality of the risks that lay ahead, Marie was pretty shocked but she was also reassured by the fact that there was a support system and contact person in place for her and all the other families so that they could check in with our progress throughout the expedition.

Building a team

Andy and Jon went through the CVs of all those who had signed up for the expedition. The team read like a Who's Who of the mountaineering world. This was the premier league of climbing and I wondered what I had let myself in for. Maciej Berbeka from Poland was one of the best and strongest mountaineers in the world at the time. He had achieved first winter ascents of Cho Oyu and Manaslu, as well as having a new route on Annapurna's south face under his belt. He had also been on K2 and Nanga Parbat, each time in winter. George Kotov, one of Russia's elite mountaineers, was a speed climber who had made first winter ascents of two 7,000m peaks in the Pamirs. Jon and Brigitte Muir were two of Australia's most prolific adventurers. Jon, who had reached the summit of Everest in 1988 via the south side, was coming along with his wife in the hope that they could make the first ascent by a couple from the north side.

Norman Croucher, an inspirational double amputee who championed disability and rehabilitation, had climbed many high mountains in the Alps and the Himalaya. There were three professional French climbers who had climbed all the great north faces of the European Alps, along with two of Finland's finest climbers and some other talented English climbers who had achieved great success around the world. I was happy to see that Ang Rita from our Ama Dablam expedition had been chosen as sirdar to organise all the logistics in Nepal and to be our link between the government officials in Nepal and Tibet. I knew he would be meticulous, not just in his organisation of equipment but also in his choice of the four Sherpa climbers who would supplement our team. I had built up a great relationship with him and knew he was someone I could trust and who would have my back.

Also joining our climbing team would be an independent four-man team that was carrying out advance research on a NASA/Guinness Research Foundation-sponsored project that involved a skydive from 40,000m. Nish Bruce was planning to attempt to break the World Record for the highest jump from the edge of space, and would be testing equipment along with team members Harry Taylor, Brian Tilly and scientist and astronaut Dr Karl Henize.

Brian Tilly had been an active member in the Special Forces while Nish and Harry had been members of B Squadron 22 SAS Special Forces wing that was involved in active duty in Northern Ireland in covert counter-terrorist operations against the Provisional IRA. Both Harry and Nish were regarded as among the Special Forces' most talented climbers and had been involved in successful ascents of major mountains throughout the world. Knowing my republican views on Irish unity, Jon Tinker took me aside and had a quiet talk about his concerns regarding any possible rows that might erupt when we were on expedition due to the opposing views that the men and I might hold. I assured him there was nothing to worry about.

A further boot camp was held in Scotland in March 1993. Twelve of our team stayed in a rented house and we spent ten days climbing, socialising, talking and seeing how we got on together. Each day, a hard route was chosen for us to tackle. I was amazed at the quality of people's climbing and what surprised me even more was that I was able to match their skills. I struck up a good rapport with those present, especially George Kotov and Maciej Berbeka. The meeting also gave me a chance to rekindle my friendship with Ang Rita, who had travelled from Nepal to meet with the team. It was only after this boot camp, when I finally felt I had the confidence needed to climb Everest, that I confirmed publicly I was joining the 1993 International Everest Expedition.

Back at home, I built a support team to help me prepare for the trip. Con and the lads in Kerry helped me with my training and pushed me to my limits physically. I gave public talks on my climbs as part of a fundraising drive and developed a core of loyal supporters. At one talk, I met Joe O'Leary, a schoolteacher and fellow Corkman who was eager to be part of my team at home. He was a very keen hillwalker and we quickly became close friends. In fact, Joe became liaison officer in Ireland on all of my future expeditions.

While I was training in Scotland, the Irish Everest team flew out to Nepal. Just over ten weeks later, on 27 May 1993, expedition leader Dawson Stelfox reached the summit. It was a great moment for mountaineering on the island of Ireland and I listened to and read every media report I could get my hands on. When the team returned home, I rang Dawson to congratulate him on his and the team's outstanding achievement. I asked about the route he had taken, as it was the same one I intended to climb. He was very forthcoming with details and I was really appreciative of his knowledge. This was the first Irish team to climb Everest and Dawson was the first Irish person to stand on the summit of the world's highest mountain. As he held dual nationality, he also claimed the accolade of becoming the first Briton to climb Everest via the north-northeast ridge.

One in four

When I decided to climb Mount Everest, the statistics were that the risk of dying was one in four. In total, 395 people had reached the summit while 112 people had died on the mountain, a statistic that I'd have been a fool to ignore. Many of my family and friends advised me against attempting to undertake the climb, worried that I might die. But I had faith in my ability; I had done the training, I had acquired the skills and knew that I was ready.

But it wasn't just my body that had to be trained for the climb; I also had to ensure that I had the right mindset for such a hazardous undertaking. To ensure that fear didn't undermine my focus, I read every account of every ascent of Everest that I could get my hands on. I spoke to people who had already summited the mountain and learned about the circumstances in which those who hadn't made it back down had died. I found out the exact location of accidents and the reasons why these accidents happened. By staying focused on my goal, by being informed and prepared, by knowing the risks involved and, most importantly, by having faith in myself, I conquered my fears. If one in four died, then three out of four would survive, and I was going to do everything in my power to ensure that I was one of those.

EVEREST (NORTH SIDE) 1993

Leaving Cork Airport on the first leg of my journey to Nepal felt simultaneously like a celebration and a wake with family and a few friends who'd come to see me off. They were there to support me even though they were all anxious about what lay ahead. The image of my sons' innocent faces looking up at me made me even more determined to return safely. My mother – always a woman of great faith – gave me a holy medal of the Sacred Heart. 'May God protect you,' she said as she put it around my neck. As I went through the departure gate, everyone was crying – tears of joy, tears of fear, tears of love – and I felt a keen awareness that this could be the last time I would ever see them if things went wrong.

Once we were airborne, all anxiety and doubt had to be left behind. There were many things that could go wrong, but I knew I had done everything I possibly could to prepare myself and now I needed to keep a positive mindset. I thought of Mallory and Irvine, those early explorers who lost their lives on Everest and whose legacy is still shrouded in mystery, with no one knowing if they were, in fact, the first people to set foot on its summit. Since their expedition in 1924, many more had come to the mountain and returned to tell the tale and I kept thoughts of them to the forefront of my mind. As the plane touched down at Tribhuvan International Airport in Kathmandu, I knew there was no turning back.

I had flown to Nepal a week earlier than the rest of the team in order to get some acclimatisation time before the expedition began. I was collected from the airport by Tsiring Bhim Bhandur, a young Nepalese Sherpa I'd first met two years earlier on our Ama Dablam trip. He had come back to Ireland with us and had worked for me in Cork until the early summer of 1993 when he returned home. Our plan was to do some hiking in Langtang, a region to the north of Kathmandu. We also visited the site where the plane in which Mark Miller had been a passenger had crashed. While there, I paid my respects to the memory of the young man whose passion to climb Everest mirrored my own.

On our return to Kathmandu, I made my way to the hotel where our team was staying. A large, noisy group of over twenty people was gathered in the foyer. I had already climbed with seven of them and introduced myself to the rest. During the four days it took to get all of our gear cleared from customs, I got to know the rest of my team-mates along with climbers from other expeditions, all of whom gathered in the Thamel area of the city. I also re-acquainted myself with Kathmandu, visiting some monasteries and praying with Buddhist monks for protection while on the mountain.

After our equipment was cleared, checked and accounted for, we loaded it up and set off in a convoy of trucks and four-wheel drives on the Araniko Highway out of Kathmandu and headed for the Chinese-controlled Tibetan border. Even in good weather, this is regarded as one of the most dangerous roads in Nepal because of its incredibly steep slopes where there are regular landslides and bus plunges. We were on the road in the middle of one of the worst monsoons to hit the country in eighty years, with reports stating that over 4,000 people had perished due to flooding, rockfalls and landslides. As we inched our way onwards, we wondered if we'd survive the trip.

After an exhausting and nail-biting journey, we turned off the highway and decamped to Tatopani to do a ten-day acclimatisation trek. This turned out to be one of the most uncomfortable, agonising treks I'd ever done. It rained non-stop for the duration and we had to deal not alone with dangerous landslides but also with leeches that crawled up our legs and sucked our blood like vampires. They were a nightmare and some nights we got no sleep as they invaded our tents and crawled on our bodies. The only way to detach them from our flesh was to burn them off or to pour salt on them, which caused them to release their tentacles. One found its way up to my scrotum where it sucked so much blood it grew to the size of my thumb; getting rid of it proved quite a challenge. Despite the discomforts, our band of weary adventurers took it all in our stride as we trekked to over 5,500m and prepared our bodies for the climb ahead.

Road to Hell

After ten sodden days we got back on the Araniko Highway and finally crossed the Friendship Bridge that spans the Sun Kosi River linking Kodari in Nepal and Zhangmu in Tibet. After the friendliness of the Nepalese, the Chinese guards' presence was abrupt and hostile. This desolate border town, clinging to the side of a gorge, was a chaotic collection of tin shacks, wooden huts, shops, brothels and border-related offices. We had to spend a few days here sorting out our papers and trying not to piss off the officials, who looked as if the only time they were happy was when someone was pissing them off. It was the most godforsaken place I'd ever been and it was easy to see why groups of climbers looking for official sanction to enter Tibet provided a diversion for the bored guards.

The relief we felt at leaving Zhangmu was replaced by white knuckles and ice-cold fear as we faced into what is rightly known as the 'Road to Hell'. Reputed to be the most dangerous road in the world, this near 40km stretch between Zhangmu and Nyalam is notorious for accidents and fatalities. We were silent as our convoy made its way up the 6m-wide dirt track that was cut from the mountain and fell off for hundreds of metres to one side into the deep Sun Kosi gorge below. The other side of the road was no less dangerous as landslides made their way down the mountain and onto the road. Because of the heavy rains, all the earth was moving; at one point, a landslide passed just in front of our truck, hauling entire houses and some people in its dirty brown belly. We were helpless and could only watch in shock at what was unfolding before our eyes. On four occasions, the road became impassable and we had to unload all our gear, which the porters then carried over the debris to vehicles that were trapped on the other side of the blockade. Once the expedition members made their way across, the drivers turned the trucks and we were able to continue our journey.

We finally reached Nyalam, a one-street hovel of a village with Chinese propaganda blasting over a Tannoy system at the downtrodden Tibetan inhabitants. Chinese soldiers and guards were everywhere in a country that has been under siege since the 1950s when China settled millions of its own people among the indigenous Tibetans, in effect bastardising the race and making them subservient.

It was a relief to get out of Nyalam and to finally get onto the flat, desert terrain of the enormous Tibetan plateau – the highest in the world – from where we could see the misty peaks of some of the world's biggest mountains in the distance. Beyond the plateau, we reached the foothills of Everest's north side and overnighted at 4,390m in Tingri village before continuing on a 70km dirt track through the Ra-Chu valley.

Seven hours after crossing the Lamna La Pass we arrived at Rongbuk, the highest Buddhist monastery in the world at an altitude of just over 4,980m above sea level. The monastery stands like a solemn sentinel at the gateway to Everest's north face. We were hoping to get a clear view of Everest, but the bad weather ensured our objective was still covered in a shroud of cloud. Prayer flags added colour to the bleak, majestic landscape and acted as a reminder that there was much to be prayed for at this altitude.

Since the 1920s, climbers have visited the monastery, mainly seeking the monks' blessing before commencing their expedition. That was also our intention when we met the holy men and participated in the traditional prayer ceremony requesting protection before we started our climb. We asked the monks to perform another puja for us at Base Camp so that we could again seek safe passage as we made our way up the mountain known to Tibetans as Chomolungma.

Base Camp Tibet

Having received the monks' blessing, our caravan of vehicles travelled the final 8km to the East Rongbuk Glacier where Base Camp was located. Here, on a flat expanse of frozen and snow-covered mud, we unpacked and set up what would be our home for the next two months in the company of several other groups, including teams from China, Korea, Spain, Greece and India. A part of the 5,000km Himalayan range, itself home to 150 of the highest peaks in the world, and standing at 8,848m – 9km up in the sky at a height that jet planes fly – Everest demands respect. As we settled into life at Base Camp and gazed upwards at the mountain's standard bathroom-size summit, we had time to think about the dangers we would encounter over the coming months.

Every expedition can expect to deal with avalanches, rockfalls, landslides, crevasses, jet-stream winds, storms, −40° temperatures and the dreaded Death Zone – that place above 8,000m where humans' ability to survive is severely compromised and where the human body literally starts to die because of oxygen intake deficit. If we were very unlucky, we would have to deal with pulmonary oedema, cerebral oedema or thrombosis – all potential killers. But we were ready for what lay ahead and used all potential dangers to sharpen our focus on staying safe and alive.

My tent partner for the expedition was Maciej Berbeka. As well as being one of the world's top high-altitude climbers, he was one of the most gentle and humble people I'd ever met and we became lifelong friends. Maciej was three years older than me and mentored me in all he knew. He told me how I should pace myself at high altitude, explaining that those who rush and move beyond their limits nearly always get altitude sickness. I also formed a strong bond with the whippet-thin, chain-smoking, vodka-drinking Russian, George Kotov, who was around the same age as Maciej. In the following weeks, the three of us spent a lot of time on the mountain together, setting up camps and fixing ropes on the upper reaches of Everest.

Our hopes for good weather disappeared in the heavy snowfall which kept us Base Camp-bound for a week, playing havoc with our schedule. We could do little but sit and wait for the weather to improve. This time was not fruitless, however, as I was always happy to socialise and these days gave me a chance to get to know my team-mates better. We were a motley group of twenty-three individuals from all corners of the world and all walks of life. There were a lot of strong personalities with firmly held opinions that ensured very lively discussions on diverse issues, from climbing to the environment, politics, religion and life in general. These talks stirred a longing in me to learn more about other races and cultures. What was remarkable was that no matter how much our backgrounds and beliefs diverged, we all wanted to climb Everest and all differences faded in the light of that shared goal.

The push begins

I woke suddenly one morning, four days after arriving at Base Camp, sensing something was different. The air felt clear and bright sunlight penetrated the fabric of my tent. I dressed hurriedly and emerged to join the others who had also come outside to check the break in the weather. As I gazed skywards, I could see Everest in all its majesty for the first time. I was mesmerised more by the fact that I was standing there, looking at the mountain, than by the actual mountain itself. It didn't look half as dangerous as I'd expected; in fact, I had been a lot more awed when I first saw Ama Dablam. I felt that, as long as I didn't have serious problems with altitude, this climb would be doable for me. That said, I knew the risks, and they were significant. I knew that Everest's power was greater than mine and that I had to remember that; complacency and overconfidence had no place on this mountain.

The good weather meant that we could start stocking the camps. We divided into three groups. I was with George, Maciej, Jon and Brigitte Muir, Jon Tinker and Thierry Reinhard, a French climber. Our group, along with three Sherpas and thirty loaded yaks, led the way to ABC at 6,400m. We were sluggish after the enforced break at Base Camp and it took us three days to cover 22.5km. Over the following days, the remainder of the team arrived, as well as a further sixty yaks laden with gear and food. Then the snow returned with a vengeance and we were again tent-bound, although this time at a higher altitude. Five of our team experienced some difficulties and returned to Base Camp to recover for a few days. Immobilised by the weather, the rest of us had to dig deep into our skills of patience and forbearance. Another week passed before, finally, the weather cleared. The decision was immediate – the push towards the top would begin as quickly as we could pack our rucksacks.

It was punishingly hard work pushing the route through from ABC to Camp 1 at 7,060m on the infamous North Col. Jon again split us into three groups, with the team I was on being first to lead out and fix the ropes on the dangerous headwall that leads to the Col. This section of the climb is avalanche prone and is the region where the highest death toll is recorded. We cautiously pushed through, ever conscious of the unstable snow. Each glance upwards was accompanied by thoughts of thousands of tons of snow suddenly deciding to follow the laws of gravity and come thundering down and, most likely, wipe us out. A slip here without being fixed to a rope and you would become a human toboggan on an endless death ride.

Having run the gauntlet of this risky section, we were elated to arrive safely at the North Col. We were now firmly in the upper reaches of Everest. From here, weather permitting, the top of the mountain could be reached with the establishment of two further camps – one at 7,900m and the final camp at 8,300m. Over the next five weeks we would make switchback climbs to these camps to allow us to get fully acclimatised for the summit attempts. We pitched our tents and rested for the night before descending all the way to Base Camp to recover from our efforts at altitude.

Battered on Everest

While I rested with my team-mates at Base Camp, other members of the team were stocking Camp 1. After a few days' well-earned rest we were on the move again but were soon stopped in our tracks by the afternoon's heavy snowfall. It was only after our fifth visit to Camp 1 that there was a sufficient break in the weather for Maciej, George and me to move further upwards and establish Camp 2 at 7,900m on the north ridge, a vast snow-covered rock slope. As we travelled slowly and cautiously over the treacherous mixed ground there were times when I felt that getting to 7,900m was beyond my capability. I gasped for breath in the thin air and prayed that I would not slip and that an avalanche or rock fall wouldn't descend on us.

We pushed on and after eight brutal hours we finally arrived at the ridge where we established Camp 2, setting up two tents facing each other on a small, exposed platform. We strapped our thin skin of manmade material to the rock face and hoped that the wind would not blow us off the mountain during a restless and bitterly cold night.

The next morning we exited our tents in piss-poor conditions with none of us feeling happy as we climbed steeper ground and plodded through deep snow. Then, after only an hour out and a 110m height gain, all three of us stopped, struck by an eerie feeling; it was as if we were picking up on some instinctive message that was warning us to turn back. We decided to take heed and get the hell down from our high point of just over 8,000m. Our slow but steady drop to ABC took the entire day and shortly after we arrived there, the entire area between 7,538m and 8,153m on the mountain avalanched. Chomolungma had vented her power and destroyed our previous week's work. Camp 2 was obliterated and our tents, sleeping bags and gear were buried under the massive debris. However, Jon had a really good relay system in operation and, the following day, the next team, who were stationed at Camp 1, set off to re-establish the second camp.

After long hours of climbing and considerable effort, Camp 2 was erected and stocked but the work was no sooner done than more bad luck arrived. Jet-stream winds, descending to 7,900m at over 100mph, ripped the tents at Camp 2 from their moorings and swept them off the slope like kites. Luckily, there was nobody in them. We were really getting a battering but were not yet willing to give up. For five weeks in total, we struggled to gain a foothold at Camp 3. Chomolungma, it seemed, was not going to make our ascent easy.

Death on the mountain

By 3 October, and over forty days on expedition, it was time to reassess the situation. So many days had been lost to heavy snowfall and storms and now the weather window was closing. Everyone was called back to ABC where we had a strategy meeting. We knew that tough decisions had to be made, and it was agreed that not all the team would be able to make a summit attempt. Jon set down the criteria for choosing who would make the first attempts. These included the ability to carry a heavy pack up to Camp 1 and the ability to sleep at Camp 2 without oxygen. There was a preference for team members who had already been at 8,000m in the previous weeks. The general consensus of all, including Jon Tinker, was that the first to go for the summit would be Maciej and Lhakpa Nura Sherpa, followed by George and me with Babu Chiri Sherpa, known to all as Ang Babu.

Outside of Lhakpa and Ang Babu, Maciej, George and I were the only ones who had slept at 8,000m. If we failed in our attempts, the others would go into a relay system for a shot at the summit until the weather window closed. George made the decision to wait for the next group of climbers to make his summit attempt, which meant that I, along with Ang Babu, would be going directly after Maciej and Lhakpa. The moment had come and I knew I was ready for the challenge.

That following day, at ABC, as I packed for my summit attempt, I noticed a change in Karl Henize's demeanour. His movements were slow and ponderous and his breathing was shallow. He didn't look well and when I asked him if he was okay he replied that he was just a little tired. The next morning, 4 October, I was up early and preparing to leave ABC when I met Karl again. He really looked shagged; he was staggering and his chest was heaving as he struggled for breath, so I got a chair for him to sit on. After a while we walked to the mess tent where I told Jon about what I had seen. He was sure that Karl had pulmonary oedema. As we discussed the best course of action, all thoughts of going for the summit disappeared with the shock of knowing that a colleague might die. However, Jon said he believed that Karl would be alright and that I should head for the North Col.

I couldn't stop thinking about Karl as I set off on my own towards Camp 1. When I arrived there, I met with Norman Croucher and the two Finnish climbers. We called ABC to let them know our location and to find out how Karl was doing. The news was bad. His condition had deteriorated and there was now a full-scale rescue taking place to get him to Base Camp, a two-day trek away. He had been placed in a Gamow bag and was on oxygen to help him breathe. We knew this was not good and all of us at Camp 2 made the decision to postpone our summit attempt and descend to help in the evacuation effort. Having been in mountain rescue, I knew all hands would be needed to ensure a speedy descent to Base Camp.

The following morning, 5 October, I caught up with the rescue party at about 5am at our mid camp at 5,700m on the East Rongbuk Glacier, only to find that Karl had died in his sleep at 1am. Everyone was devastated; the astronaut was liked by all who'd met him and his death felt like a body blow. Another name was added to the list of men and women who'd lost their lives on this mountain.

Karl had stated that if he died on Everest he wanted to remain there, so, in a solemn and surreal ceremony, we buried our friend in a crevasse, with extracts from the Bible read at the icy tomb on which we placed his NASA cap. It was hard to believe that someone who had flown into outer space on the space shuttle Challenger in 1985 had lost his life while carrying out a scientific experiment at 6,400m.

Summit-bound

When we returned to ABC, the mood was sombre. Jon called a meeting and it was agreed that we'd go ahead with our summit attempt. On 7 October, after one day's rest, eleven of our team pushed up to Camp 1, all with summit ambitions on what would be our last push. The first teams had already been picked – Maciej and Lhakpa followed by Ang Babu and me. We would also fix the ropes and be followed by George, Jon and Brigitte Muir, and Harry and Pavo, the two Fins. On the morning of 8 October, Maciej decided he would go from Camp 1 at 7,000m straight up to establish Camp 3 at 8,300m as he and Lhakpa were feeling very strong. They would be accompanied by Lama Sherpa, one of the expedition's high-altitude staff, as a load carrier as far as Camp 3. The plan was that the rest of us would go to Camp 2 at 7,900m and rest until the following day when Ang Babu and I would make our way to Camp 3 in advance of our summit attempt. Jon, as leader, was to co-ordinate everything from Camp 1. Then, out of the blue, he decided that he would push up to Camp 2 with the team.

It was clear and bitterly cold as a large group of us set off before dawn and the climbing was a physical test of our endurance. That evening, Jon approached me and said that he wanted to continue up next day with Ang Babu to be in place to support Maciej and Lhakpa on their return from the summit. I agreed without thinking, happy just to be in place and feeling strong enough for the next summit attempt, for which I would now partner up with George. The plan was that we would catch up with Ang Baba on our ascent while Jon would descend with Maciej and Lhakpa on their journey down the mountain. On 9 October, Maciej and Lhakpa reached the summit of Everest, having forged a new route from the north ridge which shaved a few hours off the climb. I was delighted for the team, and especially for Maciej, who had become a close friend.

Waiting in vain

Jon and Ang Babu left early that day to wait at Camp 3 in support of our summiteers. At Camp 2, George and I awaited further instructions from Jon as to when we should head up to the next camp, but none came. On their descent, the new summiteers called to our tent. In the course of our conversation, they said that Jon was going for the summit, taking the slot I was meant to have. We couldn't believe it. As he was the leader, there was very little we could do. On 10 October, he and Ang Babu reached the summit. That day, those of us who were at Camp 2 descended to Camp 1 and the following day we arrived at ABC where we waited for the summiteers to return.

As we awaited their arrival, there was disquiet among the members of the team – me included – that I had effectively been denied a summit attempt by Jon Tinker. It had always been my clear understanding that George Kotov or I, along with Ang Babu, would be the climbers following Maciej and Lhakpa, and this is what everybody else understood too. When I challenged Jon on the issue, he broke down and cried, knowing that he had broken his promise. He apologised to me and the team for what he had done. Jon had failed twice previously to reach Everest's summit and explained that he allowed his summit ambition to override the earlier team decision regarding the order of climbers making a summit attempt.

There was no more time to go up the mountain again; the weather window had closed and the yaks were due at ABC on 14 October to collect all our gear. Jon said he was planning a return trip and asked if I would consider joining the team. My anger subsided as I thought about the opportunity of another chance at the summit. After seventy days pushing my body to its limits, I realised that I might not have gotten to the top of Everest this time anyway and, despite what had happened, I still liked Jon. I understood that, next time round, he would have no personal summit agenda, so I shook his hand and said I'd be back.

The weeks I'd spent on the mountain had been a life-changing, eye-opening, mind-exploding experience for me. I'd climbed to over 8,000m, into the Death Zone; I'd been part of a successful expedition; I'd witnessed huge avalanches and the horrific effects of high-altitude sickness; I'd sat out weeks of bad weather in tiny tents tied to the mountain and I'd met with fascinating people from all over the world. Not bad, I thought, for a dreamer from Cork. There was no doubt in my mind that this was the life I wanted.

PART THREE

THE SEVEN SUMMITS

A MAGICAL WORLD UNFOLDS

As I departed from the airport in Kathmandu after my 1993 Everest bid, the seeds of a plan had already taken hold in my mind: I would climb the Seven Summits – the highest points of each of the seven continents. This multi-climb expedition in Nepal, Antarctica, Russia, Argentina, Tanzania, Alaska and Australia would be my vehicle to travel the world as an adventurer. I was fascinated by the stories I'd heard from other climbers about their home countries and the places they'd travelled to during their adventures. Listening to them was like a geography, history and sociology class all rolled into one. I had flunked most subjects at school but now I was learning in a way that set my brain on fire.

Before I'd started climbing, my head had been firmly stuck in bricks and mortar and spreadsheets; I was ignorant of the wonders of the world but now that I had tasted its diversity, I wanted to expand my mind and experience as much as possible.

My family accepted that, for me, not reaching Everest's summit was like a job half done and that I would be going back. What they didn't know, until I started talking about the Seven Summits, was that I wanted to become a full-time adventurer. After the Everest trip, I was absolutely convinced that I would never again sacrifice my life to work, something I had done for as long as I could remember.

For those closest to me, this attitude change was hard to accept. I was born into a working-class family where we got up early and worked hard. I had been very happy to follow that tradition but now, here I was, telling them I was going to be a full-time adventurer. I was talking about living life to the full and quoting the Buddhist monks who said, 'Life is not a rehearsal; it's a performance'. They thought I'd lost the plot altogether. 'Cop yourself on' was a refrain I got used to hearing. My father, ever the conciliatory one, said, 'Son, you have huge talent, why don't you bring it back to business?'. They all hoped, and assumed, that I'd get over my delirium in time, but I had no intention of rebuilding the walls of security and predictability that my newfound life had demolished in such a short time. For me, there was no going back.

DENALI 1994
NORTH AMERICA

I've always believed that when you put your wishes out into the wider world, you get the help and support you need. And so it happened that, shortly after I started talking about the Seven Summits, I got a call from Mick Murphy, our Ama Dablam summiteer. He was heading to Alaska to climb Denali, also known as Mount McKinley, and invited me to join the team. I said yes straight away; North America's highest mountain at 6,190m was going to be the first of my Seven Summits.

Throughout the next seven months, I kept my head down, working at my business and training as hard as I could, climbing every weekend in Kerry and continuing as a member of mountain rescue. The plan was to fly to Anchorage in June 1994 with the team, which included Murphy as leader, Corkonians Con Collins, Phil O'Flynn, Finbarr Desmond, Kate Pollock and Barry Keane, Northern Irelanders Clive Roberts and Garth Pearson, and me. Mick arranged all the logistics and everyone paid for their own trip.

On 1 June, we flew to Anchorage. Alaska was Last Frontier country and I couldn't wait to see it. I had done quite a bit of reading about its history, and during our time in the capital I went to the natural history museum where I saw a polar bear for the first time in my life. It was about 3m in height and I was blown away by the majesty of the animal. Another must-see in the city was Chilkoot Charlie's Bar, a stop-off point for most climbers on the way to

Denali. We met hard men on their way back from the Klondike, and hunters and trappers in from the outback and looking for some human contact. After a couple of days exploring and relaxing, we loaded our gear into a crocked-out bus and drove to the wild, timber shack-filled town of Talkeetna, about 120km north of Anchorage.

We were booked in for a few days' stay at the bunkhouse of pilot Doug Geeting, a Californian who'd settled in Alaska. He made his living providing accommodation for adventurers and workers and flying them to the most inaccessible parts of the region. We didn't have any problems with his aviation skills, but the bunkhouse was as rough as I'd ever seen. Con Collins and I decided it wasn't for us and booked into a log cabin near the river's edge. The other team members visited us regularly; they weren't too gone on the bunkhouse either, it seemed. Mosquitoes were the only blight in what was otherwise an idyllic setting where we had a fantastic few days fishing, white-water rafting and checking out the local wildlife.

We were well chilled when Doug flew the team in one of his Cessna 185s to Denali Base Camp, located at 2,194m on the Kahiltna Glacier, the longest glacier in the world. During the one-hour flight, the lushness of the Alaskan Tundra was replaced by the stunning rock- and ice-filled gorges of the Alaska Range. Flying so deep into mountainous, snow-covered terrain had a magical feel to it and it was thrilling to land on a white runway. Denali is one of the only places outside the Poles where your expedition starts the minute you get out of the plane, so once we'd collected our gear and tied it to our sleds, we said goodbye to Doug and skied off.

A deceptive calm

Long views across the Kahiltna Glacier showed stunning peaks protruding out of the glistening snow during almost twenty-four hours of sunlight. However, we weren't duped for a moment by the serenity of the scene before us. We knew Denali's reputation for sudden, raging winds and massive temperature fluctuations. Just before we'd left Talkeetna, we had heard about two Korean climbers who had frozen to death days earlier while they were climbing an ice route to 4,572m. Apparently they didn't have proper gear or provisions. Later, some American climbers we got to know came across a lone Ukrainian halfway up Denali suffering from exhaustion and over-exposure. He was wearing a construction site hard hat and had little other gear. Luckily for him, the Americans took him into their care and gave him shelter and hot drinks in their tents until a rescue helicopter could safely land and pick him up five days later when the winds calmed. Two other climbers fell down a steep slope while attempting a traverse at 5,181m. The woman died, while her partner lost all his fingers due to frostbite. All these incidents reminded us that we had to be ever-vigilant.

We had decided to climb via the West Buttress Route which, depending on the weather, would take us around twenty days. But first of all we had to set up our tents and say hello to the others teams at Base Camp. I loved chatting and was very adept at breaking the ice, usually by telling a story or singing a song. For me, being in places like this was all about getting to hear stories from the people I met. While climbing and reaching a certain point on the Earth's surface was the goal, meeting new people was what brought joy to the journey. It was my first time in a land where it was as bright going to bed as it was getting up, but physical tiredness after our first day's trek ensured the light didn't keep me from sleep.

The next morning we got ready to head up Denali, though – oddly – the first steps of the climb are a descent down Heartbreak Hill, aptly named because there are few who don't feel heartbreak at the end of a twenty-day climb when, totally exhausted, they have to dig deep to climb up this hill. I was pulling a sled over snow and crevasse-ridden terrain for the first time in my life and it was excruciating. The team was tightly roped together in case anyone fell into the giant ravines and it took several hours before we got a good flow to our system but, eventually, we started gaining ground. With Heartbreak Hill behind us, we started upwards on the first of many steep, crevassed rises. We slogged through unforgiving terrain until, six hours later, we reached the basin area at 2,346m, just below Ski Hill, where we set up Camp 1. There we unloaded our sleds and headed down to Base Camp again, hungry and in need of a good night's rest.

Although Mick Murphy had organised the logistics and was the de facto leader, decision-making was by consensus. We split into smaller groups and Con Collins and I quickly formed a pairing. Con was super-fit and I liked his determination. We immediately devised our own approach to climbing the mountain. We decided we'd get up very early, sometimes just after midnight, because the ice was harder then and it made it a bit easier to move while pulling our sleds. The others mostly got up around 6am and put in their day's pulling then. Because I was making a film of our climb, Con and I had extra gear, including solar panels and cameras, and all that additional stuff necessitated an extra carry to each camp. For the next week, we went up and down the mountain, setting up Camps 2, 3 and 4, and dropping down each night to the previously set-up camp. The slog was relentless but the ascending and descending helped with our acclimatisation. At 4,330m, we could pull our sleds no further and left them behind us, for which we were both very thankful. My back had often felt as if it would snap in two from the effort of pulling and hauling.

Weather window closes

We set up Camp 4 at 4,330m in an area known as the Ice Bowl. Then we climbed a further 550m up to the ridge line at 4,880m to acclimatise before returning to camp. When we got back, the others had arrived and it was agreed that we would rest there for a few days before ascending any further. Then, about 3pm, we got a call from the park ranger who was stationed in a hut at Base Camp for the duration of the climbing season. He said there was a storm coming in within the next forty-eight hours and the bad weather could last several days or weeks, he couldn't say which. It was hard to believe; we had come so far and were badly in need of rest and now we had only a forty-eight-hour weather window.

We discussed the risk involved before agreeing that the strongest would go for the summit immediately. Con, Mick, Finbarr and I were confident that we were fit enough to move quickly to the top and down again within the two-day period, although the danger of not being fully acclimatised played on our minds. We were very focused as we prepared for this unexpected challenge. As we worked quietly, we overheard a conversation between the American climbers in a nearby tent. 'Do you think the Irish guys are still back in Chilkoot Charlie's, knocking back beers?' one of them asked. We'd met them in the bar in Anchorage where they'd been impressed by our partying abilities. Not so much by our climbing, it seemed, although, subsequently, they didn't make it to the summit.

Our four-man team embarked up the mountain at 9am on 13 June, ten days after we'd set foot on the Kahiltna Glacier. Our plan was to make a single push to the summit, 1,860m above us. We encountered some incredibly exposed and steep climbing at the Crow's Nest along the final section of the west buttress, but we were satisfied with our progress. Then, out of the blue, there was an unmerciful clap of thunder. We looked around and our eyes riveted onto a vast bank of snow below us that had avalanched and fallen over the sheer, western side of the mountain. Sobered by the sight, we set up camp and rehydrated for a few hours. At 6am, we were on our upward journey again on a rising traverse to the 5,547m Denali Pass. Progress was slow and hard and all four of us suffered from significant loss of body temperature. Finbarr said he felt very unwell so he and Mick decided to rest while Con and I forged ahead.

The race is on

On the ridge, the atmosphere became even colder and harder to tolerate but then we saw the clouds gathering. That helped us focus on speeding up and getting to the summit: the race was on. We put our heads down and pushed on. At some point I looked up and said, 'Look! We're almost there!'. But it was Archdeacon's Tower, a false summit. Disappointment hit us like a dead weight, but we kept on and soon reached the exposed plateau known as the Football Field. We were now only 213m from the summit, but first we had to climb a 122m headwall; an unwelcome challenge at this point when we were fighting against time and an incoming storm.

Once we got to the top of the headwall, the last 91m provided an easy walk to the top of the High One, Denali's nickname. At 2.45pm on 14 June, Con and I stood on the top of the highest mountain in North America. This was the first of the Seven Summits under my belt and I was delighted but there was no time to celebrate. We had to get to the safety of our tent at Camp 5 at the Crow's Nest as soon as possible. As we started our descent, we could see black clouds rumbling in from the north. About an hour later, we met Finbarr and Mick below the summit ridge. 'We're going to rest for an hour here and then make for the summit,' Mick said as Finbarr lay flat on the snow. Neither Con nor I liked the look of the latter who appeared to be exhausted. We continued down and it was nearly 5.30pm when we reached the Crow's Nest, almost too exhausted to melt water to drink.

About 7.30pm, snow began to fall heavily and two hours later there was still no sign of our team-mates. By now, Con and I were very worried about the lads, so we put on our gear and headed back up the mountain. Within a short time, we met some other climbers who said they'd seen our team-mates descending. We returned to our tent to wait for them. Around midnight the pair arrived at the camp in the company of a Swiss climber who was also a doctor. They'd both made it to the summit but Finbarr, who was suffering from acute mountain sickness, had no memory whatsoever of having been there.

After a few hours of rest, we broke camp next morning and headed down. Finbarr was weak and confused and needed constant monitoring at we descended to Camp 4 at 4,330m. We rested and recuperated in our tents in the Ice Bowl. That evening the storm arrived in a fury of snow that obliterated the landscape and created walls of white wherever we looked. For eight days we remained snowbound at the camp, unable to move. We spent all that time shovelling snow so that we could get out of the tents for a bit of fresh air and to meet with the other climbers who were also stranded. We made the most of it and gathered each evening in a communal tent where we had great fun, singing and telling jokes and stories. On 21 June we held a midsummer party, attended by all the Camp 4 'prisoners', who ranged in age from fourteen to seventy-three.

Our food supply was getting dangerously low, so we made the decision to go down on 23 June no matter what the weather was like. After digging ourselves out of the 1.5m wall of snow that surrounded our tents, five of us started the descent to Base Camp. Garth had descended days earlier, before the storm started, and Mick stayed at Camp 4 with Phil and Clive, who wanted to try for the summit once the storm had blown over. However, their attempt, three days later, was scuppered at 4,937m by a second storm.

As we made our way down, the storm was still blowing, draining us of what little energy we had left. We finally reached Base Camp at 4pm after more than eight hours of hard going. Luck was on our side finally, and one of Doug Geeting's planes appeared at the Base Camp airstrip shortly after we did. We were in it like a shot and back in Talkeetna in sixty minutes, light years away from the snowbound world on the High One.

Because of the second storm, it was several days before our remaining team-mates and our gear could be brought out from the mountain. The rest of us hung out in Talkeetna where the Fairview Inn became our regular haunt. We were having a few drinks there one day when a grizzly bear-like man swung open the double doors, walked in and checked in a rifle, a side gun and a large knife. He joined us and we drank until 4am. He was a hunter-trapper and had been alone in the outback for several months. When he finally got up and left the bar, he walked across the main street and hopped into a rusty tin can of a plane with the doors falling off. He took off down the main street in a cloud of black smoke and a death rattle that shattered the morning quietness. He was one of the many fascinating people we met who lived in this remote region. Many were running away from the hustle and bustle of modern-day life while others were there because of the oil and gold extraction work.

Climbing Denali had given me opportunity to experience this world while also achieving the first of my Seven Summits, and for that I was grateful to the High One.

KILIMANJARO 1995
AFRICA

I climbed the snow-capped 5,895m Kilimanjaro – Africa's highest mountain and the highest free-standing mountain in the world – with my friend Joe O'Leary in January 1995. We left Ireland just after Christmas Day on a multi-flight trip, eventually arriving in Arusha, the capital city of the Arusha Region in Tanzania. The 40° heat and humidity hit us like a brick wall and sweat poured off us as we made our way towards Peter, our expedition organiser and one of the friendliest people I'd ever met. We loaded our gear on his old, open-top Land Rover and set off for our hotel in the city. The drive offered a snapshot of the region; as the sun set in a glorious swirl of oranges and reds, we looked at the people on either side of the dusty road, living in tin shacks, selling their wares, eating, chatting and laughing. We could feel their energy and zest for life as we drove along and it was love at first sight for me.

Joe and I spent a few nights relaxing in Arusha before Peter collected us again. With our gear loaded up, we had a three-hour drive to meet our guide and get everything sorted for the trek. Regional laws demanded that you use a local guide and porters when climbing Kilimanjaro, whether you needed them or not. Although we'd planned to do the climb on our own, we knew this was a way of creating local employment and supporting the community. When all was sorted, we set off on our five-day trek on the Marangu Route, also known as the Coca-Cola Route because of its popularity. We started walking once we entered Kilimanjaro National Park, situated at about 1,800m.

There are five different micro-climate zones as you make your way up Kilimanjaro, each lasting for approximately 1,000m. The first is a dense, green, sweltering rainforest where the humidity was unbelievable. Its narrow winding paths are walled in by tall, glistening, vine-covered trees. After a six-hour trek we arrived at a clearing where there were a number of huts. We spent our first night at the Mandara Hut along with several others, rising early next morning to trek through the final part of the rainforest, which ended at 3,000m. At this point, we emerged into the alpine meadow region where grasses and wildflowers grew in great profusion. We had a very pleasant day's trekking through this area and spent the night at the Horombo Hut.

Our third day on Kili had us walking through another new terrain, which was like a lunar landscape. This boulder-strewn belt of glacial gravel and rocks has little vegetation and a very dry atmosphere. During the day we passed the 4,000m point and the effects of altitude began to kick in. I was okay but Joe got a headache and began to find the going tough. We stayed at the Kibo Hut that night where we noticed the temperature had gotten much colder. We went to bed early, around 6pm, as we were setting off at midnight for the final leg of the journey. The plan was to be at the summit to see the sun rise over the great African plains; this meant we had six hours to make it to Uhuru Peak.

We dressed for the Arctic conditions that were ahead of us, putting on down pants, jackets, fleeces, hats and gloves. We had been told that we wouldn't need such extreme clothing, but we had done our research and knew how cold it might get. In fact, we met a group on their way down who'd had to turn before reaching the summit because of the cold. It was −10° as we made our way over scree to the crater rim. Although the gradient wasn't significant, the climbing was tough enough at this point due to the altitude.

At Gilman's Point our guide stopped. 'This is it. We're at the top,' he said. We'd heard about this trick that the guides sometimes play, trying to convince trekkers that this point is the top of the mountain when it is, in fact, 215m below the real summit. Guides pull this stunt because it shortens their journey by a few hours and, if the trekkers don't know any better, they are happy to lead them down and start getting the next group up. We knew we weren't at the summit and told our man where we wanted to go – Uhuru Peak.

High up, near the top of Kilimanjaro, we saw the most beautiful sunrise either of us had ever witnessed, the light a melding of red and orange and gold. The sky was blue above us while a perfect blanket of cloud covered everything below us. At 10am on 4 January, we arrived at Uhuru Peak, the real top of Kilimanjaro. I had the second of the Seven Summits under my belt and it was great to share the moment with such a close friend.

The lure of Kili

I knew I wanted to return to Kili. I loved travelling and climbing, and in Tanzania I saw an opportunity to make this viable for myself. I started thinking about bringing groups from Ireland to Nepal and Kilimanjaro. Such trips would allow ordinary people to achieve something special by reaching Everest Base Camp or the summit of Kili. They would also learn something about the wider world and if they were inspired to help less well-off people, that would be a great bonus.

The following year, I was back on Kilimanjaro leading a large group in aid of the Rehab Foundation. An employee had heard me talking about taking groups to Kili and approached me. She wanted to fundraise for the organisation, and I said I'd organise the logistics for the trip. We expected a handful of people to show interest and were gobsmacked when over 100 names came in from all over Ireland.

Along with my friend Joe O'Leary and some others, I put together a training programme of trekking and climbing weekends in Kerry. During those, people got an idea of what the trek would be like and whether or not they'd be able for it. By the end, we had thirty-three ready to climb the mountain and another eleven who would do a cross-country walk with members of the Masai tribe before climbing Ol Donyio Lengai, an active volcano. I was delighted that my older son Brian was also coming along to climb Kili, making this an extra-special trek for me.

We left Ireland in July 1996 for our three-week trip. Everyone had a personal reason for being there and I was touched by the human stories they brought with them. During our time in Tanzania I could see the mountain working its special magic on the expedition members, healing them and bringing calm and acceptance to their lives. I was reminded of my first climbs in Kerry and how they had helped me many years earlier.

The group gelled incredibly well, so much so that, to this day, they still meet up regularly in Ireland. I, too, made a lifelong friend on this trip when I met up with fellow Corkman Gerry Walsh. Since then, I have been back as many as fifty times with my adventure company, leading over 1,500 people, and have a second family among the guides and porters who work with me. Over the years, my groups have raised funds for many schools and orphanages in the region. For many, Kili is their Everest and for me it is a joy to share in their achievement.

EVEREST (NORTH SIDE) 1995
ASIA

It takes the best part of sixty days to walk to the top of the world, most of it spent in a place where humans are not meant to survive. Following my 1993 trip to Everest, I couldn't rid myself of the memory of us having to bury Karl Henize and leave his body in an icy grave, never to return to his family. His death affected me profoundly. He was someone I had sat down with and laughed and joked with in the days before his passing. No one expected him to die, especially as he wasn't climbing high up the mountain. But then, all of a sudden, this courageous and adventurous man was gone.

It really bothered me that Karl's fate could also be mine, yet my resolve to go back to Everest never waned. Since the first time I climbed Carrauntoohil, I had been infatuated with the world's highest mountain. During my first attempt to climb it, I'd felt a spiritual connection to Everest and a huge desire to stand at the highest point in the world that I could not rationalise. Although Karl's death rattled me, it also made me focus even more intensely on what I needed to do to give myself the best chance of surviving.

I wasn't fully sure if Jon Tinker was going to honour his promise of offering me a place on the next team he was leading to Everest but, true to his word, he contacted me in the early months of 1994 to let me know he'd received a permit for another international climb on Everest's north ridge for March 1995. He asked if I wanted to be part of the team; my answer was an immediate yes. The agreement was that I would pay $7,500, half the cost of the previous expedition; this was Jon's way of making up for what had happened two years earlier. I didn't have any issue going back to Everest under his leadership. He was a good logistical person and we both knew there would be no repeat of what had happened in 1993 when he took my summit attempt slot. At that time, it was hard for him not to succumb to the temptation of summit fever when he was already so far up the mountain and had two failed attempts behind him; I understood that though I didn't condone it.

In Ireland, the public was very interested in the whole Seven Summits Challenge, and Everest in particular, and that interest played no small part in ensuring that I had very little problem getting sponsorship for the project. BOC Gases, a British company that was getting a foothold in Ireland at the time, saw the Seven Summits Challenge as a collaborative sponsorship opportunity and agreed to come on board. The only caveat was that I had to summit Everest first. The deal, which covered over 50 per cent of all my remaining expedition costs, meant that I could now concentrate fully on my training, which was a huge relief. It was great to be working with a team that was equally passionate about the project and that could drive the promotion of my series of adventures around the world.

A storm gathers

BOC appointed a PR agency to look after marketing and they identified the project's unique selling points: if I completed the full Seven Summits Challenge, I would be the first person from the island of Ireland to do so and if I reached the summit of Everest I would be the first person from the Republic of Ireland to stand on that high point. The PR people sent out a press release stating that 'No Irish climber from the south of Ireland has yet put their foot on the summit of Everest and no Irish flag has yet been placed on the world's highest point'. I was happy with the wording, as I felt it reflected the reality of the situation. The Irish media was really fired up by my Seven Summits Challenge and *The Pat Kenny Show*, in particular, was very interested in following the story. When Pat Kenny interviewed me, he asked whether I would raise the Irish flag on the summit of Everest if I reached it. I answered that I would be proud to do so, as an Irish person and a citizen of the Republic of Ireland. That, the radio host responded, would be the first time the Tricolour would be raised on Everest.

Nothing about the comment struck me at the time, but between then and my departure for Nepal, a storm started brewing that would rumble on for years. The 1993 Irish Everest Expedition had not raised the national flag on Everest's summit. In fact, the team – made up of climbers from Northern Ireland and the Republic of Ireland – had taken a decision before heading to Nepal that they would not be raising any national flags, most likely arising from the complex historical political situation in Northern Ireland. Instead, when he reached the top of Everest, Dawson Stelfox left a pennant listing the names of the expedition sponsors. I understood and respected this course of action. The media, however, sniffing out a good story on the topic of nationality and identity – always a contentious subject in relation to Northern Ireland – were not going to let go of this one. It was my misfortune to unwittingly get caught up in a discussion where there are no easy answers and certainly no single right one.

The question now being publicly discussed was, if I reached Everest and raised the Tricolour, would I, in fact, be the first or second Irish man on its summit. A country's fractious history had come knocking on my door. The answer was clear to me: the first person from Ireland to reach the top of the world's highest mountain was Dawson Stelfox. But my opinion wasn't heard above the argument and controversy that rumbled on and culminated in an allegation of bigotry being made against me in *Everest Calling*, the book detailing the Irish team's 1993 expedition. The author took the precaution of not mentioning me by name, referring instead to 'a climber from Cork who planned to be the first Irishman on top of Everest'. It was a low blow.

It didn't end there; in fact, this was just the beginning of a long and sustained questioning by the Irish fraternity of almost every achievement I had during my career in adventuring. What was known as the 'fraternity' was made up of a small but clearly defined group of skilled and experienced mountaineers who, for years, had shaped climbing in Ireland. Their love of the mountains was huge and their aim was to promote what they saw as best practice in climbing, and much of what they achieved was admirable. But, as with most groups that dominate within a specific area for a long period, they were inclined to dismiss those who didn't come through what were deemed as the official training channels.

As far as they were concerned, I hadn't served my apprenticeship. Additionally, I was closely associated with Con Moriarty, who was like a red rag to a bull to the fraternity.

To them I was a maverick coming out of nowhere and now, here I was, reputedly saying I was going to be the first Irishman to summit Everest after less than five years of climbing. Such a short period of apprenticeship was unprecedented and they didn't like my attitude, although they never bothered to find out exactly what training I had done or what capacity for learning I had. I heard that doubts were being cast on my ability to climb independently and that I was part of a commercial guided expedition. This really pissed me off, but my father encouraged me to ignore the naysayers. 'Don't take any notice of what people are saying. You just do it your way and keep following your passion. You can't demand their respect but, in time, they will respect what you are doing,' he advised.

It was a hard ask, but I didn't have the time or the inclination to dwell on such negativity and, in time, my father's words proved prophetic.

Irish puja

My family's fears for my safety were more acute this time round. It's not for nothing they say that 'ignorance is bliss'. On my first expedition to Everest their fears were more general, but when I got back and someone I knew had died, it changed their understanding utterly. Marie expressed her concerns to me and I found it a lot more difficult to leave her and the boys for this expedition. Nonetheless, they all came to the airport in Cork to see me off on 27 March 1995. I was amazed to see a crowd of over 500 friends and supporters, along with members of the national media, gathered to wish me well. This was very different to my departure in 1993, when only close family and friends had been present, but BOC Gases had done their PR work well and I was happy to honour my part of the deal and engage with the media. As I exited the departure lounge, my family cried and hugged me. My mother, as ever, gave me a holy medal to wear – her version of a puja – and promised to keep a candle lighting until she saw me again.

I knew my responsibility was to ensure I returned home safely but I also knew, after seeing how Karl had died, how easy it was to become one of Everest's death statistics. As soon as the plane took off and I was on my own, I focused on getting into the zone that I needed to be in. I banished any anxiety I had about the expedition and used the flight time to deal with my fear, using it to keep me sharp. I knew I had developed significantly as a climber since 1993; two years earlier, I'd had some doubts about my ability at high altitude but with all the climbing at altitude I'd done in the intervening time, I was confident that I was as prepared as anyone could be for Everest's Death Zone.

Team-mates

When we touched down in Kathmandu, my friend Tsiring was there to meet me again and I spent two days with my adopted family. He insisted on me accompanying them to their local temple, where he requested that twelve monks pray for my safe return from Everest. It was an incredibly moving ceremony and very special to have private time like this before joining my team-mates at the Hotel Thamel. This time round there were sixteen climbers from nine countries. I knew about half of them, including expedition leader Jon Tinker, George Kotov, Jon and Brigitte Muir from our Everest 1993 expedition, and Mike Smith who I'd gotten to know through Jon while climbing in Scotland.

Some of those I hadn't met before were the exceptionally talented Turkish climber Nasuh Mahruki; Patrick Hache and two other French professional climbers; Mike Chapman from Melbourne; twenty-two-year-old Australian James Allen, also from Melbourne; and Kelly Armitage, a Canadian doctor who doubled as the team doctor. There was also a very colourful Alaskan cowboy, Bob Hemstead, and Jeff Shea from San Francisco, as well as two other English climbers that Jon knew. The majority were mountaineers with significant experience of high-altitude climbing under their belts. We were joined by sirdar Ang Rita and four of his strongest climbing Sherpas – Babu Chiri (Ang Babu), Lhakpa Gelu, Lama Jangbu and Tshering Dorje, as well as our cooks Dawa and Pasang. We were a bunch of like-minded adventurers from around the world with one focus – the summit of the world's highest mountain.

Mid-air terror

Unlike the 1993 expedition when we travelled by truck to Tibet, this time we flew from Kathmandu to the city of Lhasa, the capital of the Tibet Autonomous Region. It was a great relief to hear that we would be flying over the Road to Hell instead of driving on it. My relief, however, was short-lived. We had just settled into the flight when, suddenly and violently, the plane careered into a downward spiral as if it had been sucked into a vortex. The air hostesses and their trolleys came crashing down the aisle and their screams filled the cabin.

I looked out the window and saw one wing move several feet upwards before bending as far downwards. I was convinced this was the end and that it would just be a matter of seconds before the wings snapped off and we fell into oblivion. In the midst of the terror it struck me as ironic that we were planning to climb a dangerous mountain but now we were going to die before ever setting foot on it. Then, suddenly, things calmed a bit and the plane began to right itself. It was still pretty rough, though, and the flight diverted to Chengdu Shuangliu International Airport in China's Sichuan Province. I was never so happy to get off a plane in all my life.

During the three days we had to remain in Chengdu, waiting for a break in the weather, I took advantage of the unexpected opportunity to explore the city until we were able to make a successful flight to Lhasa. The Tibetan city was nothing more than a tatty metropolis except for the Potala Palace, a thirteen-storey museum and World Heritage Site which boasts over 1,000 rooms. It was the residence of the Dalai Lama until the fourteenth incumbent fled to India during the 1959 Tibetan uprising.

It was a relief to leave the city, where the oppression of the Tibetan population was evident everywhere. From Lhasa we drove in a caravan of jeeps and trucks across the Tibetan plateau and up the mountainous dirt tracks until we reached the monastery at Rongbuk, where we had butter tea and prayers with the monks before travelling the final few kilometres to the bottom of Everest.

Appeal to the deities

We were a large group of over twenty people and, with all our yaks and porters, we resembled a circus pulling into the multicultural village that was Base Camp, which was home to a total of ten teams from all around the world. It was hard to stand at the base of the tallest mountain on Earth and not feel its power, both physical and supernatural, almost as if it had a will of its own. By this time, I had become more keenly aware of the fact that it wasn't just my ability to climb mountains that would determine my fate; I knew that you could do everything to be efficient and strong and still get killed on Everest. I had become very interested in the psychology of the Sherpas and their attitude towards the mountain, their belief in auspicious days and their reasons for always doing a puja before a climb. They weren't fearful about their own ability to climb; their anxiety came instead from their belief in gods and goddesses that could be kind or vengeful. Even though their deities weren't mine, I really began to accept – in a way I hadn't done before – that no matter how hard you train, there are always elements over which you have no control.

Everyone had a great welcome for the Rongbuk monks when they arrived at Base Camp. A wooden pole rose from the altar that the Sherpas built and the monks tied a white scarf and a sprig of juniper tree to it. The tree has sacred qualities for the Sherpas and its pungent, cleansing scent filled the air as branches were burned during the ceremony while the monks prayed for good weather. They also prayed that the spirit of Chomolungma would look kindly on all about to climb her flanks. Grain and butter were offered as sacrifice while water and rice were liberally scattered. At the end of the puja, the monks told us that Chomolungma had approved our challenge: the time for action had arrived.

On the trek to Advance Base Camp, I was moving faster and feeling fitter and more confident, covering in one hour the amount of terrain it had taken me two hours to travel in 1993. At Mid Camp at 5,700m, where we had buried Karl Henize, we stopped to say a prayer. I looked for the stone that marked his grave but couldn't find it. The terrain had changed in the intervening years, reminding me that nothing on Everest ever remains the same. It was a stark reminder to me not to be complacent.

Once we set up camp at ABC, the long, arduous weeks of slog up and down the mountain began, setting up camps, stocking them and fixing ropes in preparation for our summit attempts. The weather was mixed and we had to endure a few storms that really drained our energy, but we persisted and eventually the camps were completed.

Jon Tinker drew up a list of dates for summit attempts and allocated them to the team. The first team of George and Nasuh, Brigitte and Jon Muir would leave on 15 May, with James Allen and me following on 16 May. At twenty-two, James was one of the least experienced climbers in the group. He had joined the expedition with the Muirs and he and I shared a tent for the duration of our time on Everest. For me, it was very important that the personality of the person I was spending most of my time with was a good match for mine. James' outlook was positive and passionate and I enjoyed sharing my knowledge with him and found him to be an eager learner who was hungry for success.

Doomed attempt

On the morning of 16 May, when we set out from ABC, I was feeling very confident. We reached Camp 1 at 7,000m on the North Col in the early afternoon. The next day, we moved to Camp 2 in perfect conditions. George and Nasuh reached the summit that day, the first of our teams to do so. The Muirs had also been due to go to the summit from Camp 3 but they'd had to return to the North Col because Jon was feeling ill. On their descent, George and Nasuh stopped at our campsite to wish us the best for our summit attempt. We settled in to get a good night's rest before pushing upwards the following day. Everything was going according to plan until, suddenly, nature decided to exert its power. Jet-stream winds, blowing at over 100mph, came at us with force. We sat in our tent with no way up or down past the path of the winds.

For two long days we remained there, not knowing if the thin fabric of our tent – our only protection against exposure and hypothermia – would withstand the onslaught. Then, after forty-eight hours, the wind died as suddenly as it had started. By now, however, my energy was depleted and I knew this particular attempt was doomed. Going down was the only way I could recover. It was time for hard decisions; I said that if we went down to ABC we'd give ourselves a better chance of recuperating fully. James agreed and we descended, absolutely shattered after two days of being belted by storm winds at altitude. Once we vacated the tent at Camp 2, I knew there would be others waiting in line and we would lose our summit position as another wave of climbers took our place now that there was a break in the weather. However, we weren't long gone when jet-stream winds hit Camp 2 again and this time it was totally destroyed. The rest of our group, situated at the North Col, also descended to ABC to await the next weather window.

Moving upwards

We rested for a few days until the weather improved and the teams started to advance up the mountain again. The weather held and Jeff Shea, Lhakpa Gelu and Tshering Dorje, who had left ABC on 21 May, reached the summit in perfect weather on 24 May. They were followed by Patrick Hache, Bob Hemstead, Lama Jangbu and Ang Babu, who also summited in perfect conditions on 26 May. Brigitte Muir, Mike Smith, James and I were the last wave to go on what was to be the final summit push. Jon Muir had to forfeit his attempt due to illness, so Mike partnered with Brigitte.

James and I adopted a different strategy to them for the push, leaving on 24 May for Camp 1, where we had a good night's sleep. The following day we pushed to the higher of the two camps on the north ridge at 7,800m. We wanted to get as high as we could on the mountain to make it easier to get to Camp 3 early the following day, thereby giving us plenty of time to rest before our final ascent. Brigitte and Mike left ABC on 25 May and skipped Camp 1 altogether, stopping at the lower Camp 2 at 7,600m, 200m below us. We planned to meet at Camp 3 on 26 May to head for the summit together.

We had a restful night at Camp 2 on 25 May and the following morning at 6am we radioed ABC for a weather update. We were told that storms were predicted to hit the upper reaches of Everest on 29 May. That was our weather window to get to the top and back down to safety. We couldn't afford to waste time or energy now. We each packed two bottles of oxygen and regulators. Each bottle was estimated to give six hours of oxygen on a regulator setting of three, and we did not intend to use oxygen until we were above Camp 3. I reckoned it would be a nine-hour ascent to the summit, so I was happy we had enough cover for a safe ascent although it would be tight on the way down. This was a calculated risk, but I felt it was achievable.

We double-checked to ensure the bottles were full and that the masks worked. We also packed eight small gas cylinders, for boiling water and cooking, and some boil-in-the-bag meals. Foolishly, we decided to leave our sleeping bags at

Camp 2, having decided to travel as light as possible to save energy. We were now depending on our one-piece down suits, which were reputed to protect the wearer in temperatures as low as −40°. As we exited the tent we were confident but also fearful at what the next forty-eight hours had in store for us in Everest's Death Zone.

Entering the Death Zone

It took us three hours to get to Camp 3 at 8,200m. Arriving early at 11am gave us plenty of time to prepare ourselves physically and mentally for what was ahead. This was the highest I'd ever been on a mountain, and I could feel the toll that being in the Death Zone was taking on my body. It was harder to breathe and all movement was at a snail's pace. I knew we needed to hydrate as much as possible and though I had no appetite for either drink or food, I forced it down. We were both freezing as we sat in our tent with no sleeping bags; the down suits weren't as good as the marketing proclaimed. We didn't want to dwell on the cold, so we kept heating snow to make hot drinks and tried to get as much rest as possible before our midnight journey started.

I nodded off but was startled out of my half-sleep by a thud of something hitting against the tent. When I raised the flap I saw Bob Hemstead, the Alaskan cowboy, lying half dead on the snow outside. We dragged him inside and gave him a warm drink and when he recovered a bit, he told us what had happened.

On his ascent, when he was about 50m from the summit, he slipped on hard ice, falling head-first down the slope he'd just walked up. He couldn't self-arrest with his ice axe and his fall continued until – miraculously – he was snagged on a rocky outcrop at the edge of a 1,000m drop. He clung there, upside down and shouting for help, knowing that he was in the last-chance saloon. Luckily for him, Ang Babu and Greg Child, a climber from another expedition, heard him. They knotted pieces of rope together and threw the lifeline to Bob who, defying all the odds, was able to tie it around his body so that those above him could pull him to safety.

He was shaken but his determination to get to the summit wasn't, and the three made their way to the top of Everest where, despite now having a fractured hip, Bob performed the highest rope trick in the world. This was something the crazy cowboy was doing on each of the Seven Summits. By the time he fell against our tent, he was spent but lucky to be in the company of other climbers who were strong enough to accompany him on his descent. Bob's story was mind-boggling at many levels, mostly at the one where we realised that a simple slip on an otherwise harmless looking slope could hurl you to an icy death near the top of Everest.

Lost on the First Step

It was late afternoon when Brigitte and Mike arrived and started their preparations in a tent just above us. As darkness fell, the winds started to rise and howl in the desolate Death Zone. With the wind beating strongly against our tent, I wondered if it would be possible to continue upwards. If not, there would be no other chance this season; the weather was too unstable. I tossed and turned as a million thoughts went through my mind. No matter what argument entered my head, it was followed in seconds by an equally valid counter-argument; it felt like I was going mad.

This internal conversation was interrupted by the crackling of the radio at 11pm. It was Mike in the nearby tent, asking what our plans were. The winds were continuing to pick up and the temperature was still dropping and he wanted to know what we had decided to do. I looked at James and he looked back at me. I recognised the expression in his eyes. Without saying a word, we raised our thumbs simultaneously: our summit bid was on. 'Mike,' I said, 'we're going for it at midnight. What about you and Brigitte?' 'We'll be across shortly,' was the answer. I'd just signed off when the radio crackled again. This time it was expedition organiser Russell Brice. One of his climbers, Miko Valanne from Finland, was also at Camp 3, he explained. 'He's leaving for the summit at midnight. Can he join you?' 'Fine,' I answered.

At midnight on 26 May, all five of us headed into the darkness. We trudged slowly up the most dangerous section of the climb on a cold and star-studded night, using our head torches to light the way. To reach the summit we had three formidable barriers to climb through, known simply as the Three Steps, each posing its own particular challenge. We pushed our way up the north ridge and were feeling good as we made our way across a series of icy rocky outcrops that we had to manoeuvre through and scramble up. The climbing was easy, but dangerous because of the altitude.

After two hours we regrouped as Mike's oxygen had run out. I was surprised; either his bottle hadn't been full or he had used up four hours of it in the tent. I helped him put another one on while the others had some drinks and sorted through gear. Everyone was feeling okay as we started to move up through the broken slabs. Our next break would be in forty-five minutes at the top of the First Step at 8,564m.

Mike, James and I arrived there at 3am and radioed ABC to let them know our position while we waited for Miko and Brigitte. Twenty minutes later we were still waiting in the freezing cold. There was no sign of them so we radioed ABC again, this time looking for direction on what to do. The terrain at this stage was easy enough, with no technical challenges, and while we didn't know Miko well, we knew that Brigitte was an experienced climber for whom that section shouldn't pose too much of a challenge. We agreed to continue as we felt they must have decided to turn back. Then we began the long and precarious traverse to the next obstacle, the Second Step – the most dangerous of the Three Steps – oblivious to what was happening 150m behind us.

As they'd made their way towards the top of the First Step, Brigitte and Miko had become separated. Climbing on her own but initially having James within sight, Brigitte then had the disaster of her torchlight giving out. She didn't call out to James to wait or, if she did, he didn't hear. In the freezing cold she replaced the batteries only for the new ones to die within moments. While she was distracted replacing the batteries, she lost sight of James, who had been just ahead of her on the ridge. She thought she could catch up but with no light she couldn't see the path and decided to stay put until sunrise, when she descended to Camp 3 with the intention of coming up again on 28 May. Due to exhaustion, Miko, too, abandoned his summit attempt. Unfortunately for them, the weather changed the following day and they were forced to descend the mountain without getting that second summit chance.

A notorious crux

We clipped to a thin fixed line that a previous team had placed in the spectacular traverse, a nerve-wracking snow and ice field where the force of gravity seemed to be constantly pulling me downwards from a 60° incline on a track just wide enough to walk on. I could not see where I was placing my feet so I took my oxygen mask off to ensure I did not step off the track. I turned off the oxygen flow and, happily, it seemed to have little effect on my performance. At 6am we arrived at the notorious crux that has to be surmounted to get to the top of the Second Step at 8,610m. One wrong move here and a climber would ricochet downwards to certain death. No one comes to this section without thinking of Mallory and Irvine, who, it is believed, perished not far from this point, either while still ascending or on their descent. Like many of the lost, their names have gone into the realm of myth. I quickly reconnected my oxygen supply mask for the challenge ahead. I'd had nightmares about this section and was scared shitless going into it.

Mike led the way along a rock arête, with me following and James bringing up the rear. We were not tied to each other and used the fixed rope for protection. I moved from the traverse out onto the rock face and, as I traversed into the chimney-type crack, I dislodged a big boulder, about a metre cubed in size. *Oh God*, I thought, as it sped downwards like a missile in the direction of James' head. 'Below!' I roared, the technical term for falling rock. James looked up and jumped to one side in horror; the rock whizzed past him and down the north face, nearly knocking him from his precarious perch. I could see he was badly shaken by the near-miss. 'Are you okay?' I shouted. 'Be careful, Falvey! You nearly killed me,' he roared back. I cautiously continued.

In 1975, a Chinese team fixed an aluminium ladder on the final six vertical metres of the Second Step to lessen the extreme danger and to make it easier to gain the final summit slope. I made my way to the base of the ladder, which was fixed to the sheer rock face. Below it is a drop of such depth, it doesn't bear thinking about. To move your body from the chimney onto the ladder takes both skill and confidence; one wrong step and it's over. Mike led the way and I followed him with rock-solid determination. As I gained each rung, I wondered if I would be the unfortunate climber to pull the ladder from its stressed and rusted anchor pins in the rock. Halfway up, I looked back to see if James was following.

As I turned, I saw a body further down the slope. I believed it to be the remains of the Australian climber Michael Rheinberger, whom I had met in Kathmandu a few years earlier. He had died the previous year having finally reached the summit following six failed attempts. The sight was a grim reminder of how lethal this section of the climb was. Climbing onto the ladder is tricky but getting off it requires nerves of steel as you unclip from the top rung and make a .6m stretch across the endless abyss below before reaching the safety of a tiny ledge which offers a foothold on the cliff face.

Frozen by fear

Mike was waiting as I looked down and saw James, still at the bottom of the ladder. I tied into the fixed line to protect myself and backed out onto the cliff edge to direct him up the ladder. I knew that he had been nervous on the traverse, but now he seemed totally freaked out; he, too, had seen the dead body and this had shaken him. He moved slowly up the swaying ladder but when he got to the top rung he froze. He needed to unclip from one fixed rope and lean across the face, with the abyss below, before clipping into the other fixed line. But he couldn't make the move. I could see that he was immobilised by fear.

The summit was visible from this point; it was so close and yet, for James, it might as well have been on the other side of the world. 'Come on, James, make the move,' I shouted down at him. 'I can't,' he called back in abject frustration. Mike was complaining about the cold and kept saying that we had to continue upwards. 'Make the move, James!' I roared again. 'I can't make the move, Falvey!' he shouted up at me. 'Go without me. We agreed if I needed to turn you would go on ahead. I'm okay. I'll be able to retreat on the fixed ropes.'

I hated to leave my friend behind, so I tried again to get him to make the move. I heard Mike shout down at me. 'For fuck's sake, Falvey, we'll freeze if we stay here any longer. We have to get moving.' I looked up at Mike and beyond him at the summit; then I looked down at James. 'We have to go on,' I shouted down. He understood; there was nothing Mike or I could do if he couldn't make the move off the ladder.

Mike and I headed towards the Third Step – our final barrier. I was still thinking about James and took a final glance backwards. To my surprise and delight I saw him in the distance, moving towards us: he had made the move. When we left, he had overcome his fear and literally taken a leap of faith across the face of Everest onto the ledge. We waited for him and when he reached us he said he had frostbite. 'How the hell did that happen?' I asked. He had taken off

146

the outer of his three layers of gloves in order to get a better grip when making the move off the ladder. In that short space of time he'd gotten frostbite on both hands, which eventually resulted in the loss of the tops of two digits. But we needed to keep moving. 'Let's go,' I said as I gave him a big hug. All three of us continued up the snowy slope that led to the final Step at 8,710m. We could see the summit snowfield and, beyond it, the top of the world.

World's highest gangplank

As we walked on the narrow ridge with the entire world below us on 27 May, I knew the summit was achievable. We were crossing the highest gangplank on Earth and taking in some of the greatest views on this planet. Then, as I traversed the final 60m of relatively easy walking to the summit, I started to feel very strange. It was as if I was in a hazy dream world where there were two versions of me, one walking towards the summit of Everest and the other looking down from the sky and watching my other self.

I was scared by this feeling but kept walking; it could have been hypoxia but I really felt as if I had died and my spirit was above, watching my physical body slowly edging its way to the top of the mountain. I found it hard not to succumb to the madness that was nipping at my rational mind, but I kept putting one foot in front of the other. All the time I had the most inappropriate earworm playing round and round in my head: *Oh, I do like to be beside the seaside, Oh, I do like to be beside the sea.* I couldn't stop it. It was a song that Norman Croucher, who had been on the 1993 expedition, used to sing constantly.

Suddenly, Mike thumped me on the back. 'We made it! We're here!' he shouted. In that moment, I actually saw my two selves coming together again and it was as if I woke up. *I am here, I am really here, this is it, I'm alive!* A feeling of excitement filled every inch of my body. We had reached our goal and were standing on one of the most mythical points on the planet. I stood there, in awe at our achievement, before pivoting 360° to take in the stunning views towards the north, south, east and west.

As I drank in this rare vista, I remembered the first time I said I would climb this mountain. It was a goal – mad at the time, perhaps – that gave my life focus and a tremendous sense of purpose. I thought of my father and his advice that I should dream and dream big, but always remember that it is in the following of the dream that the success lies. I thought of my grandmother who never stopped telling me, 'If you think you can, you will'. I had ignored my critics and naysayers and had followed my dream with conviction and passion, and now I was on top of the world.

It was incredible to finally be on the summit of Everest after all the years of dreaming, planning, training and sacrifice. I got out my camera and took photos of all three of us at this incredibly special moment in our lives. I knew we couldn't spend too long here but there was one very important thing I still had to do. I reached into my breast pocket and took out the Irish Tricolour, the symbol of my country and the emblem of my tradition and culture. The flag symbolises the inclusiveness that its three colours represent – green for the Gaelic tradition of Ireland, orange symbolising the followers of William of Orange in Ireland, and white to represent the aspiration for peace between the two traditions.

I attached it to my ice axe, rose to my feet and proudly held it high in the air. 'Yes! I'm standing on top of the world! I roared. I knew I had created a bit of history: this was the first time the flag of the Republic of Ireland had been raised on the summit of the world's highest mountain. I was both proud and humbled as an Irishman, a Corkman and a Norrie to be the person to hoist it aloft.

Danger looms

I had been at the summit for about ten minutes when I heard a snake-like hissing sound which brought me back to reality. My oxygen had run dry. I couldn't shake off the fear I'd felt at the out-of-body experience I'd had earlier. I didn't want to get hypoxic and knew I needed to go down. Mike and James stayed on while I turned and started my descent. I was alone now and had to focus on every step I was taking. I thought of Bob Hemstead, who had nearly fallen to his death shortly after leaving the summit the day before. *Come on, Falvey, don't mess up now. Make the right decisions, the right moves. Concentrate. Concentrate.* These words rang through my head like a mantra. George Kotov had left two half-full bottles of oxygen at the Second Step and I wanted to get to them as soon as possible. When I found a welcome bottle and hooked up to it, it was like manna from heaven.

I waited for my team-mates and, after about fifteen minutes, I spotted them coming towards me. I could see straight away that something was not right with Mike, who was falling all over the place. When they reached me, James explained that, shortly after they'd left the summit, he had run out of oxygen. I checked through all the oxygen bottles until I found the other half-full one. We hooked Mike up and he devoured the tiny bit of life-sustaining gas. The situation was now very serious; Mike was in a bad state, falling in and out of a hypoxic sleep and showing signs of pulmonary and cerebral oedema. He had radioed Base Camp just after starting his descent and asked if someone would come up the mountain with more oxygen. Jon Tinker said there were two Sherpas at Camp 3 and that he'd dispatch them to come up to us with extra supplies and to help get Mike down. First, however, we had to get him past the Second Step to the traverse.

Because of the hypoxia, Mike could not be trusted to abseil down the sheer face of the Step of his own volition. There were two fixed lines in place; one, which Japanese climbers had fixed two weeks earlier, went straight down to the traverse below with no anchors to negotiate. I attached Mike onto that line with a figure-eight abseil descender and brought him to the edge. James assisted Mike over the edge of the vertical drop and began to descend adjacent to him. If Mike got stuck on any of the ledges, James could release him by pushing him out from the rock.

I clipped into the other fixed line that we had used on our ascent and held the abseil rope Mike was attached to, using it as a controlled brake so that he wouldn't fall. Mike knew the seriousness of his predicament and mustered every bit of energy he had to descend to the bottom of the Second Step. As we reached the end of the face, Lhakpa was approaching carrying a bottle of lifesaving oxygen. We connected Mike to a new bottle and turned the regulator up to maximum to give him a boost. Although he revived immediately, he was still in a bad way.

Lhakpa clipped Mike into the fixed line on the traverse and he started making his drunken way along the narrow path on the 60° snow and ice field. James and I had already moved some way along the traverse before stopping to wait for the two men. Suddenly, Mike slipped and fell down the slope with lightning speed. I instinctively grabbed the fixed rope and Lhakpa grabbed it at the other side of Mike. Miraculously, it held. 'Stand up and get back up on the traverse,' I shouted down to him. Mike looked up, desperation in his exhausted eyes. He stuck his crampons into the ice and used his ice axe to haul himself into a standing position on the narrow path. But he was no sooner up than he fell again and slipped further down the slope.

I thought he was gone and closed my eyes. When I opened them and looked down I saw that he was still alive, even though he lay motionless on the ice. 'Get up, Mike, you have to get up and back on the traverse,' I shouted. In a supreme act of will and painfully slowly, he stood up and again dug his crampons in to get purchase on the ice. This time, and against all the odds, he got back on the traverse. We sat him down for a few minutes' rest and were horrified to see that he was coughing up blood. He could hardly breathe and we knew we had to make a plan.

We clipped Mike's harness into a short rope, with James, who was in front, also attached to the rope and Lhakpa attached to the rear. Using this sling system, our dying team-mate could be held by both men if he fell. I moved forward in search of a path downwards. Progress was excruciatingly slow as we made our way across the traverse to the top of the First Step. It was a great relief about half an hour later to see Tshering Dorje coming towards us. He took over from James but our journey to Camp 3 was still exhausting. Seven hours later, at 4.30pm, we eventually arrived there. Russell Brice, who was waiting for his team members, took over care of Mike while the rest of us rehydrated before falling into a sleep that I never wanted to end.

The following morning we descended slowly. Mike still wasn't showing sufficient signs of recovery as we descended, stopping regularly to cough and spit up bloodied phlegm. We slept at Camp 1 and he wasn't much better the next day. I radioed Base Camp and asked for back-up support. The three of us had just made our way off the North Col onto the glacier at the bottom of the headwall when we met four Sherpas who had come up from ABC, bringing flasks of hot tea with them. Even better, they could now provide the strength and support that Mike needed and that James and I could no longer give.

We walked ahead and had just arrived at ABC when we heard that Mike had collapsed. Twelve climbers and Sherpas at the camp went to help our stricken team-mate. He was literally lifted back to the camp where he was put in a Gamow bag in an attempt to save his life. The expedition doctor diagnosed hypoxia, oedema and a punctured lung. It took several weeks of medical care before he was fit again, but the fact that Mike had survived at all was a miracle and a great relief to everyone.

We finally reached Base Camp and, despite all the traumas and challenges of the climb and descent, it was time to celebrate. I'd brought some Irish whiskey to toast our expedition and – now – our summit success. James, Mike and I were the last climbers to summit that season as the weather changed on 28 May, and Chomolungma rested for another season. Nine of our team had reached the top of Everest and it was time to go home.

I had learned in 1993 that after the high of an expedition – whether or not you reach the summit – a natural low follows and I knew that the best way to counter it was to have another goal already in the pipeline. I had just completed my third – and the highest – of the Seven Summits but as I flew out of Kathmandu, I was already planning the next one: Aconcagua.

Miscommunication

Back in Ireland, during the days of our descent and trek out from Base Camp, something of a media frenzy had taken place. Due to failed communications and a press eager for a story, it was suspected that something had gone wrong for me on Everest. I had made contact with my sponsors and Marie the day before leaving ABC for the mountaintop, letting them know that 27 May would be our summit day. This information was issued in a press release and the media expected a report on our progress by the end of that day. However, by 31 May there was still no update and journalists following the expedition smelled a good story. To add to the drama, prior to leaving Ireland I'd given an interview in which I'd said that, in the event of someone dying on the mountain, the team would cut communication until the person's family were notified.

By unfortunate coincidence, our communications system went down just as I reached the summit and the Irish media interpreted this silence as meaning that something had gone wrong. For five days, the press hounded my family and sponsors, trying to find out if I, or one of my team-mates, was missing or dead. The worst of it all was that my family didn't know if anything had happened either, as I hadn't been able to contact them myself. As I celebrated our success, I was completely oblivious to the pain and anguish they were suffering at home.

In later years I realised the selfishness of such extreme pursuits where the risks are high and the stress endured by families and friends is so unfair. I also realised, however, that without that selfishness and drive, little would be achieved.

Hometown pride

On the flight home to Cork, I finally had time and space to think about the fact that I had actually reached the summit of Everest. I was relaxing and enjoying having time to let the reality of my achievement sink in when I heard my name being called out over the plane's intercom system. The captain, having been told of my summiting by someone in the control tower at Cork Airport, congratulated me on my achievement. The announcement was followed by a standing ovation from all on board. I was a bit embarrassed – an emotion I wasn't overly familiar with.

One of the stewardesses asked me to go to the back of the aircraft after landing. I was totally shocked when the doors opened and a brass band played me off the plane. Over 100 people were gathered there, including my wife, sons and other family members. Local politicians, Minister Bernard Allen and a bunch of radio and television journalists were present, waiting to hear about my Everest success. As the cameras clicked, the Lord Mayor of Cork came forward to welcome me home. He shook my hand as he spoke. 'On behalf of the people of Cork I want to congratulate you on your extraordinary achievement.' Then he put his arms around me and hugged and kissed me. 'Son,' he whispered, 'I love you. Thanks be to God you're home safe.' My father was Lord Mayor, and this was a very historic moment for our family.

I felt overwhelmed by the love and support I received that day in my home city, and was totally bowled over when I saw over 1,000 supporters and friends waiting in the terminal. I was hugged, kissed and back-slapped into a state of euphoria.

ACONCAGUA 1995
SOUTH AMERICA

I was anxious to climb another of the Seven Summits before the end of the year and just about managed to do that, with only hours to spare, when I reached the summit of Aconcagua on 31 December 1995 with Con Collins, my tent partner on Denali eighteen months earlier. Con and I left Ireland on 11 December to climb the highest mountain in South America, with a summit of 6,961m. Located in Argentina in the Andes mountain range, Aconcagua does not require rope fixing and doesn't pose any serious technical challenge. The biggest danger is the altitude and what is known as Viento Blanco, the white winds, that blow almost constantly. We opted to ascend via the Polish Glacier Direct Route, one of the easier technical routes on the mountain where we would get some good snow and ice climbing. I was looking forward to the trip with Con, who was a good, self-reliant climber that I could trust and who was also a lot of fun to be with.

Our initial base in Argentina was Mendoza in the west of the country. Even though it is in a desert, the city is full of leafy avenues and glittering water fountains. Its cosmopolitan café society is not something that climbers are used to in their 'base' cities and it was very tempting to hang around for a few days longer than planned and sample the laid-back life that Mendoza had to offer. The area is noted for its wines, so Con and I decided that it would be a shame to leave without sampling some. While we were enjoying a few glasses, we heard about a roadhouse bar about 24km into the desert that sounded like a good place to visit. No better men than us to follow a lead like that! We got a taxi there and asked the driver to collect us a few hours later. We soon joined up with a group of Chilean workers who were singing songs and playing music from their homeland. Con and I reciprocated, giving a blast of several of our favourite Irish songs. We were having such a good time that when the taxi driver returned for us at 10pm we gave him $20 and asked him to come back again at 2am.

That was the last we saw of him, but it didn't impinge on our partying until, eventually, Con brought us both back to reality: it was now well past 3am and we were due a wake-up call at 8am to start our journey to Aconcagua Provincial Park. We said goodbye to our mates and started a long, drunken walk back to Mendoza, hoping that the taxi driver would appear at some point, but he had more sense than we had. We eventually fell into our beds around 6am and when the phone rang two hours later, I felt like hell. Con was in much the same state. We were staring at our breakfast in the hotel restaurant when some people I'd climbed with in Scotland and Tibet appeared. 'Care for a few drinks later on?' one of them asked. It was sealed; we wouldn't be travelling anywhere that day.

The following morning we felt equally bad but knew it was time to move on. We got a taxi to the ski resort of Los Penitentes, from where we visited a nearby cemetery; the majority of those buried there had died on Aconcagua. While reading the names of the dead, I got my first sighting of the Mountain of Death, as it is sometimes called. Although considered relatively easy to climb, Aconcagua has the highest death rate of any mountain in South America, mainly – ironically – because it is considered such an easy climb. People become complacent and don't realise the price that being at altitude and in severe cold can exact. I looked up at the brown and white mountain rising into the sky and hoped that our names wouldn't be etched on a local rock any time soon.

A white Christmas

We met Ricardo de Torres, our muleteer, at Punta de Vacas, from where we began our trek to Pampa de Lenas. Ricardo, a gaucho, helped us load our provisions on three mules for the journey to Base Camp. He rode on horseback while Con and I followed on foot with our backpacks. The route was a mix of arid earth and fast-flowing rivers of snowmelt. We camped for the night at Pampa de Lenas, where we got our permits sorted at the park ranger station. We were also given refuse bags to ensure we left only our footprints on the mountain, which had a huge problem with rubbish and human contamination.

The next day we trekked with Ricardo to Casa de Piedra at 3,250m. As he had done the previous night, Ricardo cooked dinner – large chunks of meat thrown on an open-air grill – which we ate accompanied by maté, the national drink. The day after that we came through the zip-narrow Relinchos Valley before reaching Base Camp at 4,200m. Ricardo and his mules departed at this point while Con and I set up our tent before introducing ourselves to the other teams at Plaza Argentina.

We rested for a day before our first carry to Camp 1 on terrain of rough moraine and icy scree. On the way up, Con suffered a lot because of a lingering back problem. The toughest part of the climb was the penitentes, an area with hundreds of 2–3m-high ice pinnacles that we had to manoeuvre through with our heavy rucksacks. After a seven-hour climb, we finally reached Camp 1 at 4,700m where we sorted our gear and took time to rest before dropping back to Base Camp. The next day we moved up to Camp 1 again and spent the night there under a clear dark sky that was lit up by a million stars. Con brought out his songbook and we sang our hearts out for an hour or so, much to the bemusement of a group of climbers from Seattle who were camping nearby.

On Christmas Eve, I dropped down to Base Camp to collect more gear while Con did a carry to Camp 2, our halfway point at 5,200m. We both returned to Camp 1 that evening, where we were joined in our tent by three Californian climbers, Eugene, Edo and Carlos, for a Christmas celebration. I'd brought some tinsel and a few miniature bottles of alcohol which we shared as we sang festive songs.

We woke to a very white Christmas Day after a particularly heavy snowfall and wondered what the hell we were doing in a tent halfway up a mountain in South America when we could have been having a lovely Christmas Day at home. We rested for the day and celebrated the holiday as best we could in our lofty perch. Over the next few days we did carries to Camp 2, just below the Polish Glacier, to position ourselves for the summit push. The daily weather pattern was that snow would start falling every evening and continue into the night. Each morning, Con and I had to dig our way out of the tent before starting the next carry to Camp 2. Luckily, there was no snowfall during the day, so we could continue climbing upwards.

Route change

On 28 December, it was time for us to head up and stay at Camp 2 before aiming for the summit. We had just reached our camp when we met some other climbers who were descending, having decided that the route was too unstable after all the snowfall. Con and I assessed the situation and, having taken into account what we'd heard from the others, we decided it would be too risky to continue up the Polish Glacier Direct Route. We could have gone down to Base Camp to wait it out as the weather was due to improve over the coming days. However, we were aware that avalanche conditions were ripe on the mountain. This meant that, even if there was a good day, there could still be an avalanche due to the vast quantities of snow that had fallen over the previous weeks.

Neither Con nor I wanted to give up on our objective of reaching the summit, so we decided to traverse over to the Normal Route on the north face where there was no avalanche risk. We were well acclimatised by now and knew that getting to the top wouldn't be too difficult from that route. We also knew that if we went down to wait for better conditions on the Polish Glacier Direct Route, we might not get to the summit at all.

Traversing through the knee-deep snow with our huge rucksacks to Piedras Blanca (White Rocks) at 6,250m was back-breaking work. Our energy was well spent after a day crossing the mountain and we slept deeply that night despite the blizzard that lashed our tent ceaselessly. The next morning we rose early, determined that this would be our summit day. We followed the well-worn trail to Refugio Independencia Hut at 6,400m. This was a very primitive structure that was in ruins but, nonetheless, useful as a haven for climbers who were in need of a rest.

From there we pushed across a 400m hard-pack snow traverse on a 30° slope towards La Canaleta. We climbed that rock outcrop onto the ridge line known as Cresta Del Guanaco, where we stopped for a short time. While we rested, Eugene – one of the Californians – appeared. He told us that his two fellow climbers had turned back earlier but he was still heading for the summit. He didn't look too good but assured us he was feeling fine and would rest up for a while. Doubtful about his condition, Con and I headed towards the mountaintop, which we could already see was very much within our reach.

Dangerous descent

At 3.30pm on 31 December 1995 we reached the summit of Aconcagua, the highest mountain in South America and the fourth of my Seven Summits. It was a great way to end the year. We looked around but saw little as snow clouds obliterated all views. Instead, we raised the Tricolour, took a few photos and congratulated each other. We were just about to head down when Eugene appeared, looking shattered and barely able to walk. It was disturbing to see someone in that state at the top of a mountain. He fell to his knees. 'I feel so bad. I don't think I can make it down alone,' he cried. 'Can I go with you?' We knew that he had broken one of the codes of mountain climbing: that of recognising your own limits and not climbing beyond them because, when you do, you risk injury, death or becoming a liability to others. We knew he was in a danger situation, suffering from the effects of high-altitude sickness, and accepted that we couldn't let him descend on his own.

Our downward pace was painfully slow as Con and I helped Eugene move through the deep snow on the ridge and down to the col below. Our next – and potentially most dangerous challenge – was getting him down La Canaleta. I took the lead as we made our way down the rock steps of the steep-angled 45° slope. While moving over a step, Eugene slipped and fell forward with such force that he flew over me, his ice axe hitting the back of my head as he went past. He landed on the ground just down from where I stood. I moved quickly and jumped on him to secure his prone body on the slope. All three of us sat to take a breather and reassess our situation. A snow blizzard started and we realised that, at the pace we were moving, it would be night before we reached Camp 3 at White Rocks. We decided that I would go down to get help while Con would stay with Eugene.

I wasted no time getting back to White Rocks, where Eugene's teammates were. Neither was fit to go back up to their friend, so all three of us went to Camp Berlin at 5,800m to radio the ranger for assistance. Further up, Con was busy ensuring that Eugene was okay. He got any extra clothing the Californian had in his rucksack and put it on him to protect him from hypothermia. Then he found a semi-sheltered spot where they sat, waiting for help. While they were there, four Spanish climbers appeared with their Canadian guide on their descent from the summit. She offered to help but the four climbers didn't want to spend any more time at altitude and continued down.

Catherine, the guide, was a fantastic help to Con, and together they were ingenious in coming up with a plan to get Eugene down the mountain. They cut the straps from their ice axes and attached them to the stricken climber's rucksack. Then they placed the drowsy man on the improvised toboggan and, with the aid of two Swiss climbers who were also descending, they shoved and pulled the Californian downwards until they reached the Refugio Independencia Hut. They were still there when I caught up with them on my way back up to help.

The further down the mountain he'd descended, the more Eugene had recovered and, after a rest at the paltry shelter, he said he felt well enough to walk down, so Catherine and the Swiss climbers departed. Con, Eugene and I made our way down – slowly but surely – to our camp at White Rocks. We were all exhausted and relieved to fall into our tents. To celebrate the New Year and the end of a very tough day, Con and I had two shots of whiskey which sent us into a deep sleep.

Around 2am, I woke to the sound of someone calling my name. I thought I was hallucinating; Con was still asleep beside me so I woke him to check if I was imagining things. I wasn't; he could hear someone calling my name too. I unzipped our tent and looked out into the dark, empty night. It was only then that I recognised who it was – Willie Benegas, the renowned Argentinian climber and guide who I knew from meeting in Nepal. He was responding to the radio call for help sent out hours earlier. He hadn't gotten the message I'd given Catherine that we wanted the rescue called off.

Willie explained that their radio had gone down just after they picked up the initial call, so they couldn't receive any further communication. He didn't mince his words: Eugene would still have to pay for the rescue call-out irrespective of whether he needed it or not. Once he checked in on the Californian, who was sleeping soundly, Willie headed back to Camp Berlin.

Con and I went back to sleep, only to be woken for a second time about two hours later. It was Carlos, Eugene's team-mate. His friend was very ill again, with a severe headache and little or no feeling in his extremities. His breathing was laboured and he had a yellow colour. It was high-altitude sickness and the only cure was to get him down the mountain.

We couldn't afford to waste any time, so we got up and dressed and all five of us began to make our way downwards. Eugene had no control over his movements and was as weak as a kitten as we descended. After twelve hard hours we reached Base Camp. Eugene's condition had started to improve only shortly before we arrived, and we were all glad of our beds that night. The easy climb that Aconcagua was supposed to be had been anything but, reminding me yet again that, on high-altitude mountains, danger is always lurking.

ELBRUS 1996
EUROPE

I wanted to do a winter ascent of Elbrus, the highest mountain in Europe at 5,642m. Situated in the war-torn Caucasus Mountains in southern Russia, between the Caspian Sea and Black Sea, the mountain has two clearly visible summits. The west summit stands at 5,642m while the east summit is 5,621m high. The main challenges are the altitude, avalanches and the temperature, which can plummet suddenly and severely. Russia was an interesting place to visit at the time, not so long after the introduction of glasnost and perestroika. When I was a youngster I had learned about – and believed – all the Russian stereotypes: that the weather was freezing; the food was horrible; the people were dour; and, of course, that Communists were the devil incarnate. 'Better dead than red,' my grandmother often said.

Despite this diet of one-dimensional stereotypes, I was really looking forward to this trip where I would be climbing with my close friend, George Kotov. We had clicked on our first meeting in Scotland in 1992. George was good fun, a great talker and a man who loved to laugh. On top of that, and despite his forty-cigarettes-a-day habit, he was a brilliant and accomplished mountaineer. We'd climbed together a number of times, including in 1995 on the Everest expedition when we'd both reached the summit. I flew to St Petersburg in March 1996, where I stayed with George and his family for a few days in a vast apartment block which had about 3,000 residents. We visited many of his

My mother, Bina, with her first-born rebel son.

Just about to be first across the finish line at the Munster Cross-country Championships in Dungarvan, Co Waterford, in the early 1970s.

On summer holidays with Mary B., my beloved Nan and first mentor, in Youghal, Co Cork.

Nan's fellow traders at the Coal Quay in Cork. She stored her stock in the area through the archway just behind where the women are standing.

My father, Tim *(right)*, on a building site on Cork's northside with his brother Jimmy *(second left)* and two employees, in the mid-1950s.

Left to right: me with Mum and Dad in 1973 on a Butlin's Holiday in Mosney, Co Meath. Dad had just made me a director of Tim Falvey & Sons at the young age of sixteen.

Cork's hilly and densely built northside with the steeple of the Church of the Ascension, where I went to daily Mass with Nan, visible at the top of the hill.

Me as a snappily dressed eighteen-year-old businessman with all the family. *Front, left to right:* Majella, Barry, Mum. *Back, left to right:* Abina, Dad, Richard, Paul, me.

Marie and I on our wedding day in June 1977, deeply in love and full of joy at what the future might hold.

We moved into Beechwood, our dream home, in Kerry Pike, Co Cork, in 1982.

Directors' meeting in the boardroom at our offices on Blarney Street in Cork in the late 1970s. *Left to right:* Frank Jackson (director, Tim Falvey & Sons), Finbar Falvey (director, Falvey Group), Kevin Reddy (director, Falvey Housing), Tim Falvey (chairman, Falvey Group), me (MD, Falvey Group), Pat Sheahan (financial director, Falvey Group).

In 1987, as I emerged from the darkest period of my life, we came to Killarney for a family holiday, the first we'd taken since my business collapsed. My sons, Brian and Patrick, are with me while the boatman waits to take us on a trip to Inisfallen Island.

Marie and I enjoying a Christmas visit to Santa with the boys at Blarney Woollen Mills in 1988.

Carrauntoohil, standing at 1,038m in Kerry's majestic MacGillycuddy's Reeks, is Ireland's highest mountain. My dream of climbing Everest was inspired when I stood on its summit for the first time. Since then, I've climbed it over 1,500 times, guiding groups of people who are always spellbound by both the challenge of the trek and the beauty of the region. *(Courtesy of Valerie O'Sullivan, www.valerieosullivan.com)*

Me crossing the ridge line from Waterville to Killarney on a three-day camp craft and skills training trip in 1988.

My friend and mentor, Val Deane, who first introduced me to hillwalking and mountain climbing in 1986, pictured at Mountain Lodge, my home in Beaufort, Co Kerry.

While getting more and more hooked on climbing in the late 1980s, I was also getting back into business and developed Falvey Homes (building one-off houses) and Falvey Housing (developing housing estates), as well as setting up a finance company, Home Loan Finance.

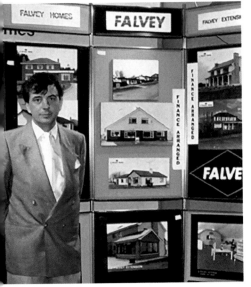

Ice climbing in Valle di Cogne, Italy, in 1991 with Pat Littlejohn and Eddie Cooper. Pat makes his way up the ice waterfall while I belay him *(left, out of shot)*.

I spent over ten years with Kerry Mountain Rescue which, under the leadership of Con Moriarty, was an incredibly progressive unit. Pictured at a training session, *left to right:* me, Mike O'Shea, Louis O'Toole, Pat Grandfield, Tim Murphy, Con Moriarty, with Carmel Cremin on the stretcher (circa late 1980s).

Left to right: Con Moriarty, Mike O'Shea and me in the Mountain Man shop in Killarney, Co Kerry, doing the final check on our food and gear for our 1991 Irish Himalayan Ama Dablam Expedition. Along with the pear drops, boxes of trifle and Tayto crisps, we had 2,400 bars of chocolate to share among six of us – 400 bars each to sustain us over a two-month period. Probably not the most scientifically based diet!

My first sighting of the snowy peaks of the Himalaya, seen through the window of the plane on our flight to Kathmandu for the 1991 Irish Himalayan Ama Dablam Expedition. Everest, in the centre, rises above them all.

Kathmandu, the gateway to the Himalaya where all of life is visible on the city streets, was a mind-blowing, eye-popping experience on my first trip there in 1991.

Pat Littlejohn *(to front)* and me *(at rear)* traversing the ridge line between the Mönch and the Eiger in Switzerland in January 1991. We reached the summit of the Eiger the following day.

En route to Ama Dablam Base Camp, I had my first encounter with Buddhist monks and learned about their philosophy and spiritualism, something which impacted significantly on my outlook on life.

Ama Dablam – known as Mother's Necklace – is one of the most beautiful mountains in the world. It stands at 6,812m and is often called the Matterhorn of the Himalaya.

Me carrying heavy loads and fixing ropes between Camp 1 and Camp 3 on Ama Dablam's southwest ridge in 1991.

Holding the Tricolour to mark the first summiting of Ama Dablam – and of a mountain in the Nepalese Himalaya – by an Irish team. On 4 April 1991, Mick Murphy was our sole climber to reach the summit. *Front, left to right:* Mike O'Shea, Ciaran Corrigan, Mick Murphy, Con Moriarty. *Back, left to right:* Tim Hickey (Base Camp manager), Kami Sherpa (tent assistant), me, Larpa Sherpa (assistant cook), Tony Farrell.

Below: With Maciej Berbeka in the Nepal-Tibet border town of Zhangmu en route to Everest's north side in 1993.

English climber Mark Miller, who set up extreme adventure company Out There Trekking (OTT) in the early 1990s. Having met Mark while climbing in Scotland, I joined OTT's 1993 Everest Expedition. Tragically, Mark died in a plane crash in September 1992 while on the way to do another expedition in Nepal.

Tightly packed into the lorry that was taking us on what is known as the 'Road to Hell' from Zhangmu to Nyalam and on to Everest's north side during the heavy monsoon season, in 1993. *Left to right:* Brigitte Muir, me, Mike Chapman.

Left: NASA astronaut Karl Henize, who had travelled to outer space on the space shuttle Challenger, lost his life due to altitude sickness at 6,400m on Everest in 1993. *(Inset)* The stone marking the place where we buried Karl on the East Rongbuk Glacier.

Sitting in Denali Base Camp on the Kahiltna Glacier with pots and pans to hand, I contemplate the snowy paradise around me, including the summit of Mount Foraker, in 1994.

Standing on the 6,190m summit of Denali (Mount McKinley) on 14 June 1994, I was happy to have the first of the Seven Summits under my belt.

The 5,895m Mount Kilimanjaro is known as the Roof of Africa. I first reached its summit with my friend Joe O'Leary on 4 January 1995, making it the second of my Seven Summits completed. Since then, I have led groups there annually on over fifty guided climbs.

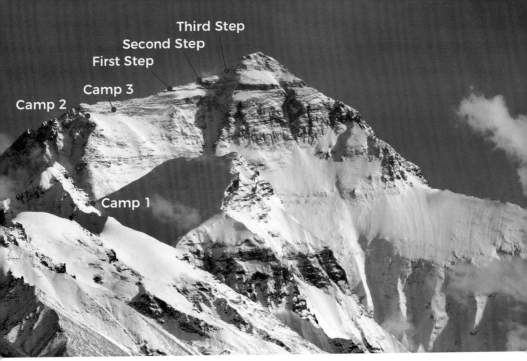

The upper flanks of the north side of Mount Everest, showing the route I climbed in 1993 and 1995.

Below: In 1996, I led a group of over forty to Kili on a charity climb for Rehab. Standing on the summit are *left to right*: Joe O'Leary, my older son Brian, me.

Right: Despite what had happened in 1993, I was happy to return to Everest in 1995 with Jon Tinker as expedition leader. He and I are pictured in the airport at Gatwick before take-off for Kathmandu.

Me en route to the higher Camp 2 at 7,900m with Camp 1 on Everest's North Col at 7,000m behind me.

Right: The notorious Second Step at 8,610m, with people ascending a rock outcrop before getting on to the ladder installed by a Chinese team in 1975 to facilitate climbers getting over the vertical barrier to the Third Step and the summit slope.

Looking back and down from Camp 2 at the North Col, along the Changtse ridge and onto Changtse Mountain (7,543m).

It was a proud moment for me at 9.10am on 27 May 1995, when I stood on the summit of Mount Everest for the first time with my friends, James Allen and Mike Smith. I now had the third – and highest – of the Seven Summits in the bag.

After climbing Mount Everest, it was a very emotional moment for Marie, Brian, Patrick and me when we met up for the first time in three months at Cork Airport, in June 1995.

I was overwhelmed at the great welcome I got at Cork Airport on my return from Everest in 1995. *Left to right:* me, Minister Bernard Allen, Gerry Donovan, marketing director at BOC Gases, my first climbing mentor, Val Deane, and Tim Falvey, the Lord Mayor of Cork – my delighted father.

Climbers approaching Aconcagua Base Camp. This is the highest mountain in South America at 6,961m.

Left: The chain-smoking, vodka-drinking George Kotov, one of Russia's elite mountaineers, was my partner on my first ascent of Elbrus in 1996. We had also been on the Everest expeditions together in 1993 and 1995.

Mount Elbrus, Europe's tallest mountain, is recognisable by its twin peaks. The higher one at 5,642m is on the left. Elbrus became the fifth of my Seven Summits when I reached its summit on 2 April 1996 during a winter ascent. Since then, I've climbed it almost twenty times.

Standing on the summit of Mount Vinson, the highest point in Antarctica and the sixth of my seventh summits, on 24 January 1997.

On 14 February 1997, my Seven Summits dream came true when I stood on the summit of Mount Kosciuszko in Australia. Although the lowest and least challenging of all the Seven Summits, this climb was very special because I was joined by three close friends and fellow rebels from Kerry. *Left to right:* Mike O'Shea, Con Moriarty, me and Gene Tangney on the summit of Kosciuszko.

After completing the Seven Summits, I travelled to West Papua New Guinea where I was honoured to spend time with members of the Dani tribe and where I got the opportunity to immerse myself in their culture and traditions.

On 20 May 1998, I led a team to the summit of Cho Oyu, the sixth highest mountain in the world at 8,201m. When team member Gavin Bate reached the summit with me, it marked the first Irish ascent of an 8,000er without oxygen. Pictured at high camp above the clouds before our summit attempt.

While our 1999 Ama Dablam team was doing an acclimatising climb on Mera Peak in the Hinku Valley in Nepal, the mountain was hit by a severe snowstorm which killed over ten people in the region. On our retreat from Mera, two local porters from another team died.

Me descending the steep Mushroom Ridge on Ama Dablam after reaching its summit on 18 November 1999, eight years after my first attempt.

Summit
Hillary Step
South Summit
South Col

Everest's imposing south face, including the south-southeast ridge, the Hillary Step, the South Summit and the summit.

Just after a puja at Base Camp, all the 2003 Irish Everest Expedition team, including the Sherpas – the unsung heroes of the mountain – gathered to celebrate the start of the climb.

The 2003 Irish Everest Expedition climbing team, which I led. *Left to right:* Clare O'Leary, Mick Murphy, me, Hannah Shields, Ger McDonnell, George Shorten.

Crossing the treacherous Khumbu Icefall after leaving Everest Base Camp is something that focuses the mind of even the most proficient of climbers.

After developing oedema at Camp 4, George had to be helped descend the mountain and was taken by helicopter to hospital in Kathmandu where he eventually made a recovery.

On our summit attempt, Clare was forced to descend from the Lhotse face due to a stomach bug while Hannah had to descend due to frostbite danger a mere six hours from the summit. I stopped at the Hillary Step, just one hour from the summit, due to developing oedema. Happily, Ger McDonnell and Mick Murphy reached the summit on 22 May 2003, making ours the first Irish team to reach the top of Everest from the south side. Pemba Gyalje and Pemba Rinzee also reached the summit that day. *Left to right:* Clare O'Leary, Mick Murphy, me, Ger McDonnell, Hannah Shields.

In March 2004, *left to right:* me, John Joyce and Clare O'Leary returned to climb Everest's south side with Pemba Gyalje (*right*).

Base Camp at Everest's south side with the Khumbu Icefall looming above.

On 18 May 2004 at 6.45am, Clare and I reached the top of the world together. In this moment, Clare became the first Irish woman to reach the summit of the world's highest mountain. Pemba Gyalje, Lama Babu, Lama Jangbu and Nang Chemmi also reached the summit that day.

Shortly after we began our descent, this shot was taken before we reached the Hillary Step. I am standing there for a moment, taking in the stunning beauty of the highest mountains in the world.

While at the top of Everest, I hit the highest puc fada in the world, remembering our national game of hurling and as a nod to all the brilliant hurlers who have come from Cork.

With our team, Clare and I descended the historical Hillary Step (8,751m), where I had almost died in 2003.

On the summit of Denali on 20 June 2005, *left to right:* me, John Dowd, Clare O'Leary, Ger McDonnell, John Roche.

On 16 December 2005, Clare O'Leary made climbing history by becoming the first Irish woman to complete the Seven Summits when she reached the summit of Mount Vinson in Antarctica. On that date, I became the first person in the world to complete the challenge twice by climbing Everest from both its south and north sides. *Left to right:* John Dowd, Clare O'Leary, me.

In November 2006, I led the largest ever group of thirty-two people on the Shackleton Traverse in South Georgia, as part of the Irish Beyond Endurance Expedition. We undertook the traverse in honour of Ernest Shackleton, Tom Crean and Frank Worsley who, in 1916, had undertaken the epic journey from Elephant Island across the South Atlantic and Southern Oceans to South Georgia to look for help to save the crew of the *Endurance*.

We had a full group of eighty-four people, including traverse and support team, on board the MV *Ushuaia*. Following our successful traverse, we sailed around the Antarctic waters, landing on various islands. The group is pictured with the infamous Elephant Island in the background.

Our group remembered the legacy of Ernest Shackleton and all the crew of the *Endurance* when we visited his grave in Gryviken, South Georgia. Shackleton died in January 1922.

In September 2007, Shaun Menzies, Clare O'Leary and I became the first Irish team to complete an unsupported ski traverse of the Greenland Ice Cap. *Left to right:* Shaun, Clare, Jon Bradshaw (whom we met while traversing Greenland and who later joined our South Pole team), me.

Clare and I training for the 2008 Irish South Pole Expedition in Tomies Wood in Killarney, Co Kerry. Over a period of twelve months, we carried heavy loads and pulled two to three tyres for up to four hours daily, between four and seven days a week.

Over a sixty-day expedition our red tents and other equipment not only provided shelter but also the only other colour in the otherwise white continent.

Our campsites en route to the South Pole.

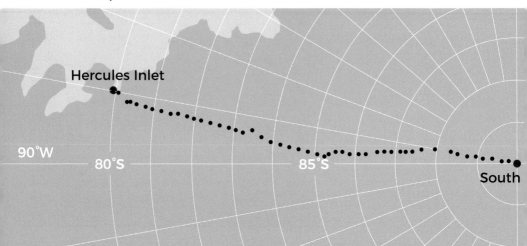

Hercules Inlet

90°W

80°S

85°S

South

Shaun resting in his tent, with a list of ailments that he had developed during his first fifteen days on the ice written on the tent fabric. These included crotch rot and heat rash on the testicles, a swollen ankle, tweaked thigh muscle, allergic reaction spots on the chin, blisters on his feet and frostnip on his ear.

Thirty-eight days into our expedition, I was in agony and on the ground after hurting my back badly. This was the most serious injury I'd ever suffered in all my years of adventuring and it brought me to my knees in more ways than one.

Every night, when the day's hauling was done and I was settled in the tent, I would take out the map of our route and mark off the distance travelled that day. We wrote every completed distance on the fabric of our tent as reassurance that we were making headway in our mammoth 1,140km journey.

On the first day of 2008, we reached 180km from the South Pole, the distance from the Pole Shackleton reached when he made the heartbreaking but correct decision to turn back in order to save the lives of his crew. Jon cut his name out of the snow to honour a man who was a hero to us all.

On 8 January 2008, we arrived at 90° south and became the first Irish team to reach the South Pole. *Left to right:* me, Shaun Menzies, Clare O'Leary, Jon Bradshaw.

My mother's prayers were answered when we returned safely from our successful 2008 South Pole Expedition. *Left to right:* Jon Bradshaw, Shaun Menzies, me, Clare O'Leary and my proud mother, Bina, pictured on our arrival from the bottom of the world at Cork Airport in January 2008.

On 2 August 2008, Ger McDonnell died tragically on K2, the world's second highest mountain at 8,611m. The previous day he had become the first Irishman to reach its summit but he died in an avalanche while descending. We spent many happy times together, including on Denali in 2005 when we reached its summit. *Left to right:* Ger and me.

In my role as executive producer on *The Summit* documentary, in Kathmandu, Nepal, in December 2008. *Left to right:* line producer and cameraman Stephen O'Reilly, director Nick Ryan, me.

Rolf Bae, my polar training partner and friend, also died on K2 in August 2008, just hours before Ger lost his life. *Left to right:* Rolf and Ger having a laugh on South Georgia during the 2006 Irish Beyond Endurance Expedition.

On our first trip to the North Pole, Clare O'Leary and I stood at 90° north on the pole in a sea of ice.

Having donned her dry suit, Clare swims across a lead in the Arctic waters.

Clare and I training on moving sea ice for our second North Pole attempt in 2011, in Iqaluit in northern Canada.

Within seconds of exposure to the Arctic conditions, ice formed on Clare's face.

Relaxing from her duties as President of Ireland, Mary McAleese reached the summit of Carrauntoohil, on a trek led by me, with a group of family and friends, including her husband, Martin *(back, first right of cross)*, daughter, Emma *(front, fourth from left)*, son-in-law Micheál O'Connell *(front, third from left)* and his father, the renowned Kerry footballer, Mick O'Connell *(back, second right of cross)*.

Left: The stories of others were my first and abiding inspiration to become an adventurer and now I love to inspire others at seminars, courses and presentations around the world.

Below: On stage at the Cork Opera House performing my one-man show, *Everest, Antarctica and Beyond Endurance*.

Left: At our boot camps we train people to push their limits.

It's an honour and joy for me to bring groups of people beyond their comfort zones and into their full potential on treks to Elbrus, Kilimanjaro, Everest Base Camp, South America, Antarctica and other destinations around the world.

Mum and Dad are always at the centre of the extended Falvey clan, which now includes four generations.

relations and while their living spaces were small, their welcome for me was huge. After a few days in the city, George and I flew south to Mineralnye Vody Airport where we hired a Lada car and a driver to take us to the Baksan Valley in the Elbrus region.

The 150km journey was broken by three militia checkpoints where the same scene was played out each time. Our convoy of twenty vehicles, with a tank in front and a tank behind our car, would be stopped by bored looking soldiers. Our driver would say a few words and there would be a curt response. Then the driver would hand over 2,000 Russian roubles – the equivalent of $1 – which I had supplied him with, and we would be waved on. This military bureaucracy was more like the stereotypical Russia I'd expected to encounter. In 1996, such behaviour was even more evident with the war between Russia and nearby Chechnya at its bloodiest. Hundreds of tanks and thousands of troops were on standby to join the war, which was taking place 250km from where we were climbing.

I wasn't too concerned at the show of military heavy-handedness although I was still relieved when we turned off the main road and headed towards the Baksan Valley. It was a lovely rural area with cows roaming freely across the roads and small villages along the route looking as if they hadn't changed since medieval times.

Jail time

We eventually reached our destination at Cheget village. At the hotel we had to hand in our identification and travel papers to be checked and stamped. As I passed mine to George, I was thinking about the plans he and I had to explore the region and meet up with some of his friends before our climb. That train of thought was brought to an abrupt halt when I heard my friend arguing with the hotel registrar. George had to explain to me what was going on; my papers, it seemed, were not in order and I didn't have the required permit to be in the Central Caucasus region.

I couldn't believe what I was hearing. It turned out that the Russian Embassy in Dublin had issued a visa listing only St Petersburg and Moscow as the places I would be visiting and omitting to give details of anywhere else. I'd assumed that each destination I was going to was written on the visa, but there was no mention of Cheget and now things were beginning to look very dicey.

The registrar had the air of someone who was grimly enjoying this moment. He said we would have to leave and that he would be informing the police of the situation but that we could spend the night in the hotel. In the meantime, he would be keeping my passport, luggage and money. I could hardly believe that my climb was in danger of failing before I had even seen Elbrus. We went to our room where George pulled a bottle of vodka out of nowhere – a trick he was apt to perform regularly – and we drank the night away.

The next morning, the police arrived and George and I were escorted to the main barracks in Tyrnyauz, the administrative centre for the region. I wasn't feeling too hopeful as we sat in a smoke-filled office before an unfriendly-looking official. He wanted to know how I'd gotten this far beyond St Petersburg without the correct papers. I hadn't known that I had insufficient permits, so I could only guess that the money I'd parted with along the road had helped me arrive at this point. I was thinking that another bribe would get me a bit nearer to Elbrus so, when I handed over my passport, I slipped a $50 note into it. This, it turned out, was a wrong move. 'You have made a big mistake,' the official said, looking at the money in disgust. He then had two police officers usher me to a cell; I was being arrested for trying to bribe an officer.

George started to talk like a man on speed and I hadn't a clue what he was saying. I later learned that he explained to the official that I was from Ireland and was climbing the Seven Summits. When the man heard the word 'Ireland' his demeanour changed from hostile to friendly and I was released from the cell. He started talking about the USSR–Ireland game at the 1988 European Championship. He mentioned Jack Charlton and Roy Keane before asking me questions about our national team. It turned out that he was an avid soccer fan. His English wasn't great and while I wasn't too sure what was being said, I replied 'yes' to every question.

The discussion continued for what seemed like ages before the official stood up, shook our hands and ordered the two policemen to drive us back to the Elbrus region. We couldn't return to the tourist hotel because I had no visa, so the official organised alternative accommodation for us at a hotel in Terskol where the residents were military and navy personnel. He told George we would be safe there and I would be able to continue with my climb without any further queries about my visa. Greatly relieved, we spent the next week skiing and acclimatising for our summit attempt.

Beaten by a blizzard

On 20 March, we walked to the AZU cable car station at the base of Elbrus and took the cable car to Mir Station at 3,658m. From there, we trekked to the Priut-11 Hut, situated at 3,960m on the south face of the mountain. Most people climb the mountain in summer when conditions are more stable and our winter ascent, while not technically difficult, would throw up challenging conditions in terms of cold, wind and elevation. For a mountain whose main route is considered a non-technical climb, Elbrus has an astonishing death rate of between fifteen and thirty climbers annually. As we slogged up towards Priut-11, I didn't have to be reminded that every mountain presents its own unique dangers. I was stunned by how cold it was; it felt colder and damper than any place I'd ever been before.

We weren't ascending for long through deep snow when we were hit by a whiteout: I literally couldn't see my hand in front of my face. The blizzard reduced visibility to less than a metre and it took us over three hours to reach the hut where we would get some reprieve from the weather. Priut-11, a three-storey aluminium-clad structure, was a primitive building but George and I looked forward to getting inside it so much it might as well have been a luxury hotel. The hut was normally open only during the summer climbing season, which began in May but, as we were the only climbers heading for the summit at the time, George had asked the caretaker to leave it unlocked for us.

We were totally pissed off when we got to the door and discovered that it was still locked. We had to get out of the blizzard so we forced our way inside. There were lots of empty bunks for sleeping on but, other than that, the place was bare. We ate and rested and tried to keep warm until 2am when we set off for the west peak of Elbrus. Yet again, we trudged through very heavy snow as we made our way towards the Pastukhov Rocks at around 4,700m. When we reached them, we were both frozen to the bone. The wind was increasing and we knew that becoming too cold was the greatest danger facing us. We talked about what to do, and decided to return to Priut to wait out the blizzard and biting winds.

We remained there for twenty-two hours, drinking tea and talking. When it came to going for the summit, both George and I knew that patience was vital. When you are close to the top, your instinct is always to want to push on for the summit, but we both knew the mountain wasn't ready and could take us out if we continued upwards. We also knew that if we continued we would be exposing ourselves to the risk of frostbite and hypothermia. A mountain, I'd always said, is not worth a finger or a toe, so we sat and waited.

At 3am the next morning we set off, glad to be on the move again. There was an ice-cold mist and we had to use a compass this time to direct us towards the Pastukhov Rocks. Through thickening fog, we reached the rocks and moved beyond them towards the saddle that sits between Elbrus' twin peaks. As we traversed north, we came into a crevasse-ridden plain. Fairly quickly, we found ourselves in another whiteout; it was way too dangerous to continue through the crevasses so we returned to Priut for yet another long, cold night. We were both very tired by now from being at altitude and from the relentless cold.

There was no way of warming up in these conditions, so George suggested we go back down to the valley to get some proper rest and to review the situation. I agreed, happy to get away from the hard conditions at this elevation. I didn't see our retreat as defeat; rather, it was an opportunity to rest, reassess and give us a better chance of getting to the summit.

Waiting it out

It was good to be down in the valley again where, though temperatures were well below freezing, the cold didn't seep into my bones as it had done up the mountain. Two days later, the sky was blue and the sun shone; Elbrus was ready and so were we. We took the cable car up to Mir Station again and, this time, the trek to Priut was pleasant, with lots of people out skiing. Although it was my third time at the hut, it was the first time that the view from that elevation was visible and it was worth seeing. There was something quietly noble about the panorama as I looked along the majestic Caucasus main ridge up to the twin peaks of Elbrus.

We rested in the hut for several hours, waiting for our 2am start to the summit. The night was dark and clear and in less than three hours we were at the top of the Pastukhov Rocks. Although the ground was good as we went upwards to the saddle, I was really feeling the cold again and wondered momentarily if I could continue. Thankfully, as the sun rose, so did my body temperature, albeit fractionally. Still, it gave me the push I needed.

We rested in the saddle before traversing under the east summit to the higher west peak. We still had a few hours of hard climbing on an icy slope which was like walking on glass. We had to take extra care here as, if we fell, it would be very difficult to break the fall with an ice axe because of the impenetrable terrain. I didn't need to look up to see the rich colours that filled the sky; I could see the crimson rays reflected on the icy ground under my feet. When we reached the summit ridge, I finally looked around me at the glistening beauty of the ice fields we had just come through and at the motionless clouds below. The summit field in front of us was broad and white, with a gentle slope to the final ice-covered peak.

Finally, on 2 April 1996, I was at the top of Elbrus, the fifth of my Seven Summits. I hugged my friend, delighted we were sharing this moment, then I took out the Tricolour and we took the mandatory summit photos. It was time to descend, but George wasn't ready yet. He reached into his bag and brought out a packet of cigarettes. He was a man at peace as the nicotine hit the back of his throat.

My first trip to Elbrus was a triumph of patience over summit fever. Subsequent trips were less challenging for the most part although my 1998 climb there coincided with a fire in the Priut Hut just as we approached it for an overnight rest. A number of people were injured and it was a miracle that nobody died in the blaze that destroyed the shelter. In the following years, I have climbed the mountain multiple times, leading expeditions of people who want to climb Europe's highest peak.

MOUNT VINSON 1997
ANTARCTICA

At 4,892m, Mount Vinson is the highest mountain in Antarctica, the coldest, most remote and most hostile continent on the planet. I was really excited about going there as I'd been fascinated by the place since devouring books on the lives of legendary explorers like Ernest Shackleton, Robert Scott, Roald Amundsen and Tom Crean. Training for the sixth of the Seven Summits was different; the temperatures and katabatic winds in the region were going to be like nothing I'd ever experienced before, and I had to prepare my body for the challenge ahead. But firstly I had to deal with the issue of funding the expedition which was costing in the region of $50,000.

With my local support team, I devised an educational project for Irish schoolchildren, based on the expedition to Antarctica, to be rolled out in a number of schools on my return. A grant application was made on my behalf, via the Mountaineering Council of Ireland, to the Department of Education and the Environment. I was on Kilimanjaro in August 1996 when I got a call from my office in Cork to say that the minister had allocated £20,000 for the project. This was great news as it relieved me of the burden of finding further sponsorship for the expedition.

As the weeks turned into months, however, there was no sign of the grant money. Then, in early November, something unprecedented happened: the MCI returned the cheque to the government department. While the main committee had approved the application and receipt of the money, the expedition committee objected and had overruled their chairman. They sent the cheque back to the National Lottery, stating that they would not give it to me because they felt the project was not worthy of support even though their general committee had approved it and had sent me a letter confirming this.

Everyone was puzzled, including the officials at the National Lottery and the government department. I was in a state of angry disbelief. Not only was this a personal insult to me, but this action, at such a late stage, meant that there was little chance I could secure expedition sponsorship for the shortfall in the weeks before Christmas and my departure in early January. I threatened to sue the MCI for breach of duty in not forwarding the funds they had agreed to administer.

I believed this behaviour to be begrudgery on the part of some senior members of the council who contended that I had introduced commercialism into Irish climbing. For years, I had heard what the fraternity were saying about me but I had always taken it on the chin and said nothing. This, however, was much more direct. I needed that money to fund both the shortfall of the expedition and the educational project, and both were now in jeopardy. Over the following weeks, there was much heated discussion between the MCI, the National Lottery office, the government department and me before the council finally agreed to accept the grant and pass it to me just two weeks before my departure.

Throughout all this upheaval, I had continued organising the logistics and training for the expedition. This included spending twenty-four hours in a giant meat freezer in Midleton, Co Cork, where I was joined by fellow 'rookies' from Kerry – Con Moriarty, Mike O'Shea and Gene Tangney. I wanted to test my clothing and gear to see how they performed in conditions of extreme dry cold. I particularly wanted to see how the stoves I'd sourced performed at low temperatures. It was a useful experiment from the point of view of ensuring that everything was working well at temperatures of $-30°$. It was also a fun twenty-four hours with my mates in a deep freeze the size of Croke Park. Our antics caught the imagination of the local and national press, who were keen to do colour stories on 'Little Antarctica', as our overnight lodgings were called.

Another world

On 5 January 1997, I flew to Paris where I met up with the other team members. I had climbed previously with Frenchman and full-time mountaineer Thierry Reinhard on Everest in 1993; I had climbed Everest with Jeff Shea from San Francisco in 1995 and had met Michael Jerjensen, a full-time adventurer from Holland, at Base Camp that year. It was my first time meeting the other Frenchman, Jean Luc Neidergang, who had already climbed five of the Seven Summits and had Mount Vinson and Everest yet to do.

We flew to Punto Arenas in Chile; from there we were taking what was considered to be one of the most expensive flights on Earth – costing in the region of $17,000 – across the Southern Ocean to Antarctica's Patriot Hills. A storm on the white continent meant we ended up having to stay put in Punta Arenas for four days, during which we saw every single tourist attraction in the largest city in southern Chile. On the fifth day, we got good news: the storm at Patriot Hills had abated and our flight was going ahead.

We were delighted to be on the move and quickly got to the airport where we loaded all our gear into the Hercules plane. Once on board, we sat on the pull-down timber seats, belted up and waited for our flight of almost five hours to begin. There were fourteen people in total on the flight – ourselves, a few other adventurers and some people who worked at the Patriot Hills base for Adventure Network International (ANI), the sole company providing support for scientists and adventurers to the interior of Antarctica. It was claustrophobic sitting like paratroopers squeezed beside the cargo in the plane, which had originally been used for transporting soldiers to war zones.

There were no windows to look out and it was great when the pilot allowed everyone to spend some time in the cockpit. Looking at the white world unfolding before my eyes, I had a sense that we were flying into nothingness. There was no scale to what I was seeing; it was as if the world I knew had disappeared and we were approaching a new, strange and pristine landscape. I had never seen anything like it before.

The process of landing the plane was enough to bring me back to reality. I have always had an irrational fear of flying and, as we approached Patriot Hills, this feeling was heightened. The landing strip was a 4km blue-ice runway on which hydraulic brakes couldn't be applied or the plane would go into an uncontrolled slide. We could hear the throttle moving back and forth as the pilots worked hard to bring the machine to a gradual stop. It was a relief when we finally halted and were able to disembark. Standing at Patriot Hills and looking at the vast expanse of white emptiness around us was surreal. So few people ever get the chance to set foot on this continent, and I felt very lucky to be one of them.

The semi-permanent camp at Patriot Hills consisted of a number of heated tents where scientists, adventurers and visitors could stay. There was a communal tent that served as a dining room and gathering area. Some of those present, like ourselves, were climbing Mount Vinson, while others were there to walk from the edge of the continent to the South Pole; others were being flown to the 89th parallel south in order to do the last degree to the Pole while a small handful were flying to the 90th parallel south for the sheer thrill of saying they had stood at the South Pole. They would then be flown back to Patriot Hills before flying out in the next scheduled Hercules. This was a phenomenally expensive flight with no five-star treatment, yet people were happy to pay the price just to set foot on Antarctica.

Out-climbing the storm

We set up our tents and stayed at Patriot Hills for two nights until the weather was suitable for take-off for our 200km flight to Vinson Base Camp, at 2,308m on the Branscombe Glacier. We flew in a small, cramped Cessna while a Twin Otter carried our gear. After the planes dropped us at Base Camp, our isolation was complete. Now it was just the five of us amid endless snow and ice. In front of us were the snow-covered Ellsworth Mountains, the highest mountain range in Antarctica. The range is bisected by the Minnesota Glacier, with the Heritage Range to the south and the Sentinel Range to the north. Mount Vinson is in the Sentinel Range and at 4,892m is the highest point on the continent.

We barely had time to take in our surroundings before our radio crackled. There was a weather alert: a system was moving in on Vinson at 914m in forty-eight hours and would move to 3,048m over the following days. We agreed that we needed to get higher up the mountain straight away.

Once our gear was ready, we hooked up to our sleds and set off to Camp 1 at 2,769m. It was a tough, seven-hour slog pulling our sleds and heavy packs over the hard ice. Once there, we set up our tents as quickly as possible. Not having slept in over forty hours, everyone was exhausted and in need of a hot drink and food. Tempers frayed when it took much longer than normal to light the stoves but none of us had energy to waste on useless recriminations. We didn't have sufficient experience of lighting stoves in continuous very low temperatures to know that the flow of the gas was being impeded by the extreme cold. As the days passed, we copped on to the fact that if we heated the funnel lightly with a candle then the gas would come through without a problem.

After eating, we quickly got into our sleeping bags for some much-needed rest. There was little to distinguish day from night in the twenty-four-hour light and we were soon up and getting ready to move upwards to Camp 2. The biggest challenge was again the sheer slog of pulling heavy sleds up towards 3,100m. The weather update meant that we needed to get as high as we could as quickly as possible.

We rested for the night and next day we left our sleds behind and carried what we needed in our rucksacks. Having negotiated our way around numerous crevasses, we moved through an area known as the Icefall. At Camp 3, at 3,692m, we pitched our tents for the night on the saddle that sits between Vinson and Mount Shinn. We were now above the storm, and as we looked down from our perch we could see the weather system below us.

Next day was our day to head for the summit. We checked in for a weather update and were told the storm wasn't expected to rise any higher. Conditions above us were perfect and we set off, roped together for safety in case one of us fell into one of the many crevasses. It took five long and exhausting hours to reach the summit ridge.

Out of the blue, Jean Luc starting arguing that we were on the wrong mountain. He was so convinced that he was right that he refused to move and held up the progress of the entire team. It took a lot of arguing – and time wasted consulting maps – to convince Jean Luc that we were, in fact, on Mount Vinson. I was finding the cold hard to bear, and standing around trying to convince someone we were on the right mountain in the middle of Antarctica did nothing to help that. My biggest fear about getting so cold was that it was draining my energy as my body struggled to retain heat. But we were within an hour of the summit at that point and, almost suddenly, we were there.

On 24 January 1997, I stood on the highest point in Antarctica. The panorama was vast and white and silent, with a sense of expansiveness that I had never experienced before. I could see the curvature of the Earth and was fascinated that a guy from Gurranabraher, a mason who had left school at fifteen, was standing in this place, holding his country's flag.

Hit by hypothermia

We quickly started downward to Camp 3, food and rest. When we got there we radioed for the latest weather update and to share news of our success. There was another storm coming in and we were told we had to get off the mountain. There was no time to lose and no time for the rest and nourishment our bodies so badly needed. A plane was being despatched to collect us within twenty-four hours. If we missed it, we were told, we could be stranded on Mount Vinson for seven days until the storm blew over.

We decided to go for it and moved very fast, not stopping at Camps 1 or 2 other than to collect what we had stored there, including our sleds. Shortly before we got to Base Camp, the clouds came in and the temperature dropped further. None of us had eaten or drunk enough over the previous twenty-four hours and, even though I could feel there was something very wrong in my body, I just kept going.

At Base Camp, we were all frozen to the core with very little energy left. To add to our problems, the sun dipped below the horizon and the temperature dropped by a further 20°. We were exhausted, freezing cold, hungry and thirsty from our long two-day retreat without rest or sleep. We only had the energy to erect one tent which we all packed into. When we tried to light the stoves they wouldn't ignite. Fully clothed, we got into our sleeping bags. To try and generate heat we huddled close together but it didn't work as we were all frozen. I could feel my core temperature drop as my body shivered uncontrollably. I could see my hands in front of my face through my frozen eyelids but I couldn't feel them as my body started to close down. As I lay there, I didn't know if I was going to survive or not.

Hours later, the tent began to change colour; I knew that the morning sun would bring some warmth and as I watched our small tent become suffused with bright light, I could feel life come back into my body and, gradually, I stopped shivering. By the time the others woke up, I had recovered from what was my first – and last – experience of severe hypothermia.

When the Cessna and Twin Otter planes appeared, I was very glad to get on board. The doctor at Patriot Hills did a check on me and confirmed the signs of hypothermia. In the rush to get to Base Camp and not miss our flight, I had pushed myself beyond my limits. I hadn't eaten, drunk or rested enough in an environment where even a 1° drop in temperature can burn up your energy reserves. I was learning that, in remote areas, it is not necessarily the technical challenges that are the problem; rather, it is the environment. I was lucky to have gotten out of it so quickly and without any lasting effects, but the experience taught me hard lessons about not pushing my body beyond what it could reasonably endure.

MOUNT KOSCIUSZKO 1997
AUSTRALIA

I didn't delay in Punta Arenas with the other team members as I was already late for a meeting with some of my oldest climbing friends from Kerry – Con, Shea and Gene. These original rookies had agreed to join me for the final Seven Summits' climb and to undertake what we called the Southern Hemisphere Expedition where we would climb Mount Cook in New Zealand, Mount Kosciuszko in Australia and Carstensz Pyramid in West Papua New Guinea. I was thrilled that, at the end of this life-changing project, some of my closest climbing friends would be with me.

The lads were already at Mount Cook Village climbers' base and tourist centre, and I made my way there after my plane touched down in New Zealand. It was fantastic to meet and catch up on all the news. Con and Gene had already been to the summit of Mount Cook via the north ridge and we intended doing a group climb to the summit via the east ridge. Our plan was to head off the following morning but when we woke, the weather had broken and for the next three days we were Base Camp-bound on the Tasman Glacier at 2,400m. It didn't bother us too much as we had great fun, the kind you can only have with old friends.

We hooked up with two other Kerrymen, Brian Galvin and Mick Quirke, who were at the village. When the weather finally cleared, I climbed Mount Cook with Brian and Mick on a fifteen-hour round trip by the Linda Glacier via its left ridge line and ticked off the highest point in New Zealand. After descending we visited all the notable sites in the vicinity, including Fiordland National Park where we climbed the 1,828m Mitre Peak, a beautiful and difficult mountain on the shore of Milford Sound. Then we got a helicopter to pick us up from the summit, just for the fun of it.

At 2,228m, Mount Kosciuszko is the lowest of the Seven Summits and the final peak I needed to climb to complete my three-year project. Located on the Main Range of the Snowy Mountain in Australia, this is the easiest of all the highest continental summits to climb, and anyone with a fairly good level of fitness can walk to the top.

We flew into Sydney and spent a few days there, seeing the tourist sites and hanging out in the city. I was anxious to get back on the road, though, so we cut short our stay in the city, hired a car and set off on a five-day trip. We shared the driving, laughed, sang, hopped ball and generally had a great time together. Finally we reached Kosciuszko National Park with plans to climb the mountain straight away but the heavens opened so we decided to wait until the following evening. I was going to be interviewed from the summit by Irish radio host Pat Kenny and needed to be in situ in the late evening because of the time difference. The rain continued all the next day, though it wasn't as heavy as previously, and that evening the four of us, along with a few Australian pals, set off up the muddy trail of Mount Kosciuszko.

We chatted and laughed all the way up a mountain that, uncannily, reminded me of Mangerton in Co Kerry, the first mountain I had ever climbed. We saw the summit and went for it. In what seemed like no time at all, I was standing on the top of the seventh of my Seven Summits: on 14 February 1997 my dream had become reality. What made this moment really special for me was the fact that I got to share it with the people I'd started my climbing career with, people who had helped me train and who had supported me throughout my Seven Summits odyssey.

There were no problems for interviewer Pat Kenny in getting a clear phone line from Ireland to the summit. He congratulated me on becoming the first Irish person and the fiftieth person in the world to complete the Seven Summits. 'How does it feel?' he asked. 'Amazing,' I answered. Having my dream come true was amazing, but even more so was the fact that in the previous ten years I'd had the opportunity to travel to some of the most beautiful and remote parts of the world; I felt truly blessed.

West Papua New Guinea

Con, Shea, Gene and I planned to travel to West Papua New Guinea to climb the Carstensz Pyramid, the highest mountain in Australasia, after climbing Kosciuszko. I was also intrigued by the local Stone Age Dani tribe, their culture and ancient way of life and wanted to learn about how colonisation was affecting a group whose traditions stretched back millennia. I was particularly intrigued by stories of the last female warrior tribe and was hoping to meet with them if they, in fact, existed.

Expeditions were severely restricted in the province and we had to secure a special permit to visit and climb in the area. We managed to secure one but, just before we arrived in the country, our permit was cancelled by the authorities. We understood that this was due to the fact that, a few months earlier, two Britons, two Dutch and five Indonesians had been kidnapped and two of the hostages had been killed. Despite this, we continued our journey, determined to see this amazing part of the world and to get as close as we could to the mountain. Through some people I knew, I made contact with Justinius J. Darby, a spokesperson from the OPM Free Papua Movement. When he heard we were from Ireland, he agreed to get us to the interior and to ensure our safety from attack from the OPM. We were willing to take the risk.

We met with Justinius in Jayapura, the capital city. He organised all the logistics and our flight to Wamena, a remote jungle town 300km from the nearest road. There we awaited a flight to the village of Illaga and the start of our trek to Carstensz Pyramid. However, just before boarding, we were told that all flights had been cancelled for the foreseeable future. We had to accept that our attempt to reach Carstensz Pyramid was over.

We spent the next few weeks deep in the jungle, living and travelling with members of the Dani. After my three friends flew back to Ireland, I stayed on a bit longer with Justinius, visiting some of the local villages and schools. It was one of the most interesting places I ever visited but a few months after I returned home, I learned that, tragically, Justinius had been killed by the Indonesian military.

My travels, and especially the weeks I had spent living with the various tribal people in West Papua New Guinea, gave me a new perspective on my own life. I knew I had much to be grateful for: I was living in a free country with good health and education systems and good infrastructure. We didn't live under the threat of avalanches, earthquakes or landslides. Compared to the challenges and deprivation that I'd seen people facing in other countries around the world, life in Ireland was very easy indeed.

PART FOUR
RETURN TO THE TOP OF THE WORLD

TAKING STOCK OF MY LIFE

After returning from my three-year Seven Summits odyssey in the spring of 1997, I had lots of new dreams and ideas buzzing in my head. I was fascinated not just by mountains but also by the people I'd met and the places I'd been. I wanted to learn more about the psychology and mindset which have driven humans since our evolution and which challenge us to succeed. My adventures were challenging all my old beliefs – personal, emotional, spiritual and psychological. My journey around the world had also rocked the core belief my grandmother had taught me, which was that making money was my main function in life. I had a keen sense that it was now time for a proper stocktaking of my life. I had too many balls in the air and it was time to reflect and reassess my goals and dreams for the future.

There was one thing I had no doubt about: after over ten years climbing throughout the world, I wanted to continue as a full-time adventurer. The hooks that had drawn me in from the beginning – travelling, climbing mountains, meeting people from different cultures and learning about their traditions, observing up close how humans follow their dreams and make them come true – were as strong as ever.

Since my business trauma and suicide attempt in the late 1980s, I and a small group of employees had worked steadily over a ten-year period to rebuild my business in housing, property development, auctioneering and financial services. The business was doing very well and it could be said that I had it all – financial stability, a successful business, freedom to travel and do my expedition, and a family that loved and supported me. But I was under huge pressure time-wise trying to keep it all together. My focus was split and I knew that, to reach my full potential, I needed to choose between my business and my adventure life. I knew my family was hoping for the return to normality of their prodigal son, and my mind was in turmoil as I looked for answers.

I took some time out and headed back to my spiritual home in Nepal to seek clarity on what to do next. After a lot of consideration, I decided to get out of the business I'd spent all my life developing and focus on my career as a full-time adventurer, guide, public speaker and author. I set up a new company, Pat Falvey Irish & Worldwide Adventures, to provide skills training and run treks and expeditions around the world, as well as offering inspirational talks, courses and seminars on personal development and the importance of teamwork in achieving success. I believed that anyone could follow their dream and fulfil their goals, just as I was doing, if they believed in themselves and learned the proper skills.

No one believed that my new dream was viable, and my family thought I was going through a midlife crisis. My responsibilities to them weighed heavily on mind and, before taking any step towards my new future, I had to figure out how I could make this work financially, especially for my wife and sons, whose material well-being was paramount for me. To ensure I had sufficient, regular income, I converted some properties I owned into rental apartments. I had office space at my home in Beechwood that I could use and, once the Falvey Group was wound down, I was free to focus fully on developing adventures to Russia, Africa, Nepal, South America, Antarctica and within Ireland.

It was very exciting to start up a new chapter in my life at forty years of age in an area I felt so passionate about. I started to build up a steady business, mainly by word of mouth, and that, coupled with the public and corporate talks I was giving, became my new source of income. There was a great freedom in not having to split my attention between two completely different sectors and, fairly quickly, travelling the world became not just my passion but also my full-time work.

Foolishly, however, I didn't focus more on my family life. I thought at the time I was taking the correct course of action, but I was sacrificing one of the most important things for my ambitions – time with Marie and the boys, and with my parents and siblings. This was time I could never recover and was something that became a source of deep regret in later years.

CHO OYU 1998

What's next? The question a journalist had asked me on my return home after completing the Seven Summits kept ringing in my ears. As soon as my financial and working life was under control, I began to think seriously about what, in fact, would be my next big adventure. Then it came to me: I wanted to climb one of the world's fourteen 8,000ers – as the mountains that rise above 8,000m are known – without using supplemental oxygen. No Irish climber had done this before and I was captivated by the challenge. I chose Cho Oyu – also known as the Turquoise Goddess – which is located 28km west of Everest on the Nepal-Tibet border. While it is the sixth highest mountain in the world at 8,201m, and one of the 8,000ers, it is known to be one of the more accessible of the high-altitude mountains and one that could, in theory, be climbed within the comparatively short time of six weeks.

When I started getting a team together for the expedition I was looking for people who hadn't climbed an 8,000er before but who had a passion for such a challenge. Con Collins, who'd climbed Denali and Aconcagua with me, was very interested. During the course of some public talks I gave, I got to know two other climbers who were interested and who fitted my criteria. Gavin Bate from Belfast and Eoin Sheehan from Sligo were young, passionate and skilful mountaineers.

All four of us got together to do some climbing and I drew up a training schedule. We were all going to have to meet very specific technical and fitness levels, particularly as we wouldn't be using oxygen on any part of the ascent. I was the only one of the four of us who had climbed an 8,000er before, but I believed that the others were sufficiently focused and willing to do the necessary training to give themselves a realistic chance of success on Cho Oyu. We got on well together and I looked forward to leading this team on an expedition where we would be totally self-reliant from the moment we arrived at our Base Camp in Tibet.

After flying to Kathmandu in April 1998, we started our five-day, bone-rattling truck and jeep journey to the Nepal-Tibet border town of Zhangmu before taking the Road to Hell to Nyalam. After crossing the Tibetan plateau, we finally arrived at Base Camp where we rested and acclimatised for a few days before putting our gear on yaks and trekking to ABC at 5,800m. From ABC, there is a clear view of the ancient glaciated mountain pass of Nangpa La, which has long served as a trade route between Tibet and Nepal. It is also the site of illegal border crossings, and we could see a stream of Tibetans moving over the pass from Chinese-controlled Tibet into Nepal. We were very disturbed when we heard gunshots and realised that Chinese soldiers were shooting at those who were crossing the pass while trying to escape the oppressive regime in their country. Sadly, there was nothing we could do.

Over the next few weeks, we started the process of stocking our camps and getting acclimatised to the thin air. Conditions were very favourable and we had no problems setting up Camp 1 at 6,400m. I'd learned by this stage, however, that on the mountains you can never assume things are going well, even when they seem to be. And so it happened that one day, just after returning from Camp 1, Gavin was attacked by a yak which ran at him, caught him under the groin with its horn and catapulted him into the air. Luckily, his injuries were no more than some torn ligaments, and after a few days' rest he was ready to get back up the mountain stocking the camps.

We were about to start our first push to stock Camp 2 at 7,200m when news filtered down to ABC that a Russian climber had died at Camp 3 (High Camp). He had been on the way to the summit with his team when he started to feel unwell and decided to return to camp while his team-mates continued. When they returned to High Camp after reaching the summit, they found their friend in his tent. He had suffered a burst blood vessel in his nose as a consequence of being at high altitude and had bled to death. It was a terrible tragedy for the climber and his friends.

We were horrified at what had happened as this man slept, having taken the right decision to retreat once he felt unwell. Death or injury as a result of an avalanche, or from getting caught up in a storm, or by falling into a crevasse, causes shock, but not surprise. But when death creeps into the tent of a climber who has done the right thing, it can traumatise others on the mountain. Of our team, I was the only one who had been in the Death Zone previously and who had experienced death on mountains. I had built up a filter to prevent such tragedies from undermining my confidence, but I noticed that Con and Eoin were particularly shaken by the Russian climber's death. In spite of that, they said there were still determined to continue upwards.

Another death at High Camp

We started the climb to Camp 1, located in a saddle at the base of the northwest ridge, and made fast progress. We stayed there for the night to acclimatise before heading for Camp 2 early the following morning. Con and Eoin had a restless night but left camp with Gavin and me the following morning. All was going well until we came to the crevassed headwall at 6,600m. At this point, both Con and Eoin, who'd been having some difficulties moving at higher altitude, said they were going back down to Camp 1 to rest and wait for our return. Gavin and I continued over the 100m headwall to Camp 2. At 7,000m, Gavin, who was getting tired, decided to pitch a tent and rest for the night while I continued to Camp 2 at 7,200m to deposit our load, pitch our second tent and sleep there for the night.

The next day, Gavin reached Camp 2 and decided to rest there overnight before descending to join up with the team again at Camp 1. I bid him farewell and made my way down to the lower camp. During the night, jet-stream winds blew in and Gavin became trapped for two days as the wind and snow cut off all routes above and below him. At Camp 1, we, thankfully, had radio contact and were able to check in with him.

On the first evening of the storm, more tragic news filtered down from Cho Oyu's Death Zone. Two German climbers had become separated after leaving the summit and only one returned to High Camp at 7,450m. An American climber, who was higher up and descending through the Yellow Band, had seen a body flying over the steep rock and ice headwall and landing in a couloir below. Without making a sound, the falling climber continued to roll down the slope before finally coming to a stop. Shock again ran through the camps and some teams decided to call it a day. With two deaths in quick succession, it was hard not to wonder who would be next. The following day, Gavin descended to Camp 1 and we all continued to ABC to rest and reassess our climb.

I understood why people wanted to get off the mountain. At the end of the day, every individual had to assess how they were feeling and how the deaths were impacting on their confidence. As the expedition leader, I knew the team was fit, sufficiently trained and well acclimatised. However, going into the Death Zone was, ultimately, a personal decision and each team member had to decide whether they were willing to take the risk. It might be my opinion that they were capable of attempting the summit, but if they didn't feel they could do it, then they had already reached their summit. However, once we talked everything through and analysed how we were operating as a team, everyone was happy to go for a summit push.

8,000er without oxygen

We headed up to Camp 1 again, where we overnighted. The following morning we were making good progress until we reached the headwall 200m above Camp 2. This was the point where Con and Eoin had previously made the decision to go back down. The headwall was again a challenge they were uncomfortable with, and they decided to descend. Gavin and I continued upwards and spent the night at Camp 2 before pushing on to High Camp at 7,450m the following day. There were spectacular views, and Gavin and I watched this show of stunning natural beauty as we ate and drank before settling down for our last rest before the summit push.

We were dressed and ready for the final part of our climb by 3am. For seven laborious hours, we climbed the steep snow- and ice-covered slope and through the 150m rock and ice section of the Yellow Band. We exited this headwall section at 7,850m as we moved onto the summit plateau.

Once on this level ground, we completed the final 350m slog to the summit in three hours, reaching Cho Oyu's highest point at 1pm on 20 May 1998. I was particularly proud to have led the first Irish team to the top of the sixth highest mountain in the world. We were also the first Irish team to reach the summit of one of the world's 8,000ers without using supplemental oxygen; it was a moment to savour. At the summit I could see Everest rising higher than any other peak in this land of unimaginably high peaks and, as I looked at it, I knew that I wanted to climb it again, this time from the south side.

RETURN TO AMA DABLAM 1999

As the dawn of a new millennium drew close, Con Moriarty and I were talking about our adventures together over the previous twelve years. We'd had some great times climbing in Kerry, Europe and the Himalaya. Both of us had been busy developing our adventure businesses in recent times and hadn't undertaken any big expedition together in a while, something we both wanted to do. We agreed that now was the perfect time for another big trip and both of us were clear about where we'd be heading: Ama Dablam, the jewel whose summit had eluded us in 1991. Neither of us had ever forgotten what is regarded as one of the most beautiful mountains in the world and now, with the twentieth century about to end, we decided that a trip there would be a fitting way to end the millennium and ring in the new one, as well as marking our friendship in a special way.

The climbing team consisted of just Con and me. His brother Denis and friend Ann Curran joined us as trekkers to Ama Dablam Base Camp. I already had plans to go to Everest Base Camp with a trekking group in October and met up with Con and the others in Kathmandu when that trip was over and after I'd climbed the 6,189m Island Peak. By this stage I had been at altitude for almost a month and was fully acclimatised. Con, however, needed to acclimatise before we headed to Ama Dablam, so we decided to climb Mera Peak in the Hinku Valley. At 6,476m, it is the highest trekking peak in Nepal and is especially suitable for those who want to get used to altitude before tackling a tougher climb. We wanted to attempt a rapid ascent of Ama Dablam, so it was important that we sorted out any acclimatisation issues before getting there.

We flew from Kathmandu to Lukla in the northeastern Khumbu region. From there we started our seven-day trek over the 3,500m Zatra La Pass into the Hinku Valley and over the 5,410m Mera La Pass to Mera Peak Base Camp at 5,310m. We had no sooner arrived and set up camp than a massive snowstorm hit the whole region, trapping us in our tents for the next three days. Over three metres of snow fell, and every few hours we had to dig out our tents so that they wouldn't collapse under the weight of the snow. But that wasn't the worst of our problems: Con was in agony with a pounding headache and on the third morning, as soon as he woke, he was showing the symptoms of someone in the grip of acute mountain sickness (AMS). Even though the snowstorm was still blowing, I knew that he had to get to a lower altitude to recover. We quickly packed our gear and got ready to move.

Tragedy on Mera

There were three other teams also stuck at Base Camp and we learned that one of their porters had died. The teams had failed to supply the proper equipment and clothing needed for travelling in this remote valley in such weather conditions, where the windchill brought temperatures down as low as –20°. Shock spread through Base Camp, and everyone knew it was time to get lower down the mountain.

Conditions were very rough as a few Sherpas and I began cutting a trail through the wall of snow. At one point I looked behind me and saw that over eighty people were following in our trail. Progress was painfully slow as we pushed waist-deep through the powder-soft snow. It was further hampered by a whiteout which reduced visibility to zero. Word then spread through the line that a kitchen boy had died. This situation was tragic but there was nothing we could do; the body had to be left where it fell. All that could be done in this unforgiving storm was to mark the area so that the remains could be brought down at a later stage.

I was heading the caravan of people and moving across a glacier when I entered a crevasse-ridden area. In the whiteout it was too dangerous to cross and I radioed Con, who was at the end of the human train. 'We can't continue on this trail,' I said, 'you'll have to turn the group from behind and find a way onto higher ground and search for another path down.' The seriousness of the situation we were in had registered with him at Base Camp despite the pain he was in; his vast experience in mountain rescue kicked in and, almost miraculously, his altitude sickness disappeared. 'Okay,' he replied, 'I'll take the lead from here.'

The entire group turned and headed back up as Con led the way across the glacier and boulder field and, eventually, down steep, snow-covered slopes. After twelve hours of cutting trail in some of the toughest conditions any of us had ever experienced, we arrived at Tangnag at 4,350m, where we had stayed on our way in. The teahouses and yak herders' huts were almost lost under heavy snow but we all rested there for the night, grateful to have shelter, hot food and water and to be at lower altitude, but mostly just to be alive.

Due to the negligence of the other teams in not ensuring proper provisions for their porters and Sherpas, the toll on the local mountain staff was heavy. Ten had frostbite, six had snow-blindness and two were dead. This loss of life weighed heavily on our minds and we wondered how their families would survive. It was hard to accept that foreign teams, aiming to keep their expedition costs lower, had short-changed their local team members and endangered their lives in the process, with tragic results. The next morning we continued down the Hinku Valley and back to the village of Lukla, where we learned that the storm had killed at least a dozen local Sherpas who lived and worked on the mountains in the Khumbu region.

Beaten down by altitude

In Lukla we talked about what had happened in the previous days. I voiced a recurring question: 'Why are we doing this? Why are we continuing with this expedition when people are dying?' We analysed every aspect of what we were planning to do and only then made the decision to continue. Collectively, Con and I had built up a vast amount of experience since we'd last attempted to reach the top of Ama Dablam and, despite what had happened in the past week, we were confident that we had what was needed to attempt to reach the summit.

Our small group of four Irish people and two locals – cook Dawa and Dorje, his helper – set out on the road to Ama Dablam Base Camp at 4,600m, where we arrived five days later. Once we were there, Denis and Ann took on the role of providing support from Base Camp. As we looked up at the stunning natural beauty of Ama Dablam, rising 6,812m into the sky, we talked about our previous visit when Con had been stalled in his climb by food poisoning and my attempt had fallen foul of a storm and wet clothing on a bivouac below Camp 3 on the Mushroom Ridge. It felt right that we were both here again, two friends who had climbed many mountains together and who were now back to tackle the one that got away in 1991.

After resting at Base Camp for a day, we started the first carry to Camp 1 at 5,650m. We unpacked our gear, made some food and relaxed as we took in the amazing views of the surrounding high mountains. Not long after we'd retired for the night, Con woke me. He had a severe pain in his head. Neither of us could believe it; altitude sickness had struck him again. All night long he suffered as the pain got progressively worse. As soon as the sun came up, he packed his gear and headed back down to Base Camp. 'I'll go down and rest for a day,' he said. As I watched him struggle downwards, I knew in my heart that he wouldn't be coming back up again. On the Zatra La Pass, at Mera Peak Base Camp and now at Camp 1 on Ama Dablam he was hit by excruciating AMS and the only antidote was to stay low.

I still didn't want to accept that this was the end of our climb together, so I waited throughout the day at Camp 1 to hear news of how he was feeling after reaching Base Camp. He didn't make the expected recovery and next day, when he attempted to ascend to Camp 1 again, he had to stop after an hour's climbing. There was no question now that he could come up the mountain. High altitude had put a stop to one of the most intelligent and skilful climbers I knew. 'There are others on the mountain,' Con said to me on the radio, 'join them and just keep going up.' I was devastated but I knew he was right; I was at Camp 1 and wasn't having any problems with altitude. Conditions were excellent and there was a good weather window. I focused on my goal – the summit of Ama Dablam – and put aside the emotions I was feeling.

Continuing upwards

After another night at Camp 1, I set off the following morning for Camp 3 at 6,400m. I was feeling strong and fully acclimatised. The route ahead had already been roped by previous teams and not having to do rope fixing, coupled with the fact that I was much more technically adept than I had been in 1991, meant that I was more confident on the ascent. I clearly remembered every part of the route, especially the crux at the Yellow Tower, from my first attempt, but I found that everything was easier this time round. Nonetheless, I was still concerned about what lay beyond the highest point I had reached on my earlier attempt.

I climbed the Yellow Tower and continued past Camp 2 at 6,000m into the gully where we had found the dead Canadian climber. To my surprise, the gully was banked out in snow from the storm, presenting some of the best snow and ice conditions I'd experienced in years. With double ice axe and crampons I scaled through this section in super-fast time, enjoying every moment of the climb. Once I was beyond my highest point of 1991, I felt an energy boost which was like a shot of adrenaline. I was past my previous 'summit' and now I looked at the top of the mountain and kept moving towards it.

I could see four climbers ahead and soon joined up with them. Dave Cummings and Kate Ross were from Scotland and were climbing with their Sherpas, Phendon and Pemba. We crossed the narrow and challenging Mushroom Ridge together before setting up camp about 100m above the ridge on the small, glacial plateau at 6,400m. The plateau, which sits below and slightly to the side of the Dablam – the serac that gives the mountain its name – was very exposed to the wind from both sides and was subsequently very cold. I was keenly aware of the temperature as I was travelling light and had left my sleeping bag behind. I had a small bivvy tent for shelter and just enough food and gas for a lightning ascent. As quickly as I could, I erected my tent and settled in for the long night.

All five of us set out the next morning at 4am. I forged ahead on my own, feeling comfortable and relaxed as I moved across the glacier under the Dablam to gain the upper ridge line to the summit. I felt like a fly alone on a big wall with over 2,200m of a fall below me; this was not a place to make a mistake.

At 8.10am on 18 November 1999, after a wait of eight years, I finally reached the top of Mother's Necklace. The view was a breathtaking panorama of some of the most iconic mountains in the Himalaya, with Everest, Cho Oyu, Lhotse, Nuptse, Pumori, Shishapangma, Makalu and the Khumbu Himal all clearly visible. As I looked at the stunning view around me, I thought of Con at Base Camp. He had led me on my first trip to this mystical region and I was sad that he wasn't at the top of Ama Dablam with me.

I reflected on how, this time round, my personal summit was so much higher and how our summits change throughout our lives. What had been a huge challenge for me years earlier had been so much easier this year. I acknowledged how lucky I was not to suffer from AMS, which is indiscriminate in who it targets.

I was brought out of my reveries by a tap on the shoulder. It was an Austrian speed climber who was testing a new paraglider. He had left Base Camp the night before and wanted me to take a photo of him as he flew off the top of the mountain. His twenty-five-minute journey to the bottom was infinitely shorter than my descent, which took two days.

It was an emotional reunion for Con and me when I walked into Base Camp. I think, without saying it explicitly, we both realised that high-altitude mountaineering wasn't an option for him. The Mountain Man, who had taught me so much and who had a natural talent for climbing that I could only stand back and admire, would no longer be my partner on high-altitude expeditions.

TIME OF RECKONING

By the end of the 1990s, I had become obsessed with adventure and for seven months of every year I was on expeditions and treks around the world. During the five months I was in Ireland, I was working as a mountain guide, inspirational speaker, personal development trainer and corporate team consultant. Finding a balance between my working and family life was proving impossible.

Marie and I had done our best to hold our relationship together, but my obsession was causing huge problems which forced us apart even though we still loved each other. The fourteen-year-old she had fallen in love with had traded in his mason's trowel and business dreams for ice axes and crampons and a way of life that was not compatible with traditional family life. I suggested that the family move to Kerry and start a new life there. But that wasn't a runner; their entire lives were in Cork.

Eventually, in late 1999, we realised that the situation couldn't continue and that we should separate; I would move to Kerry, where most of my Irish work now was. Deep down I didn't want to leave and Marie didn't want me to go either, but we both knew that my staying was causing too much pain and disruption. We didn't want to hurt each other more and realised that the best way to ensure we could still survive as a family was by living apart. It was very hard to leave my family and Beechwood. Not only were my beloved wife and sons there; my parents, siblings and their young families were also living in the area. We were a big, close-knit family and it broke my heart to go.

Mountain Lodge

The busier I got with work, the more obvious it became that I needed my own space in Kerry, not only for work but also to create a new home for myself. It was several months before I found a place that really resonated with me – a furze-covered field at the base of six of Ireland's highest mountains overlooking the Lakes of Killarney, one of the country's most popular tourist destinations. When the site came up for sale, early in 2001, I put in a bid and bought it.

In between leading trips at home and abroad, I got stuck into the block work. It had been a long time since I'd held a trowel in my hand and it felt good to be back at my old trade. By late spring 2002, the house – which I called Mountain Lodge – was ready to move into. Not only was the Lodge a place for me to live and work from, I had also built it so that it would serve as a skills training centre with accommodation. I started training weekends straight away and within a year of moving in, I'd developed de-stress weekends that ran over the summer months. Outside trainers and facilitators ran the various courses and weekends with me during which we offered hillwalking, yoga, meditation, holistic therapies and organic food. People came to the Lodge from all over the world to spend a few days learning how to unwind, de-stress and set healthier challenges for themselves.

EVEREST (SOUTH SIDE) 2003

My dream of going back to Mount Everest never left me. For years I planned to return, and set out the goals I wished to fulfil if I did. I had three main objectives: to lead the first Irish woman to the summit of Everest; to lead the first Irish team to the summit from the south side; to be the first Irish person to reach the summit of Everest from both its north and south sides.

It was not until June 2002 that an opportunity arose for me to go back. I had just returned to Kathmandu from one of my treks to Everest Base Camp when Ang Rita, my Nepalese business partner, said, 'Pat, do you want to climb Mount Everest from Nepal?'. He knew bloody well that I did, as we had spoken about this subject many times. 'Due to a cancellation, I can get a permit for March 2003, the fiftieth anniversary of the Hillary and Tenzing climb,' he continued. 'Do you want it? You have to make your mind up fast.' Even though it was only forty weeks to the start date for the expedition, I jumped at the opportunity. This was really short notice to put a team and all the logistics together but it was a challenge that excited me, so I committed to it and gave Ang Rita a deposit to hold the permit.

Having spoken regularly about returning to Everest in lectures and to the teams of people I trained, I knew a number of friends and climbing partners who I thought might be interested. I rang fifteen of them to ask if they wanted do the expedition and, to my surprise, four committed within two weeks. I had climbed with Mick Murphy, a friend and seasoned high-altitude climber, on Ama Dablam and Denali. He had also been on Everest before although he had not summited on that occasion. Over the years, I had undertaken climbs with Dr Clare O'Leary and George Shorten from Cork, along with Hannah Shields from Derry, and they all had a common goal: to climb Everest. Without too much effort, the climbing team was in place.

Building the team

Then, a few weeks later, a young man called Ger McDonnell walked into Mountain Lodge. The thirty-one-year-old engineer from a small village in Co Limerick was home on holiday from Alaska, where he worked and lived. His smile and good humour were infectious. My secretary was a friend of his and she told him I was organising a team to Everest. 'You're going to Everest and I'd like to go,' he said. 'I'm a good team player, I'm strong and you won't regret it.'

We spent two hours talking and I was totally captivated by this climber who approached life with such enthusiasm, energy and positivity. Our climbing team was sorted, but I wanted to give him a chance. His CV very much stood up to scrutiny, so I rang the others to discuss the addition of another person to the team. If I wanted to take a chance and believed in him, they were happy to go with my decision. I rang Ger the next day and confirmed him as our sixth member.

I recruited John Joyce from Tuam and Pat Duggan from Cork as our Base Camp managers. Niall Foley from my own office was our communications officer whose brief was to liaise between the team on the mountain and our families and the press. My friend Joe O'Leary took over the responsibility for equipment and rescue logistics as well as acting as family liaison officer, a role he carried out on all my expeditions. In Nepal, Ang Rita secured the Sherpa team, all of whom I had worked with before. They are the unsung heroes without whom most expeditions would not succeed. They were an integral part of this expedition and were classified as full team members.

Pemba Gyalje Sherpa took responsibility as sirdar of our Sherpa climbing team, which included Pemba Rinzee, Dorje Sherpa, Mingma Chhiri, Nang Chemmi and Nima Sherpa. Napoleon once said that an army marches on its stomach, and to ensure we would be sustained and eat wholesome food to maintain our energy I appointed Dawa Sherpa, who I had been working with since 1991, as head cook. I organised four support groups through my adventure company to come out at different times during our climb, some of whom were family or friends of the team. The first group was led by me, with the other three being led by three of my top trekking leaders – Joe O'Leary, Gerry Walsh and Mike Grainger. I also organised a sponsorship team which was headed up by Dave Twomey and Pat Fenton.

As leader, I drew up a contract and disclaimer for each climber to sign, stating the dangers and risks of climbing Everest and also outlining their responsibilities on the mountain. I requested that every person show the contract to at least one family member to ensure they also knew the risk of serious injury and even death that their loved ones would be exposed to. The contract clearly exonerated all other team members from responsibility in the event of serious injury or death on the mountain. We set up an emergency response team that was headed up by Joe O'Leary. Joe would ensure that, if anything went wrong on the mountain, families would be the first to find out directly from him.

The time period for planning the logistics was crazy: I had to order fifty lightweight oxygen cylinders from Russia, specialised food from five different countries, thirty new tents from America and specialised cold climbing gear from England, America and Canada that could cater for temperatures as low as $-40°$. In total, there were 11,200 pieces of vital equipment that had to be accounted for, which, in itself, was a logistical nightmare. Clare took responsibility for all our diet and medical requirements – a vital task – to ensure the good health of the team. The pressure to get everything together in the short window available was enormous and I had a lot of sleepless nights, but all the team worked together to make it happen.

A fascinated public

We secured funding from the Irish Film Board and RTÉ to make a documentary of the expedition, to be produced by Kevin Hughes of Wallslough Studios/M3 Productions. The Irish press latched onto the story and we garnered a lot of media coverage. Press and the public alike were captivated by the notion of an Irish team heading to Everest on the fiftieth anniversary of the first summiting.

The heroics of Edmund Hillary and Tenzing Norgay had a fascination that hadn't dimmed over the years and the public was hungry to connect with their story again.

Since the publication in 2000 of Michael Smith's book *An Unsung Hero: Tom Crean, Antarctic Survivor*, there had been a huge growth in interest in seeing ordinary people achieve extraordinary things. These stories and exploits resonated with a public who identified with people like themselves who were taking on challenges and seeing them through to completion. Our team and goals really caught the public's imagination and ensured we had massive interest and support for our expedition before we ever left Ireland.

There was another – irresistible – aspect to our expedition that drew people like magnets, particularly kids, and that was Frederick T. Bear, or Freddy as he was generally known. This toy bear concept was developed by Mary Curtin, who was a primary school teacher friend from Cork, Clare O'Leary and me. Our plan was that Freddy would travel around the world on expedition and write about his adventures. He was a perfect conduit for introducing young people to the most remote regions of the planet and informing them about its cultures, people, wildlife and birdlife at the Earth's extremities. He eventually had over 200,000 followers online and became a regular presence on future adventures.

When we arrived at Cork Airport on 15 March 2003 for our departure to Nepal, I was blown away that over 1,000 people had gathered to wish us bon voyage, with more than 500 children there to wish Freddy T. Bear good luck. This was the highest-profile expedition I'd been on to date, and the many good wishes we got at the airport made for a very auspicious beginning.

GODDESS MOTHER OF MOUNTAINS

Forty weeks after Ang Rita asked if I was interested in getting a permit to climb Mount Everest, I was back in Kathmandu with an Irish team. It took us three days to clear all our gear and equipment through a corrupt customs. On 19 March, we flew from the capital city over the lower foothills of the Himalaya on the forty-minute flight to Lukla, the starting point for our trek to Base Camp. This flight is reputed to be one of the most dangerous in the world, and landing on an airstrip built on the side of a cliff face certainly focuses the mind.

We unpacked all our equipment before checking and double-checking all our provisions and gear. We then hired seventy yaks and sixty porters and started our nine-day trek through the lower foothills of the Upper Khumbu Valley to Base Camp. We stayed in many villages along the way, living among the indigenous people and learning about their traditions and culture. We walked along the banks of the Dubh Kosi and Bhote Kosi Rivers and crossed eleven suspension bridges covered in prayer flags.

At many Buddhist monasteries we prayed for a safe journey. Each day's trek was more spectacular than the day before. Mountains projected high into the sky like massive pillars as we walked along narrow paths etched from steep hillsides. I looked at Thramserku – the mountain of the ten summits, Kantega – the saddleback mountain, Ama Dablam – Mother's Necklace, the mountain I had first come to in 1991 and whose summit I had reached in 1999. In the

197

distance, at the top of the valley, was the highest of them all – Mount Everest beckoned, its head projecting above the mighty Nuptse-Lhotse Ridge.

Base Camp Nepal

Base Camp was established at the head of the Khumbu Valley at a height of 5,380m on a moving glacier that looked like a war zone, with massive craters that looked as if falling bombs had created them. There were six other teams there when we arrived on 27 March and pitched our tents on the moving foundation. In a short time, our mess tent had become a social hub where all the other teams would come and join us for nightly chats and singsongs.

Our merry group of trekkers stayed for a night and then bid us farewell. They had become part of the team and we were sad to see them go, but we had a job to do and our focus was now firmly on the climb. All the climbers, including our Sherpa team, worked together on the glacier, perfecting the speed and performance of our technical ability in crampon and ice axe use as well as fixed-rope, ladder-crossing and rescue techniques. This helped us get the mindset we needed to tackle Everest.

We had a puja which was performed by monks from Tengboche Monastery. This was a welcome moment which allowed everyone – including non-believers – to focus on what was ahead and to pray that Sagarmatha, as the Nepalese call Everest, would look favourably on those about to climb her flanks. Base Camp was awash with colourful prayer flags as rice and food were offered to the Goddess Mother of Mountains and we all prayed that she would allow us to enter her sanctum and return safely.

Dread in the Khumbu Icefall

On 5 April we were ready to start climbing. The team's excitement was tempered by anxiety at the thought of entering one of the most dangerous sections on the mountain – the Khumbu Icefall. Situated at the foot of the Western Cwm and the head of the Khumbu Glacier, the icefall begins just 500m from Base Camp and by 2003 had already claimed the lives of thirty climbers who were unlucky to be in the wrong place at the wrong time when crossing it. We knew we had to constantly be alert to its dangers, with crevasses that open up with little or no warning and can swallow you up in an instant. Speed is of the essence when moving through the icefall, which is frightening to even the most experienced climbers as the objective dangers are outside human control. Because the area is at its most solid in the very early hours before the sun has had a chance to beat down on the glimmering ice and destabilise it, we rose at 3am to cross it while it was still dark and very cold.

Our initial climb through this nightmare zone, where there are billions of tons of ice constantly moving downhill at a rate of up to 1.2m a day, took seven nerve-wracking hours. Total concentration was demanded as we inched our way over the shaking ladders – sometimes up to seven tied together – that are laid across the yawning crevasses. As this was our first acclimatisation trek to Camp 1, we erected two tents, dumped our loads and returned to Base Camp. On the way down, the sun was shining like a heat lamp on the glacier and we witnessed two frightening serac falls just off our path. It was a great relief to get back to Base Camp and to know that we had made our first foray safely through the icefall; we now had our first foothold on Everest.

Over the next few weeks, our team made many switchback climbs to and from Camp 1 and beyond. We cut the time it took us to get through the Khumbu Icefall down to three hours as we became more acclimatised and more confident about climbing on moving ice, although we never looked at this section with anything other than respect and trepidation.

Running the gauntlet

For the entire month of April, we ferried equipment and food to Camp 1 at 6,000m as well as pushing on to Camp 2. From Camp 1 we carried heavy loads through the Silent Valley, a vast area of endless snow, deep crevasses and a massive avalanche wall on either side of Nuptse and the western buttress of Everest. All the team were acclimatising to the higher altitude even though we had to weather two storms during the month. Pemba Gyalje and I were on camera duty as we climbed, hoping to get some interesting footage for the film we were making of the expedition.

By 29 April, Camp 2 was established at 6,400m on a rocky moraine at the base of the icy Lhotse face. All provisions were in place to move on and establish Camp 3 at 7,315m and Camp 4 – our High Camp – at the South Col at 7,950m when, out of nowhere, we were hit by hard, relentless snowstorms that trapped us at Camp 2 for three days. Tension and frustration built up as we wondered if we were ever going to get away from this godforsaken spot. In terms of time and energy, I knew it was vital for us to get to Camp 3 without having to go back down to Base Camp. Then, as suddenly as it had started, the snowstorm stopped and we climbed the steep 1,000m hard-ice headwall to Camp 3. We cut platforms from the face for our tents so we could spend the night there before descending to Base Camp the following morning.

As we descended, George became very ill with high-altitude cerebral oedema (HACE). He was weakening by the minute and we knew we had to get him to a lower altitude immediately, so the entire team began a slow and worrying descent. By the time we got to Camp 1, he wanted to rest but I knew that we needed to push on down. Crossing the Khumbu Icefall was a nightmare as George – now in a semi-comatose state – attempted to negotiate the most dangerous descent area on Everest.

With great resolve and determination, he made his way back to Base Camp. The permanent medical team checked him out and put him in a Gamow bag in the hope that the controlled pressure would stabilise him, but his symptoms were so severe that the doctor recommended he be taken to hospital. Once the rescue helicopter arrived, George was evacuated to Kathmandu. We were all sad to see him go but knew that this action would give him the best chance of recovery. By this stage, we were shattered emotionally and physically and remained at Base Camp for a few days to rest and refocus on our goal.

Undone by a stomach bug

By the second week of May, we were again making our way up the mountain with the summit firmly on our minds. All of the team – eleven of us in total – made our way to Camp 2 and were on target to go to Camp 3 the following day. That evening, however, Clare got violent cramps in her stomach which left her exhausted and dehydrated. We held a team meeting and decided the majority would rest at Camp 2 for an extra day to give her time to recover. Pemba, along with four of the Sherpa team, continued upwards to stock High Camp. The plan was that they would meet us at Camp 3 the following day. The weather forecast looked good, with calm weather predicted until 20 May and jet-stream winds blowing in after that.

The next morning, Clare was feeling a bit better and all six of us headed for Camp 3. However, by the time we got to the bottom of the Nuptse face, between the two camps, she was feeling very sick again. Being a doctor, she knew immediately that she had to descend. She also knew that, with the short weather window that was forecast, she wouldn't get another chance at the summit. It was very emotional to see this woman who I'd trained and climbed with over the past few years having to make the hard but correct decision to retreat. Dorje Sherpa accompanied her as she slowly made her way back to Base Camp where she made a full recovery.

A losing battle

Mick, Ger, Hannah, the Sherpa climbing team and I all met at Camp 3 and continued towards High Camp at 7,950m the following morning. En route, Hannah was very tired and was starting to feel intensely cold. In the previous weeks, she'd noticed that she was more susceptible to the cold than the rest of the team and was subsequently very wary of getting frostbite. To try and ease the pain, Pemba and I attempted to get her circulation moving by rubbing her gloved hands and placing them under our armpits for heat. She kept going and we reached High Camp at the South Col at 11am. After we erected our tents we settled in for a long day of preparation for our summit attempt. We had fifty cylinders of oxygen in place with enough food and gas for two days. There were four other teams at the South Col with us, all focusing on their summit night.

We rehydrated and rested as best we could as we mentally prepared ourselves for what was to come. More than ever before, we now had to conquer our fears of what the night might have in store for us in Everest's Death Zone. We all made a satellite phone call home to reassure our loved ones we were okay. At 9pm, we exited our tents in our down suits and boots, carrying our harnesses, technical gear, some food, three litres of water and three cylinders of oxygen each. Two of the strongest Sherpas from each team had left an hour earlier to fix ropes in the harder sections of the climb. The night was a cold $-35°$ with a moderate wind. As we set off, we felt strong and positive about the journey ahead.

A few hours in, however, the winds increased and moving became a real struggle. Several teams turned back but we still felt strong enough to continue despite the tough conditions. Then, after eight hours of battling through high winds, we had to abandon our summit attempt just as we reached the south-southeast ridge below the Balcony at 8,400m. The rope-fixing team ahead of us had also turned as the ridge above was impassable in the high jet-stream winds, which had not been mentioned in our forecast. Disappointed, we returned to High Camp, leaving all our spare oxygen at our highest point.

Forced to descend

After three hours' rest we had to decide whether we would wait out the bad weather or descend from High Camp. Because the weather window was closing, we knew that if we went down it would be the end of our summit chances. A serious consideration was whether or not we had enough supplemental oxygen for a longer stay in the Death Zone. We knew that we needed four bottles each on a summit attempt and calculated that we'd used fifteen bottles already. This meant we still had thirty-five full bottles left. We decided to stay; it was a high-risk strategy but everyone felt that they had the energy for another push upwards. We knew, however, that we had to ration the remaining oxygen and stay off it for as long as possible while we were sitting in High Camp.

As the winds died down, the immediate forecast was that there would be no further weather window after 21 May, so we made our plan to leave High Camp for our second summit attempt at 9pm that night. We estimated that it would take up to thirteen hours to reach the top of the mountain and that we had enough oxygen and time for this final attempt. My biggest concern as we set off at the planned time was whether the energy we had as a team was enough to see us safely up and back to High Camp. The first summit attempt in atrocious conditions had been exhausting, and we had now spent thirty-six hours at 7,950m and over 8,000m where, even when you aren't moving, your energy is being burned just trying to breathe. But everybody was going well as we moved upwards and I felt reassured.

It was cold with little wind and we progressed fast onto the Balcony and the start of the southeast ridge, where we changed our oxygen cylinders. As we moved along the ridge, Hannah said she was getting very cold again and was feeling the onset of frostbite. At –35°, she didn't dare take off her gloves to check. No climber wants to risk frostbite, particularly someone like Hannah, who works as a dentist. Having been in the Death Zone for so long, it was getting harder to keep warm and now, at 8,450m, she decided to descend. It wasn't an easy decision, especially as she was just under 400m from the summit. Two of the Sherpas – Nang Chemmi and Mingma Chhiri – turned and accompanied her on the emotionally tough walk down the mountain.

Watching Hannah descend was shattering for the team. She had put in a Trojan effort over sixty days on expedition and to have to turn just five hours from the summit was very tough. Our objective of having the first Irish woman on the summit of Everest was no longer a possibility.

In death's grip

Pemba Gyalje and Mick went ahead to ensure the fixed ropes were in place at the Hillary Step. Shortly afterwards, Pemba Rinzee, Nima Sherpa, Ger and I continued for the summit, with Ger bringing up the rear. After a while, he passed me and asked if I was okay as he thought I was moving slowly. I hadn't realised that I'd slowed down but Ger's comment, and the fact that he was now stopping to wait for me, alerted me to how sluggishly I was moving.

When I looked at my watch I knew there was something wrong; I had enough high-altitude experience to know where I should have been on the mountain by that stage. At the South Summit at 8,749m, just 99m from the top of Everest and one and a half hours' climbing away, I told Ger, Pemba Rinzee and Nima to go on. Nima, who had worked with me on nearly all my expeditions for over ten years, stayed with me. When I checked my oxygen cylinder I discovered that there was nothing coming out. In fact, since our last cylinder change, four hours earlier, there had been an obstruction caused by some ice that got stuck in the valve. By the time I got it fixed, it was past my own turning point of 9am so I decided to sit and wait for the team to return.

Shackleton's quote, 'Better a live donkey than a dead lion', sustained me during that time although I still wondered why I had run out of steam with the summit so tantalisingly close. I felt that I should have been able to operate without oxygen, but maybe it was Sagarmatha telling me she didn't want me at the summit this time round. I wasn't angry or sad that I wasn't going to get to the top of Everest; after all, I told myself, I'd been there before and now I had led the first-ever Irish team up the south side of the world's highest mountain

203

and it looked as if we were going to have a few summiteers. My plan now was to reserve whatever oxygen I had left until the team returned and to use it on the descent.

I felt okay as I sat and waited, watching the sun rise high in the sky, not realising that I had already entered one of the most dangerous places I'd ever been and that, very soon, my life would be hanging by a thread. Unknown to me, I had become hypoxic and, minute by minute, I was becoming more and more like a very drunk person, oblivious to the fact that I was losing control over my own ability to act. On top of that, the batteries in my radio had died due to the cold so no one at Base Camp could contact me; if they had, they might have noticed that I wasn't fully with it.

After two hours, Mick appeared. He had reached the summit with Pemba Gyalje and was on his way back to High Camp while Pemba waited at the top for Ger. I was thrilled with his news and hugged him, explaining that I was waiting for the others in case they needed any support on the way down. To Mick, I seemed my normal self; he didn't notice anything strange about my behaviour and asked why I wasn't going for the summit, remarking that there was still time. As we chatted, I started to think I was feeling fine again. *Maybe I just needed that little bit of encouragement*, I thought, before deciding to get up and go up the mountain. Very quickly, my desire to reach the top of Everest became overriding; I had summit fever.

I told Nima I was heading for the summit and he said he'd come with me. As I moved slowly towards the Hillary Step we met some people on their way down. I was attached to the fixed rope and one of the descending climbers unclipped his security to pass me on a narrow ledge. He didn't clip in his back-up security on the other side of me and slipped suddenly as he passed me and started to fall down the face. I instinctively reached out and held him in a tight grip. Something about the suddenness of the movement woke me from my hypoxic stupor to the reality of my situation: *What the hell am I doing here? I need to get down.* The climber I had just rescued thanked me and continued downwards, still shocked at what had happened. I was now in shock myself and, realising that ascending was a mistake, I told Nima I was turning back and that he should continue on his summit bid.

As he made his way upwards, I started to move downwards but it was exhausting and I really had to focus to get my body to take the next step. I lost

204

my peripheral vision and clipped into the rope, trying to feel for a foothold that I could no longer see. Everything was blurred. I knew I was in danger but I couldn't allow myself to panic. An inner voice guided me: *Be careful on the ridge. You need to get down fast.* But I had zero energy and after a few steps, I'd sit down for a rest. It was so nice to just sit and do nothing. Every time I sat, a feeling of euphoria came over me and I wanted to stay put. Then I'd hear the inner voice again: *If you don't keep moving down you will die. You have to get to a lower altitude.* That voice forced me to get up and take another few steps before I sat down again, my energy spent.

I had no idea how long it took but, eventually, I reached the South Summit, where I sat down again. But I knew I had to keep moving so I stood up again and started making my way down the southwest ridge like a blind man, using the fixed line like a Braille rope. Ensuring that I always had one of my protections attached to the rope, I stumbled my way downwards, all the time fearing I'd fall off the side of the mountain.

The next thing I knew, Ger, Pemba Gyalje, Pemba Rinzee and Nima were standing in front of me. Ger and Pemba Rinzee had reached the summit while Nima had turned just before the top point as the others were descending at that stage. Ger immediately saw that there was something radically wrong with me. 'Pat,' he said, putting his hand on my shoulder, 'I think you're in trouble.' He had seen the complete lack of energy in my eyes and told me that I had to stand up and get moving. At that moment the four men knew that they had a massive challenge on their hands. We were almost at the top of the highest mountain in the world and they wanted to help me get down. But they couldn't carry me; all they could do was encourage me and support me. On seeing their concern, something clicked in my brain and I willed myself to move.

For the first time in my life, as I stumbled down the Death Zone, I doubted my ability to survive. This self-doubt frightened me much more than the challenge of moving itself. I needed to eliminate doubt and focus on surviving, so I thought of my family and locked onto the memory of my sons, just as I had done many years earlier on a dark night in Cork when I wanted my life to end. I knew that if I stopped, it would be almost impossible to start again and the men would have to leave me behind. I was unbelievably weary but I heard Ger's voice: 'You have to keep going and get down. You need to get back to your family. Keep moving.'

All four stayed with me as I stumbled towards High Camp. As soon as we came off the fixed ropes there was a complete whiteout and visibility was reduced to zero. We couldn't see where High Camp was and for thirty minutes we sat and waited for a clearing in the weather. When it came, we got a bearing for the camp and walked towards it as quickly as we could. I was never so happy to have a tent to fall into.

The next morning we started the long descent and I began to recover. We made it to Camp 2 at 6,400m, where we stayed for another night. Although still exhausted, I was feeling better the further down the mountain I went. The following day we reached Base Camp, by which time I was fully recovered and finally able to get some perspective on what had happened to me. What I realised more than anything was how lucky I'd been. If the weather had been any worse or a bad storm had blown in, I might not have made it down. I also knew that without the help and support of my team members, my chances of survival would have been cut to a life-or-death margin.

Promise to return

Four members of the team – Mick, Ger, Pemba Gyalje and Pemba Rinzee – had reached the summit of Everest on 22 May 2003 and we were all safely down so it was time to celebrate. I was very happy for those who had stood on the summit and was also satisfied personally at having led the first Irish team to that high point via the south side of Everest. Dawa Sherpa, who was a very talented cook, made a chocolate cake for us and we partied as hard as we could on the icy moraine at Base Camp.

Before leaving, Clare approached me and expressed her desire to return. She felt that she hadn't given it her best shot and could summit if given another chance. She wanted to know if I would lead another expedition to this mountain. I immediately agreed. On the descent, I'd been reflecting on what had gone wrong and I, too, wanted another shot at reaching the summit of Sagarmatha. I immediately contacted Ang Rita in Kathmandu, telling him I wanted him to seek a new permit for me. This expedition wasn't yet fully over and plans were already in place for the next one.

Instead of trekking out of Base Camp, we decided to treat ourselves to a helicopter ride to Lukla before flying to Kathmandu, where George was waiting for us since he'd been evacuated a few weeks earlier. Several friends and family members were also in the capital, waiting to meet and party with the team.

The Nepalese government had arranged an extravagant celebration to commemorate the fiftieth anniversary of Hillary and Tenzing's historic first summiting of Everest. All those who had summited Everest over the years were invited to a formal ceremony at the Hyatt Hotel, where we were presented with a memorial medal of honour by the King of Nepal. Some of the world's top climbers were also there, including Reinhold Messner, Doug Scott and Peter Habeler. The great man himself, Edmund Hillary, aged eighty-four, was also present. I was awed to be in the presence of so many of my heroes and it was a superb end to what had been a challenging, exciting and successful expedition for the 2003 Irish Everest team.

As we were about to leave Nepal, Ang Rita confirmed he had secured a permit to climb Everest in spring 2004. 'Book it,' I said.

EVEREST (SOUTH SIDE) 2004

This time round, I decided that the team was going to be small as I didn't want to be pressurised organising logistics for a bigger group. The climbing team consisted of three people – Clare, John Joyce, who'd been our 2003 Base Camp manager, and me. John wanted to get as high as he could on the mountain, and I was confident that he was an able mountaineer who would be happy not to climb beyond his limits. Clare had been my climbing partner on Everest in 2003, when I'd found her to be an enthusiastic and strong climber who had huge self-belief that she could go all the way to the top.

We were very lucky in terms of sponsorship for the expedition when Lowe Alpine, Spórt Corrán Tuathail and the giant pharmaceutical company Wyeth came on board. At the time, Wyeth was completing a multi-million euro factory and was bringing a new product to treat arthritis to the market. I worked closely with its HR director, Larry Kelly, on developing 'Operation Everest', the strategy of which involved the staff seeing themselves as a team sharing a goal and identifying the completion of the building and successful launch of the product as their 'Everest'. Their timescale for completion was tied to the training and climbing timetable for our 2004 expedition.

With a smaller climbing team, the expedition organisation was much easier to manage and by March everything was in hand. Our support team included Base Camp manager Adrian Rahill and assistant manager Sheila Kavanagh while our technical man was Niall Foley, with Joe O'Leary in charge of logistics in Ireland. We chose 17 March – St Patrick's Day – to depart from Cork Airport and hundreds of well-wishers came to see us off. The mood was celebratory; everyone was buoyed by the prospect of Clare becoming the first Irish female summiteer of Everest. But as we prepared to say our final goodbyes, the mood among family and close friends became more sombre. They knew we'd both had difficulties in 2003 and that, even though we'd trained and prepared as well as we could for this new expedition, dangers were always present when climbing the world's highest mountain.

Clare's father, Kevin, spoke to me just as I was about to go through to departures. 'Pat, will you make sure that my daughter is okay?' he said. His request brought home to me the emotional turmoil that families go through when their loved ones are on expedition. 'I'll do my best,' I replied, 'but Clare is a woman of her own volition and very strong. We'll work as a team and won't take any dangerous actions. We have a plan and are prepared to come off the mountain if it isn't working.' I knew that Kevin wasn't the only one who had concerns; all our family members had, but none of them wanted to stop us pursuing our dreams and goals. As we left the terminal, it was time to put any doubts out of our minds. From the moment we got on the plane, our only focus was the climb and our survival.

Earthquake threat

We arrived in Kathmandu and settled into my usual haunt, Hotel Thamel, for the next few days. Even though the team was small, there was still a huge amount of organising to be done before we left the city. We had three teams of trekkers joining us over the duration of the climb and I needed to ensure that all was in order for them. Pemba Gyalje was again our climbing sirdar and we had four other climbing Sherpas on the team – Lama Babu, Lama Jangbu, Lhakpa Gelu and Nang Chemmi.

The first group of ten trekkers arrived and we enjoyed a few nights on the town in Kathmandu before flying to Lukla on 24 March. From there, we began a nine-day trek to Base Camp through the Khumbu Valley with its colourful villages and friendly locals. On 1 April, after a glorious trek, we arrived at Everest Base Camp. Our Sherpa team had arrived before us and had completed most of the initial heavy work, including levelling our site and setting up the tents. We had a meal with the trekkers before they headed back the way they'd come and we settled in for a long stay at the foot of Everest.

There were about eight teams from around the world at Base Camp, as well as a few groups who were there to film. David Breashears, the well-known American climber and videographer, was filming a sequence for *Into Thin Air* while a team from Discovery Channel was shooting a six-part documentary on Everest and the Sherpa culture. The ground under us was busy too; every now and then we could feel it move. An earthquake had been forecast for 2004 although there were no specifics on the exact date. We kept in regular contact with our weather forecaster in Seattle to get up-to-the-minute scientific predictions.

I had to put thoughts of an earthquake to the back of my mind because we needed to get started on the process of acclimatisation. We spent a few days practising ice techniques on the Khumbu Glacier and I could see that we were all performing well on the ice and snow. We were fitter and more experienced that we'd been the previous year, which was reassuring as I knew that speed would be of the essence in making this a successful expedition.

A close encounter

On 8 April there was a puja ceremony during which the monks prayed for an auspicious and safe climb for all the teams about to climb Everest. That night, heavy winds caused us to cancel our first crossing of the notorious Khumbu Icefall. Instead, we remained at Base Camp, where we celebrated Clare's thirty-third birthday and prepared to say goodbye to Niall, who was heading home after setting up our communications system.

The following day, 12 April, we finally made a hazardous and sobering five-hour journey across the icefall, arriving safely at Camp 1, situated at 6,248m at the entrance to the Western Cwm. John was exhausted and rested for the day while Clare and I walked a further 300m across the gradually inclining glacier towards Camp 2. By the time night fell, we were all exhausted and in need of rest before returning to Base Camp. Sleep, however, proved elusive as our camp was hit by heavy snowfalls, with up to 500mm of snow falling on the mountain overnight.

During the early hours of the morning, John was hit by stomach cramps and was in our makeshift open-air toilet cubicle at 5.30am when we all heard a massive explosion coming from further up the mountain that literally rocked our camp. It was a huge avalanche that had started over 1,000m above us and was now thundering down the mountain. We had been very careful to pitch Camp 1 out of what we believed to be the main avalanche route and thought we'd be relatively safe from the objective danger that was now speeding down the mountain.

I got my camera and opened the tent door to take some photos. To my horror, the debris of the avalanche had stopped a mere 100m from our tent. I jumped back inside as a great 30m wave of icy dust came towards us, not able to tell if we were facing a direct hit that would most definitely bury us in a snowy grave.

John was still somewhere outside as the spindrift flew past the tent. Seconds later he appeared, looking like a real-life snowman and still trying to pull up his down suit. As soon as the danger passed, we all laughed at the predicament that he had found himself in. Behind the laughter, though, was a keen awareness of just how lucky we were to have survived. We decided to avoid sleeping at Camp 1 again during the expedition, opting instead to go straight from Base Camp to Camp 2.

After breakfast we made our way down the mountain for a few days' rest. Back at Base Camp, John started to feel unwell and after being assessed by the doctors there he was diagnosed with AMS. He was still able to move and made his way to the village of Lobuche at 4,940m. From there, he was helicoptered to Kathmandu as he felt the risks were too great to continue. Now that our team-mate was gone, Clare and I regrouped with our Sherpa team and restructured our plans.

Pushing beyond our limits

From 17 April to 17 May, the team worked hard to prepare for our summit attempt as we acclimatised and stocked Camps 2 and 3 and, finally, High Camp at 7,950m for our summit attempt. We made twelve more precarious switchback journeys, ascending and descending the Khumbu Icefall. I really hated that place; it terrified me and we had a few near-misses with blocks of ice the size of houses falling around us. It brought me completely out of my comfort zone each time I entered that chamber of horrors where my skills as a climber meant nothing. There, everyone was at the mercy of an uncontrollable power of nature. The ice field just kept moving downhill and nothing ever remained the same for long. We were in constant fear of falling into a crevasse as we crossed rickety, unstable ladders, or of having a towering, overhanging serac collapse on us as we crossed under it.

These were not the only dangers outside our control that we had to contend with; heavy snowfalls had made the Western Cwm and Silent Valley above Camp 1 dangerous places to be. Massive avalanches were constantly pouring down the steep faces of Everest and nearby Nuptse. This year, I was witnessing some of the biggest and most powerful avalanches I had ever seen in the area.

Physically we pushed our bodies to the limit, carrying heavy rucksacks as we stocked the camps. Recent *National Geographic* research showed that carrying a heavy rucksack above 6,000m was the equivalent, hour on hour, of carrying a person of your own weight on your back at sea level. We were constantly under pressure, fighting the inevitable tiredness that is always with you when you are breathing Everest's thin air. There were days when we just wanted to give up and go home as we weathered snowstorms, high winds and whiteout conditions where you couldn't see your hand in front of your face. We had to contend with temperatures that moved from +28° to –40°. There were times we feared heatstroke from being burnt by the sun's ultraviolet rays; at other times frostbite was a real risk.

There were further dangers that played on our minds as we climbed – pulmonary and cerebral oedema, thrombosis and loss of peripheral vision. I was much more aware of these due to what had happened to me the previous year. We also had to conquer the fear that comes with knowing that many climbers have lost their lives in their attempt to stand on the summit of Sagarmatha; we did not want our names added to that list.

We also experienced amazing beauty during our trips up and down the mountain. I felt honoured to be in such an amazing landscape that was once at the bottom of the sea and which, through the power of tectonic forces, had been pushed to the top of the world. When I found a fossil of a sea creature one day I sensed the true power of Sagarmatha and again felt the spiritual connection with this mountain that I'd experienced the first time I'd stood on her summit in 1995. Even though we wanted to quit at times, we always maintained our self-belief and never lost focus on our objective of standing on the summit. We kept pushing upwards with resolve and accepted the hardships we had to endure to see our goals become reality. Then, after sixty days of climbing, dreaming and facing down risk and danger, we were ready for our summit push.

A waiting game

On 17 May 2004, we arrived at High Camp on the South Col, one of the most desolate and windswept places I'd ever been. Lhakpa and Lama Babu Sherpa had arrived first and erected the tents. They were in the process of melting ice for hot drinks by the time Pemba Gyalje, Nang Chemmi, Lama Jangbu, Clare and I arrived just before 1pm. It was such a relief to be there. After years of training and the previous year's failed attempt, both Clare and I were finally at a point where our goal was within reach. But we knew that Everest isn't sentimental; if we were to get to the top of the mountain, we could leave nothing to chance.

Over the next eight hours, we rested and rehydrated, fully focused on the task ahead. I radioed Adrian at Base Camp for the latest forecast. We were told that the jet-stream winds were predicted to hold off for another twenty-four hours before descending on the mountain. I was hoping this was correct and that they wouldn't hit the mountain sooner.

Eventually, the darkness we'd been waiting for fell and at 8pm the intense silence was broken as the radio crackled into life. It was Pemba. 'Come in, Pat. What are you and Clare doing?' Clare said nothing as she raised her thumb. There was a short pause before I spoke. 'Come in, Pemba, we'll be ready to head out in an hour. What are you and the rest of the team doing?' 'We are going too,' he replied. The decision was made; the entire team was ready to go to the summit.

Death Zone dangers

At 9pm we gathered outside our tents, feeling both anxious and excited about the challenge ahead. The night was clear but the winds were stronger than forecast and the windchill made it was a very cold −35°. Our adrenaline was pumping as we headed into the dark abyss knowing we were now facing the most dangerous part of the climb. We had a 10am turning time at the latest, no matter what.

While reaching the summit was our goal, staying safe was our priority.

About an hour out of camp, we passed the only other team that were summit-bound that night from the south side. The 69-year-old Bolivian-American Nils Antezana and his guide, Gustavo Lisi, were moving very slowly on the South Col with their two Sherpas. Nils, who was behind the other three, was hunched over and resting on his ice axe. We were alarmed to see someone whose movements suggested that they shouldn't be in the Death Zone of the world's highest mountain. As I passed Gustavo and the Sherpas, I gave a thumbs-up which Gustavo returned; I took this as a sign that everything was alright.

At 8,400m, we passed the body of Scott Fischer and said a prayer for the well-known climber who had died while descending from the summit in May 1996. His death, along with those of eleven others that year, precipitated a sustained and angry debate on the subject of commercial climbing on Everest. We then proceeded onto the Balcony and the start of the southeast ridge, where we changed our oxygen cylinders. Very mindful of the trouble I'd gotten into the previous year with a blocked valve, I made sure there was no snow or ice restricting my oxygen flow as we headed higher into the Death Zone.

It surprised me at this point to discover that we were two hours ahead of our schedule. Twilight turned to sunrise and my heart rose. We were the only people on the ridge as dawn broke across the highest gangplank in the world. The views were spectacular as we continued to make great progress.

At the point where I'd nearly died the previous year, I stopped for a moment and looked across at the heavenly sight of Lhotse, feeling stronger than I'd ever felt at over 8,000m. Clare and Pemba were ahead with me following behind, thoroughly enjoying every minute of the climb. At the South Summit, I clipped into the fixed line and approached the Hillary Step. As I reached it, I had a very clear memory of the climber I'd caught and held from falling and how this action had awakened me from my hypoxic stupor. This year, I couldn't have felt better. At 8,790m, the Hillary Step is renowned among mountaineers: a 12m near-vertical rock and ice climb and the last real challenge before reaching the top of the world. When I got beyond this final barrier, I was on the summit slope with only 200m to go. Nothing, I knew, was going to stop me now.

Close to heaven

A feeling of excitement rose from the pit of my stomach and filled my heaving chest as I walked on the narrow summit ridge with thousands of metres of fall-off on either side of me. I was cautious as I moved forward, inching my way to the top of the world and stopping every few steps, in awe of where I was. Then, almost suddenly, I was there.

We had reached the summit at 6.45am on 18 May and were standing on the most mystical place on the planet. I felt a surge of joy and pride; joy at the team's success and pride in Clare, this young doctor who had become the first Irish woman to set foot on Everest's summit. All the team – Clare, Pemba, Lama Babu, Lama Jangbu, Nang Chemmi and I – hugged as we realised the magnitude of our achievement. We took in the awesome panorama around us. Other 8,000m peaks protruded through white puff clouds into the sky but none were higher than the point we were standing on.

I was very relaxed and didn't have a repeat of the out-of-body experience that had thrown me so much when I'd stood on the top of the world in 1995. As I looked around, I took a moment to reflect on my life and how my dreams and goals had taken me to amazing places and allowed me work with great people. I thought of all the people I knew who had died pursuing their dreams on the world's highest mountain. Then I focused on the people with me and knew that, without them, I would never have succeeded in achieving the three objectives I'd set out in 2002.

As we sat on the summit I put my hand into my breast pocket and took out the Tricolour. After placing it on my ice axe, Clare and I held it aloft, happy to acknowledge our country in our achievement. Then it was time for a bit of fun; I took out a hurling stick and sliothar and hit the highest *puc fada* in the world. The previous year, Ger McDonnell had hit a sliothar from the South Col and I'd promised him that, if possible, I'd bring a hurley to the summit on this expedition and hit it from there. As the small ball flew off over the top of the world, I saw the telltale signs of jet-stream winds blowing our way: it was time to head down.

Death at the top of the world

On our descent, which began at 7.30am, it was as if we were in the calm eye of the storm that we could see blowing all around us, with the strongest wind to our right and just beyond us. Around one hour later, just below the South Summit, we came across Nils Antezana and Gustavo Lisi with their two Sherpas again. Incredibly, they were still heading towards the summit despite the strengthening storm. Not only were they moving very slowly, Nils was unstable on his feet and seemed, from our vantage point, like a dead man walking. At the speed they were going, I reckoned that it would be at least noon before they reached the summit, far past a safe time to turn for a weak climber. There wasn't anything I could do; stopping in the Death Zone to convince someone else of your opinion – especially someone who didn't know you from Adam – was a non-runner.

We continued on our descent and arrived into High Camp at 12.30pm. Absolutely shattered, Clare and I went into our tent and fell asleep. I woke sporadically over the following hours and wondered if the climbers we'd met on our descent were on the way back. Around 5am the following morning, Pemba came to our tent and woke Clare and me. He was already stripping the camp for our descent and told me that he'd given some of our oxygen to two Sherpas – Mingma and Big Dorje – when they'd struggled into camp around 11pm. He'd helped them into a tent and given them something to drink. The Sherpas told of two 'crazy men' who, they said, had continued to the summit long after they should have turned back.

While they were telling the shocking story, shouts were heard coming from somewhere beyond the camp at 11.30pm on the night of 18 May. Our Sherpas went out and found a climber lying in the snow; it was Gustavo Lisi, the Argentinian guide. They helped him back to camp and gave him some oxygen before guiding him to his tent. As soon as I heard this, I went to the tent where I could hear Gustavo on his satellite phone talking to someone. It turned out that, by the time he came out of his tent, his webmaster was already updating his website with the news that *'Gustavo has conquered Everest!!!!'*. When I spoke to him, he said that they'd had to leave Nils Antezana higher up on the mountain.

By now, there were severe winds above us and heading back up the mountain was not an option that those who had descended from the summit could consider;

it was just too dangerous. The Sherpas from Gustavo's team were totally wrecked and looked as if they'd hardly get down the mountain, never mind go back up in search of the missing man. I went to Victor Saunders, an English guide who was at High Camp and who'd had to retreat from his summit attempt the previous day. He, too, was exhausted, as were his Sherpas, so they couldn't safely go back up. I rang Base Camp and got a weather update. It wasn't looking good and I thought the best thing was for everybody to descend.

Lama Jangbu from our team accompanied Gustavo from High Camp to Camp 3 while Big Dorje and Mingma made their way down with our Sherpa team. They told a story that horrified all of us when we heard it. They said that they were very angry with Gustavo because he had continued upwards even though he and Nils were going far too slowly. They said they had all reached the summit but, on their descent, Nils slowed even further. When they reached the Balcony on the south-southeast ridge at 8,350m, they put him sitting in an alcove at the top of this section and continued downwards. As they walked away from him, a very weak Nils reached out and caught one of his team-mate's legs, pleading with him not to go. As soon as I heard this story, I phoned Base Camp to let them know that there was a climber missing, presumably – by now – dead. This was a nightmare scenario but there was nothing we could do for Nils Antezana.

As we descended, the winds hit the mountain with ferocity. Because of our fast ascent, we managed to get below them and out of danger. Others were not so fortunate that day; fifteen climbers reached the summit and four died on the way down. Along with Nils Antezana, three South Korean climbers – Joon-ho Baek, Min Jang and Mu-taek Park – all aged in their thirties and climbing via the north-northeast ridge, died of exposure.

When we reached the Khumbu Icefall, visibility was about 10m. Everyone was glad this was our last time facing this particular challenge. On the other side of it, our support team waited to meet us and accompany us back to Base Camp, where we arrived at 11am. It was a relief to be down and safe, having reached the summit of Everest. I had also fulfilled two more important personal goals by leading the first Irish woman to the summit of the highest mountain on the planet and by reaching that same summit from the south side; it was a moment to celebrate. Our final group of trekkers rolled into Base Camp on 21 May and we shared a meal before beginning the long trek from Base Camp to Lukla the following day.

From there we flew to Kathmandu on 26 May, where Clare and I met up with Michael Kodas, a climber and writer who had been on Everest while we were there. When news of the disappearance of Nils Antezana broke, he had been contacted by his daughter, Fabiola, to help her find out what had happened to her father who, by now, was presumed dead. Kodas, who I didn't know, had heard that we had seen Nils on both our ascent and descent. He wanted to meet with us to piece together the details of the Bolivian-American doctor's last hours.

It was heartbreaking to see what this woman was going through as she struggled to find out what had happened to her beloved father. It brought home to me, yet again, how difficult it is for the families of those of us who spend so much of our time risking our lives doing something even we don't always understand.

A new goal

As we had made our way down from Everest's summit, I had been thinking that it was time for me to ease down my high-altitude expeditions and look to the Poles, which had long fascinated me. But then Clare turned to me and asked what I thought she could do next. I replied that no Irish woman had yet completed the Seven Summits Challenge and that she should take on the project. She loved the idea and asked if I would lead the climbs. Impulsively, I said I would, immediately ending all thoughts of slowing down. The Irish Seven Summit Challenge was born before we had reached Everest Base Camp.

THE SECOND SEVEN SUMMITS

By 18 May 2004, Clare already had three of the Seven Summits in the bag, including Everest in Asia, Kilimanjaro in Africa and Aconcagua in South America, so it was natural for her to want to achieve the goal of becoming one of only a handful of women to complete all seven. I hadn't hesitated when she'd asked me to undertake the challenge with her because I couldn't resist the chance to lead someone I had mentored and respected for so long in such an iconic climbing project.

We had two objectives: to have the first Irish woman climb to the summit of all the highest peaks on each of the seven continents and for me to become the first person in the world to complete the challenge twice while summiting Everest from both its north and south sides. I had a heavy workload for the rest of 2004, with guided trips to Russia, Tanzania, Nepal, South America and Scotland lined up, but I was still up for the project, which we estimated we could complete by the end of 2005.

In May 2005, we flew to Alaska with the other members of the team – John Roche from Limerick, John Carey from Cork and John Dowd from Kerry – to climb Denali, the highest mountain in North America. We met up with Ger McDonnell in Anchorage, where he was living with his partner, Annie. Ger was joining us on the climb and had arranged the logistics for the expedition. We sorted all our gear at his home before heading for

Talkeetna in his campervan.

Once our permits were in place, we flew to Base Camp on another hair-raising flight through the narrowest of mountain passes before reaching the wide expanse of the Kahiltna Glacier. In the twelve years since I'd last been here, I hadn't forgotten either the beauty of Denali or the capriciousness of its weather. They say it is so unpredictable that all you can do is turn the dial and wherever it stops is what you might get. It can be a very harsh mountain to climb, and we didn't know that we were about to get caught up in one of the worst storms to hit the region in years. Initially, though, the weather wasn't bad and we moved steadily from Base Camp at 2,200m up through Camps 1, 2 and 3, travelling at night when the ground was firmer so we could avoid melting snow bridges and falling into crevasses.

We had just settled into Camp 3 at 4,330m when a massive storm hit that lasted for almost two weeks. Every morning we had to get to work with shovels to clear the snow that covered our tents. We built 2m-high walls around the tents to protect us from the wind and snow and had to create igloos in which to cook and eat over the two-week period, during which over three metres of snow fell. It was tough sitting out the storm and trying to find the patience to wait yet another day, but I had seen too many climbers die in avalanches so we waited until the risks had eased. Then we started running low on food stocks and realised that if there wasn't a break in the weather we would have to descend rather than risk starving at Camp 3.

The price of making up for lost time

Finally, the winds died down and the snow stopped falling. We had lost a lot of time and our flights home were booked for four days later. John Carey decided to leave the mountain as he couldn't risk missing his flight. The remaining five team members stayed and made the decision that, due to time constraints, the only chance we had of reaching the summit was if we launched our attempt from Camp 3 and didn't spend a night at Camp 4 en route. The seventeen-hour ascent from Camp 3 was tough, but we had kept up our fitness with all the daily shovelling during the storm.

When we reached the summit at 10am on 20 June 2005, Ger pulled out his bodhrán and played a celebratory tune. Then we raised the Tricolour before moving off that beautiful spot without delaying too long. We descended quickly, stopping only to clear our camps in what turned into a thirty-six-hour marathon. We were totally exhausted as we pulled our gear up Heartbreak Hill and back towards Base Camp. I was severely dehydrated but we hadn't had time to stop and melt snow for hot drinks on the way down as we didn't want to miss our flight back to Ireland. My thirst was so excruciating that I'd started to eat snow on the descent.

When we finally reached Base Camp we were knackered and a guy from another team gave me a bottle of water. I was so thirsty I drank the entire contents in one go. Almost immediately, I had an anaphylactic reaction from drinking the water on top of having eaten freezing snow. My throat and tongue swelled and my airways closed. My heart was racing as I started to vomit and I feared that I was going to choke to death. Thankfully, the reaction abated after a couple of minutes. I learned a lesson that day: to never again allow myself become dangerously dehydrated and to avoid eating snow or ice. It was a wake-up call to me that, even with all my experience, I could make such a stupid mistake and put myself in danger.

In spite of all the delays, we made it off the mountain in time to get our plane back to Talkeetna. Ger drove us to the airport in Anchorage and we made our flight back to Ireland with just twenty minutes to spare.

Within two days of returning home, I was back on a plane, heading to Kilimanjaro with a group. After that, I had a three-week break before starting what felt like a whistle-stop world tour of the final three summits of the highest mountains in Europe, Australia and Antarctica. We reached the summit of Elbrus in mid-July with a team that included Micheál O'Connell, Michael Storey, Gordon Browne, Tim O'Connor, Richard Oakley, Micheál Cunningham, Katie O'Connor and my Russian climbing partner Natasha Bashkirov. Now there were just two more summits left; in November 2005 we climbed Kosciuszko in Australia before travelling to Antarctica in December with John Dowd, who'd also climbed Denali with us. Mount Vinson was the seventh and final mountain in our Seven Summits project.

Disastrous weather

Flying into Patriot Hills was as spine-tingling as it had been the first time I had come to this white land. The mess tent was full of the same mix of scientists, wealthy visitors and those, like ourselves, who were heading off on expedition. We set up our tents at Base Camp on the Branscombe Glacier and prepared our gear for our first carry to Camp 1. The forecast was for heavy snow and gale-force winds, but we were taking no chances and built 1.5m-high by 1m-wide snow walls around the tent for extra protection. Our plan was to spend the night at Camp 1 and set off early next morning to bring provisions to Camp 2 at 3,100m before dropping down again to 2,769m to carry more provisions to stock our camps.

The following morning, however, there were serious signs of bad weather and we decided to stay put. As the hours passed, the winds grew ferocious and soon we were in the middle of a deadly storm. It was difficult to relax while surrounded by such a violent natural force that beat ceaselessly against our tent, but we did our best, chatting and playing cards. We were constantly on the alert for any change in the winds or any threat to our skin-thin protection, which was the only line of defence between us and a gale-force wind in temperatures of $-35°$.

Suddenly, a massive block of snow, lifted and blown by the wind, hit the tent with great force. 'Grab the poles to steady the tension!' I shouted. All three of us moved and pressed against the outer sheet of the tent to try to ease the pressure being put on the poles. They held, but then a second block of snow collided with the tent directly on one of the poles, which cracked under the pressure.

John and I put on our down suits and went outside to try and fix the tears on the tent. The conditions made it almost impossible to move and even though we had our protective goggles on, we couldn't see anything in the blizzard. While we were trying to fix the tears with duct tape, and Clare was working inside providing counter-tension, a third snow block was flung at the tent and cracked another pole. Then two more poles snapped and shot through the outer layer of the tent. The fly sheet was ripped in four places and the tent was beyond repair.

It was clear that our situation was now very dangerous; we had no protection and, on top of that, we were all exhausted from our exertions. The only thing we could do was use the fallen tent as a bivouac shelter until we recovered and could move again. We crawled between the tent walls, put on every item of clothing we could find, got into our sleeping bags and lay close to each other for the next twenty-four hours as the storm continued unabated. Every two hours, we had to leave our bivvy to shovel away the spindrift that was threatening to bury us in a snowy grave. The following day, with the winds dying down, we knew we had to go back down to Base Camp. We were totally wrecked, as was our tent, and our stove had frozen so we couldn't even melt snow to make hot drinks.

It took five hours to descend and we spent the next two days recuperating at 2,308m and waiting for a break in the weather. When it came, we headed up to Camp 1 again, where we rested briefly before continuing to Camp 2 at 3,100m with our sleds and supplies. We left the sleds behind and traversed the gentle slope to Camp 3 at 3,692m where we rested for the day to ensure we were fully acclimatised and ready for our final climb to the summit.

Double firsts

The day was clear as we roped together and started the five-hour slog over ice crevasses to the summit ridge. Once there, an hour's walk along the ridge brought us to the top of the highest point in Antarctica on 16 December 2005. It was the final summit of our Seven Summits project and we raised the Tricolour to celebrate Clare's achievement in becoming the first Irish woman – and the fifteenth female ever – to complete the Seven Summits, and my achievement in becoming the first person in the world to have completed the challenge while reaching the summit of Everest from both its north and south sides.

Clare, John and I spent about fifteen minutes on that high point, and as I looked out over the vastness of Antarctica I thought of the early explorers who had come to this great white continent, all of them my heroes: Roald Amundsen from Norway, the first man to reach the South Pole; Robert Falcon Scott, the Englishman who was beaten to being first there by thirty-four days and who died of starvation with four of his men on the return journey; Ernest Shackleton, one of the greatest leaders ever and a man who never achieved any of his dreams. Then there was my favourite adventurer, the unsung hero Tom Crean, an ordinary man from Annascaul in Co Kerry.

All three of us drank in the panoramic beauty before starting down the mountain on the long journey home. As we descended, Clare asked what had, by now, become a routine end-of-expedition question. 'What's next?' 'The South Pole,' I answered. 'Would you be interested in joining me?' 'Yes,' she replied without missing a beat, 'I'd love to.'

PART FIVE
THE WHITE CONTINENT

ORDINARY MEN AND WOMEN: EXTRAORDINARY FEATS

What was to become the Irish Beyond Endurance Expedition had been germinating in my mind for a number of years since I'd started to turn my attention away from the world's high mountains and towards its lowest point: Antarctica. Convinced that people are capable of achieving much more than they think they can, I wanted to take a group of ordinary men and women and train them to do something extraordinary. On every trip I was leading, I saw the struggle and self-doubt in people, followed by the growing self-knowledge and joy as they journeyed up Kilimanjaro, Elbrus, Aconcagua and to Everest Base Camp, constantly challenging themselves to go beyond their comfort zones.

I had four objectives for the expedition: to lead a group of ordinary people across the Shackleton Traverse; to go beyond 88° 23' S, the point Shackleton and his men had reached in 1909 during the Nimrod Expedition and which, at the time, set a new Farthest South; to lead the first Irish woman to the South Pole; and to lead the first Irish team to the South Pole.

I had long been fascinated by the legendary stories of the adventurers of the Heroic Age of Antarctic Exploration, especially the expeditions of Shackleton, Scott and Amundsen. I was intrigued by what drove these men to adventure to the most remote regions of the world. Shackleton, in particular, captured my imagination because of his leadership style. When he and his men became trapped on the ice in the Weddell Sea for ten months, the story of their survival under his leadership was astonishing and inspiring.

At the same time, I was also growing in awareness of the unsung heroes who accompanied these great leaders, and learned that many of them were Irishmen, with several from my home county of Cork and adopted home of Kerry. In addition to Kerry's Tom Crean, there was Robert Forde, Patrick Keohane, Tim and Mortimer McCarthy, all Corkmen who worked on the ships that went to the bottom of the world during the great age of polar exploration. These were ordinary men who achieved extraordinary feats of survival and endurance, pushing themselves to their very limits.

I knew that polar adventures presented physical and mental challenges that were totally different to what I had become used to on high mountains, but I wanted to pit myself against my own limitations and explore what was needed to endure the harsh conditions on Antarctica's unforgiving landscape.

The biggest risk

The Irish Beyond Endurance Expedition was the riskiest – both financially and physically – and most ambitious I had ever undertaken. On paper, however, the first part – leading a group on a traverse of South Georgia – looked feasible. With an expert team of six leaders I would lead a group of ordinary people in the footsteps of Ernest Shackleton, Tom Crean and Frank Worsley on the ninetieth anniversary of their famed crossing of South Georgia in a desperate attempt to find help to save the crew of the *Endurance*.

Before I started looking for the traverse team, I needed to charter a big ship to bring us to the island and provide a full rescue service if needed. I chose the MV *Ushuaia*, a US Navy ice-strengthened vessel converted specifically for navigating Antarctic waters whose charter cost, including thirty-eight crew and staff, was €650,000. The ship had eighty-four berths, seven of which were set aside for the team leaders. The remaining seventy-seven berths were available both for the traverse party and for people who wanted to go on an Antarctic adventure cruise. The sale of these berths, plus the amount paid for training by the traverse team, would raise €880,000, enough to cover the cost of the ship, insurance and logistics and part-fund my South Pole expedition.

I had to come up with a €150,000 deposit to secure the ship and had to produce a bank guarantee to secure the balance, which was due within four months of booking. I had just paid off the mortgage on my home in Kerry but I remortgaged it and signed personal guarantees, something I'd sworn I would never do again in my life. This was a high-risk financial venture and I was scared, but greater than any fear was my commitment to the project and my belief that it would work despite being told regularly that it was off-the-radar mad.

There was no doubt that the Beyond Endurance dream was a big one and I needed a good team to help me deal with all the logistics and training. A group of five people got together with me in Kerry and we did what I always do when I have a new dream or goal – we imagined what it would look and feel like; we talked about it and then we made a plan. Other than our own absolute belief in the idea, we hadn't a notion what the response would be, but with the ship booked and the training team in place, the time came to test the public interest in the expedition, so we put out an ad that read:

Wanted
Ordinary men and women for hazardous journey to Antarctica.
Cold, dangerous and adventurous. Training provided to minimise risks.
Join us on an adventure of a lifetime.

Objectives
1: Traverse of South Georgia: 6 required
2: Adventure cruise to Antarctica. 64 required
3: Trek to South Pole: 4 required

The wording of our ad was inspired by Shackleton's original advert when he was recruiting a crew for the Endurance Expedition:

MEN WANTED
for hazardous journey, small wages, bitter cold, long months of complete
darkness, constant danger, safe return doubtful, honor and recognition
in event of success.

Unprecedented response

We were totally unprepared for what happened next: we had over 2,500 responses, with 750 of those for the Shackleton Traverse. We were astonished, as we'd thought we would be lucky to get forty people interested in the traverse. This huge response was unprecedented and reflected the enormous fascination Irish people had with the Antarctic and its heroes.

Now we had a new challenge: to whittle down the list to those who were really willing to do what was necessary to see their dream come true. An application form had to be sent to every single respondent, which created an administration nightmare. The upside was that I now knew that the expedition wasn't going to break me financially. The first thing that knocked the numbers down was the cost, details of which hadn't been included on the website or in the press. There was no way of softening the hard edge of what we were selling. This expedition was going to cost – financially, physically and psychologically – and only those whose want was strong enough and who were prepared to make the necessary sacrifices would be selected.

Within a short space of time, the number of people who were serious about training for the traverse was down to 145. This still presented a big logistical problem as I had initially secured a permit from the governing authorities of South Georgia and the South Sandwich Islands for just six people to do the crossing. The question now was how we were going to cull 145 down to six. We had put a very intensive training programme together and knew that the numbers would most likely drop significantly during that, but I didn't think they would drop as low as six.

I contacted David Nicholls, the chairman of the technical committee for expeditions to South Georgia, and explained our dilemma. David, who was based in Scotland, believed that the training programme would serve as an effective culling ground. 'But what will I do if they all pass?' I asked. 'That won't happen,' he replied. Then, almost on a whim, he added: 'We know that you will train all those who pass to the necessary standard and we'll give you a permit for that number, whatever it is.' That promise gave me some breathing space as we began the training process.

Making the cut

The first job for my team of trainers was to carry out a general fitness assessment on each applicant. We looked not only at the physical fitness and technical ability of participants, but also at their mindset and how they reacted psychologically to stress, challenge and working in teams under conditions where trust among members was vital. Survival, we told them, was often decided by mental, and not physical endurance.

As the training progressed, some people opted out of their own volition. For many of them, the boot camps were the most challenging thing they'd ever done in their lives and they learned about their own limits and how far beyond them they could go. By the end of the four boot camp training sessions in Kerry, the number of people left was down to forty-five.

Our final training took place over seven days in Norway under Fram, a polar training and adventure company run by Rolf Bae and his wife, Cecilie Skog. I had first met Rolf while climbing Aconcagua in 2003, when I was immediately taken by his drive, ambition and passion. We became friendly and joined forces to offer specialised polar training and travel for my Irish teams. Rolf's expertise and experience were impressive: in 2000, he completed what was then the world's longest ski journey by crossing Antarctica with Eirik Sønneland; in 2005, he skied from the ice shelf to the South Pole with Cecilie; and in 2006 they both reached the North Pole unsupported. With that expedition, she became only the thirteenth person in the world to reach all three Poles, including the North Pole, South Pole and Everest.

The skills Fram and my team taught the traverse hopefuls included crevasse rescue techniques, polar camp craft and survival skills. Part of the training was a four-day mountain trek that was similar to the terrain, altitude and conditions that could be expected on South Georgia. The trek was very tough and the pace relentless; people were pushed beyond what they thought they could endure, yet nobody wanted to give up. Eventually, twenty-five people made it onto the team. Throughout the months of training, we'd worked on developing self-leadership in the participants. This meant that when the time for the final assessments came, most of those who didn't make the cut instinctively knew why, and understood that the assessors had made the right call, hard as it might have been to accept it.

I also had to organise the logistics, which were significant; in terms of equipment alone, thousands of individual items had to be packaged and shipped out to Argentina before the team flew out. Because of the size of the South Georgia expedition, I thought it would be a good idea to make contact with the Argentinian ambassador to Ireland before we left. About two weeks before our departure, I went to Dublin and met the ambassador at the embassy. He promised that if we needed any support while down there, he would be happy to help out. It was some comfort to know we had this connection if anything went wrong. Another relief was that all the berths on the *Ushuaia* sold out fairly quickly; it was good to know that the roof over my head was secure.

Shackleton's legacy

On 6 November 2006, we arrived in Tierra del Fuego with a final group of eighty-four, including the twenty-five-person traverse team plus seven guides, fifty-three adventure cruise members and a film crew who were making a four-part documentary on the expedition. At the capital, Ushuaia, there was some concern when we realised that our traverse gear, which we'd shipped from Ireland weeks earlier, had not arrived. After three days and a lot of enquiries, I learned that customs were refusing to release the gear. Finally, after much discussion and a backhander, the problem was sorted and the gear delivered to the dockside, where it was loaded onto the MV *Ushuaia*. On 9 November, with Captain Jorge Aldegheri at the helm, our ship set sail towards the island of South Georgia.

This was the place Shackleton had come to ninety years earlier, searching for help to rescue his crew. For almost ten months, the *Endurance* had been trapped in ice on the Weddell Sea. Eventually, when the ice broke up and their ship sank, the crew got into the lifeboats and made their way to Elephant Island. They found bleak refuge on that piece of rock; after a few days, Shackleton realised they couldn't survive there indefinitely. He knew that he needed to do the seemingly impossible and find help.

He chose five men – Tom Crean, Frank Worsley, Harry McNish, Timothy McCarthy and John Vincent – to make the unimaginably harsh and dangerous journey in the *James Caird* across the South Atlantic and Southern Oceans to South Georgia, where he knew there were whaling stations. The remainder of the *Endurance* crew waited on Elephant Island, not knowing if they would ever see Shackleton again or if they would eventually all die there.

That sixteen-day crossing has become the stuff of legend. Having survived horrific storms in high seas, the six men landed, half dead, on the uninhabited southwest side of South Georgia where their boat was wrecked. Now they faced a new challenge: how to get to Stromness whaling station on the northeast of the island. His men were malnourished, frostbitten and exhausted and Shackleton knew he had to take a gamble: they had to cross the unknown and uncharted crevasse- and glacier-filled interior of the island. He chose Crean and Worsley, the two strongest men, to make that crossing with him.

At 2am on 19 May 1916, the three men started an epic thirty-six-hour journey, eventually arriving at Stromness where they met human beings other than the *Endurance* crew for the first time in almost two years. A rescue was raised and, by the end of August, Shackleton was on another boat sailing back to Elephant Island to find that the men he'd left there almost four months earlier were all still alive. Not one member of the *Endurance* died during that expedition, sealing Shackleton's legacy as one of the greatest-ever expedition leaders.

Traversing South Georgia

We passed through the treacherous Drake Passage, which, thankfully, was uncharacteristically calm. During our four-day sea journey, we went through a dry run of the traverse with the team – thirty men and two women who ranged in age from twenty-one to sixty. We erected tents on the ship's deck, simulated crevasse rescue, rehearsed what to do in case of a storm and did a final gear check.

The morning of 13 November was bitterly cold as we stood on the ship's bridge and watched South Georgia come into view. We looked across the sea at snow-capped mountains that reached into and under the water. The island is known for its vicious weather and the forecast for the coming days was not good, with winds ranging from twenty-five to forty-five knots. But we were at the point of disembarkation and knew that if we didn't get off the ship, the expedition wouldn't happen. A decision was made and at 7am, our traverse team set foot on land at King Haakon Bay, the same point where Shackleton and his men had arrived, ready to begin the expedition we had trained so hard for during the past year.

There was no time to lose, which meant we didn't get a chance to take in our stunning surroundings and the Antarctic wildlife around us. We got off to a good start thanks to a break in the weather which gifted us blue skies and no wind. North of the Shackleton Gap we reached the first snow-covered ground. Having put on our snowshoes, we roped together in teams of five or six and trekked for four hours, crossing the Murray Snowfield where dark clouds began to form and winds started to blow.

By late afternoon, as we approached the Trident Ridge, the cloud cover was very heavy and visibility down to 15m, with winds gusting at 40–50kmph. This section was our first real trial as the team dragged their sleds over the top. By the time we got to the bottom of the other side of the ridge – the one Shackleton, Crean and Worsley had slid down not knowing what was at the bottom – the winds had picked up further and were gusting at 70–100kmph. By now, a wet and heavy snow had started to fall and soon we were all soaked through. We set up camp as quickly as we could and got into our tents while the wind howled around us. But the storm grew stronger and it wasn't long before tent poles cracked, a worrying development as these were brand new extreme storm-force tents. We did our best to repair what we could so that everyone was sheltered while the storm continued overnight.

Early next morning we assessed the damage and found that six tents were damaged beyond repair so I made a call to the *Ushuaia* to request replacement ones. We were due to reach Fortuna Bay at the end of our second day and Captain Aldegheri said we could make the pick-up at 7pm. The weather was still very bad, with strong winds that slowed the team while packing up and delayed our start. At the head of the Crean Glacier, the winds became even stronger – several people were knocked over and one sled was blown away; the area's katabatic winds were really testing us.

With wind speeds of up to 90kmph, we made slow progress across the glacier, covering only 3km in three hours. In the afternoon, however, the clouds lifted and we got our first clear view of South Georgia. The Crean Glacier was piercingly beautiful in its rugged whiteness but the going was tough and some team members got very tired. This was worrying as we still had about seven hours' trekking ahead of us before we reached camp.

We all got a lift, however, when we spotted Fortuna Bay from Breakwind Ridge. That was our destination for the night and having it within sight was a great boost. When we heard the welcoming sound of the *Ushuaia's* horn we knew they had us in view and were urging us on as we made our descent. It was much later than the appointed 7pm when we got to the beachhead where we collected the spare gear from some of the ship's crew. As soon as camp was set up and our new tents were secure, we all fell into an exhausted sleep.

The next morning was mercifully windless though still overcast and cold. Before setting off we were joined by all the support team from the ship. They had spent the previous days sailing around the area and stopping off at some of the islands and bays to look at the wildlife. It was a truly special moment when everyone came together as one big team to make the final 8km trek into Stromness. We were all emotional when we saw the ghostly whaling village and imagined the families that had lived here and what they must have thought when they saw three men appearing out of nowhere almost a century earlier.

After re-boarding the ship, we sailed to the settlement of Grytviken, where Ernest Shackleton was buried in 1922, at the request of his wife, when he died suddenly from a heart attack while on another Antarctic expedition. Standing at his grave, we joined together in a semicircle, raised the Tricolour in honour of the Irish men who had been to this place before us, and sang the national anthem before a lone piper played 'Amazing Grace'. I felt humbled, not only at the thought of what Shackleton, Crean and Worsley had accomplished on South Georgia, but also at what this team of ordinary men and women around me had accomplished by completing the Shackleton Traverse.

Partying at the bottom of the world

By evening we were back in the comfort of the *Ushuaia* with our expedition complete and a twelve-day adventure sailing in the Antarctic waters ahead of us. That night – and every night afterwards – we partied, drank, danced and sang as if our lives depended on it. During the days, we cruised along the Palmer Archipelago through the Neumayer Channel and on to Port Lockroy where we landed. We saw the wonder of Antarctic wildlife in all its glory – from gentoo and king penguins to sheathbills, terns, skuas, blue-eyed shags and seals.

We had one final port of call: Elephant Island, that bleak piece of ice-covered rock that was home to the *Endurance* crew for nearly four months while they waited to be rescued. Not many people get to land there, and our arrangement was for the full traverse team to be taken on Zodiacs to the island. However, as we approached, our captain decided conditions were too dangerous to make multiple landings on the island at Cape Valentine. In the end, only one crossing could be made, carrying some crew and expedition leaders including Clare O'Leary, Ger McDonnell, Rolf Bae and me.

It was a very special moment to stand on the rough, dark rock of that island where, ninety years earlier, twenty-two men never gave up on either themselves or their master. Being there really brought home the extent of their courage and will to endure against all the odds.

This part of the Irish Beyond Endurance Expedition taught me an important lesson: we are all ordinary and it is only what we do that makes us extraordinary. I had spent well over a year training and travelling with people who wanted to step outside their comfort zones and do something extraordinary, and they had succeeded. I learned that anyone with the desire and ambition to do something, and the determination to follow their goal, could achieve their dream as long as they committed to training and ensuring they had the right skills and were part of a great team. I also learned that I loved inspiring and leading people on their journey from the ordinary to the extraordinary.

PREPARING FOR THE SOUTH POLE

From the time I first mentioned leading a team to the South Pole, Clare O'Leary confirmed herself as a team member. Ger McDonnell also committed to the expedition. We wanted a team of four and I was confident that the South Georgia project would contain the final team member. One of the traverse team stood out from early on: Shaun Menzies, an IT consultant in his early forties, who showed real commitment and passion for the training and the traverse and who emerged as someone who was ready for a bigger challenge. Born in England of Irish parentage, he lived and worked in Dublin. After I spoke to him about joining our small team, he confirmed that he was up for the adventure.

The individual cost was around $60,000, a significant sum for each one of us. While the money and sponsorship needed to be sorted out, the main focus for the team was the training, which was brutal and harsh but vital to ensure our survival in Antarctica.

In February 2007, we were all disappointed when Ger said that he couldn't raise the funds to cover his costs and had to make the hard decision to step down from the team. We knew we'd miss him, not just for his physical strength but also for the warmth and joy he brought with him wherever he went. It would have been a great plus to have someone on the team whose positivity would bring other members through the tough days we knew Antarctica would throw at us, but it wasn't to be.

Ger soon turned his thoughts to the Himalaya, and later in the year he joined a Dutch-led team that was planning to climb K2, the world's second highest mountain, the following year. He had attempted to reach its summit in 2006 and had been badly injured by a falling rock. He'd always wanted to go back and saw this expedition as an opportunity to become the first Irish climber to get to the top of what many consider to be the world's most dangerous mountain.

An expedition of 100 marathons

Throughout the early months of 2007, Clare, Shaun and I trained in Kerry and Norway. The challenges ahead of us were both physical and psychological. The unique task of skiing to the South Pole is that you start at point A and have to walk to point Z, the Pole – a journey of 1,140km – with nothing between you and your goal except a sea of white. I quickly learned that it was an entirely different world to high-altitude climbing, which has a social aspect whereby you meet up with other climbers and teams and where Base Camp often offers something approximating the comforts of home. Walking to the South Pole would provide no such comforts; whoever was on the team would be the only human beings we'd meet once our journey began.

As part of the logistics, we had to specify our date of arrival at the Pole, when we would be picked up by one of the infrequent outward flights which mainly carry scientific personnel. If we weren't at the Pole on the appointed date, the pilot would pick us up from whatever point we were at; there would be no question of hanging around for us to finish the expedition.

This meant that, on a sixty-day expedition, we had to cover 23km daily across some of the harshest terrain on our planet. That timescale allowed for approximately ten days for rest days and the unexpected such as accidents, injury or illness that would slow us down or keep us tent-bound. We had to ensure we were fit for the journey; that our gear wouldn't let us down; that mentally we were prepared not just the harshness of the terrain but also for the repetition of doing the exact same tasks every day, from day one to the final day. I knew each of us would have to dig deep psychologically before we ever left Ireland to ensure that, when our bodies grew weary, our mindset would pull us over the line.

Our energy input and output was key to the success of the expedition. Every day we had to move, not just to cover ground but also because temperatures were so cold in Antarctica that stopping – even for a few moments – would cause our core temperature to drop and our sweat to freeze. The threat of hypothermia and frostbite was huge and potentially fatal so, unless we were in our tents, we had to be moving constantly. To keep moving, we had to keep eating. The food we would eat on the expedition was vitally important so, donning her doctor's hat, Clare spent a lot of time researching and analysing our precise dietary needs for the trip. Working with Professor Phil Jakeman, head of the Department of Physical Education and Sport Sciences and the elite athletes' programme at the University of Limerick, she learned that each day's trek on to the South Pole would use up the same amount of energy as if we were running two marathons.

I found it hard to get my mind around the fact that we would expend the energy needed for 100 marathons during our time on the ice. The science took into account the weather, the amount of ground we would cover each day and the fact that each person would be hauling a sled weighing around 100kg over difficult terrain. Every item of food and gear would have to be calculated and weighed in advance because every extra gram would demand more energy to haul. We really focused on getting our nutrition right so that our bodies would work optimally in an environment that took no prisoners. We also had full body check-ups to find if we had any hidden weaknesses that might be exposed during such a tough expedition. It was vital that anything that could jeopardise us on the way to the Pole was rooted out in the months beforehand.

Between 2006 and 2007, we travelled to Norway eight times for cold weather and polar skills training. One of my biggest learning curves was in cross-country skiing. When I started, I was falling after 20m and couldn't ski down a minor slope without flipping over. Small kids whizzed by as I lay in the snow. *If they can do it, so can I*, I'd think. I loved learning all these new skills; not only how to ski, but all aspects of polar survival and how to be efficient in every task that we did, from cooking and how to erect and take down a tent in the shortest time in the worst of katabatic winds, to how to build an igloo and how to pull a sled across rough terrain.

In Norway, I grew to love the landscape of snow and ice and pure cold, excited by the fact that I was pushing my limits a bit further every day. I dreamed about the remoteness of Antarctica and the South Pole and the fact that we would have nobody to depend on except ourselves. I relished the opportunity to prove that we could do it.

238

TURNING FIFTY

In 2007, I turned fifty. Something about reaching that age and entering a new decade prompted me to stand back and do something I hadn't done in a long time – have a proper look at my life and how I was living it. What I saw shocked me: I was obsessively busy. In the previous six months alone, as well as organising the logistics for the entire trip, I'd led the Beyond Endurance Expedition to South Georgia. I returned to Ireland only to leave almost immediately to lead a group on Aconcagua in Argentina. During that time, I was totally immersed in training for the South Pole expedition while simultaneously organising and leading trips to Kilimanjaro and Everest Base Camp.

Financially, I was taking risks that close friends and family were telling me were outrageous. When I looked at how I was spending my time, I saw that all the money I was making was being poured into expeditions. I'd never thought of retirement or what I would do if I couldn't continue with the life I was leading.

Physically, I felt very strong but turning fifty brought home to me the fact that I was no longer young and couldn't predict what the future would bring in terms of health. Those who loved me had supported me over the years on all my expeditions. They knew that if they tried to restrict me, it would be like putting me in a box. Although they trusted that I was good at calculating risk and was a very efficient self-leader, they still worried every time I went on expedition. The fact was that the selfishness that drove me to continue was part and parcel of the personality trait that allowed me to focus fully on minimising risk by obsessively training and learning the skills I needed to survive.

In 2007, however, I started to see the impact my lifestyle was having on those closest to me. I wasn't seeing anywhere near enough of my family, especially my sons. I wasn't listening to my close friends who told me that I needed to slow down. I finally understood what all these people who cared for me had been telling me for years: I had no balance in my life. My goals had become my obsession, to the point of demanding that everything – and everyone – not associated with them was sidelined.

At fifty, I realised that I had lost sight of what was most important, not just in my life, but in everyone's life: family and friends. I was very familiar with the sacrifices I was making to pursue my goals but I'd never before stopped to consider the huge sacrifices my lifestyle was inflicting on family and friends. I had taken them for granted and assumed they would always be there, waiting for me to return, not just from my adventures, but from this life where there really wasn't any place for them.

Too much sacrifice

One day, around this time, my son Patrick said something to me that stopped me in my tracks. 'We are very proud of you, Dad, and we love you. You have done amazing things but you've missed out on a lot of time with the family. You've missed so many important days and events in our lives because you were busy or away on expedition. This really hurts us still and we'd like if you spent more time with us.' The truth of his words hit me like a hammer blow.

For the first time in my life, I understood the enormity of the sacrifice my family had made, and were continuing to make. When I saw the pain I was causing, I decided I had to do something about it and make reparations. I needed to show them that I really wanted to change and take up the position that I, as a father, husband, son, brother and friend, had disregarded for so long. I remembered the words of a poem by Robert Service that I had come across years earlier and that resonated with me in an uncanny way:

240

There's a race of men that don't fit in,
A race that can't stay still;
So they break the hearts of kith and kin,
And they roam the world at will.
They range the field and they rove the flood,
And they climb the mountain's crest;
Theirs is the curse of the gypsy blood,
And they don't know how to rest.

I saw myself in every line of this poem. I loved my adventures but often wondered why I was always moving on to the next thing. Sometimes it felt as if nothing would be enough for me. The last verse of the poem, especially, was my idea of a nightmare future:

He has failed, he has failed; he has missed his chance;
He has just done things by half.
Life's been a jolly good joke on him,
And now is the time to laugh.
Ha, ha! He is one of the Legion Lost;
He was never meant to win;
He's a rolling stone, and it's bred in the bone;
He's a man who won't fit in.

I feared that I could end up a lonely old man, with nothing but my past achievements for company. I also saw how selfish and unfair I'd been to those who loved me and who I'd taken for granted. I saw that I'd never had any balance in my life, even from my youngest days, and that the lack of balance had exacted a very high price.

I had to change and learn how to treat the most important people in my life with the love and respect they deserved. It wasn't too late to build the many bridges that I needed to build. I wasn't going to give up going on expedition, but I would make sure that my time at home was given to family and friends. I set myself a goal: to make up to Marie and my sons for all the hurt I'd caused them over the years.

Changing my mindset and the lifestyle I had when I was in Ireland was difficult and I knew that achieving this goal wasn't going to be easy. Even harder was finding my place back in the family unit; they had lived for so long with my absence that my presence, even though they wanted it, was hard to adapt to. But we were all committed to our family and never doubted that it was underpinned by a love that the years hadn't diminished.

When I wasn't abroad, I began to go home to Beechwood once a week to work from there. This allowed me to connect in a more meaningful way with Marie, our sons and my wider family. I faltered many times and caused more hurt and disappointment but, each time I failed, I tried again to fit into this family unit where I belonged and was at my happiest. It would be an ongoing journey but, thankfully, our love for each other meant that we were all committed to the long haul.

GREENLAND ICE CAP TRAVERSE 2007

The intensity of our training for the South Pole Expedition increased during the summer with a trip to Norway in early June 2007, where we completed a fourteen-day, 300km skiing trek. Six weeks later, Clare, Shaun and I travelled to Greenland with the intention of completing the first Irish unsupported ski traverse of the Greenland Ice Cap, the second largest ice cap in the world. This was a journey of 660km that would take around thirty days of man-hauling across one of the most active glaciers in the world. It was our final immersive training for the South Pole and a hugely challenging adventure in itself.

Because we were doing the traverse towards the end of summer, a lot of the crevasses on glaciers were open, making it very difficult to find crossing points and making the ice fields more precarious. This terrain was as close as we could get to what we would experience at the Pole and it served as a great testing ground for our skills and endurance. I knew that, after the Poles, Greenland presented some of the toughest snow and ice terrain in the world, particularly since global warming had started melting the glaciers, turning increasing numbers of ice fields into melt-water rivers.

We flew there on the last day of July, having shipped out our gear a few weeks earlier. The next day, a small propeller plane took us across the country to the east coast and the village of Kulusuk. As we flew over the polar plateau, we could see multiple glacier lakes and streams, as well as open crevasses, especially at the start and end of our intended route. This was a cause for concern, but it was better to know what was ahead of us so we would be prepared.

The small population at Kulusuk was made up of Inuit people, many of whom were out whaling when we arrived. We met up with an international team there – led by Charlie Paton, a former Royal Marine – that was also attempting a crossing of the ice cap. The team consisted of two Belgians, an American and an Englishman, Jon Bradshaw, whose father was Irish. Jon had been cycling from London to New York but when he arrived in Greenland he found the terrain wasn't suited to cycling so he decided to ski across instead. I really liked his personality and his quirky sense of humour and could see straight away that he was competitive and driven in a good way.

We spent the next few days sorting out our gear, which weighed in at approximately 100kg each. In addition to our individual fibreglass sleds, we were bringing two extra-light plastic sleds to carry the lightweight but bulky gear. We needed to avoid packing the main sleds too high and making them more prone to flipping over on the ascent to the plateau.

Having seen all the open crevasses on the overland flight, we took the opportunity to do a bit more practice on our crevasse rescue skills. We also checked our roping plans to make sure that we would be roped in such a way that, if one of us fell in, a sled wouldn't follow. By the following Monday, we were ready for the two-hour sea journey on old fishing boats that took us to our starting point at the Apuserserpia glacier snout at Nagtivit.

Relentless grind

Following a fairly rough sea ride and four subsequent hours of man-hauling, we made camp on the glacier by 9pm. Charlie Paton's team was trekking with us for five days as we ascended the glacier and it was good to have more people around to keep our spirits up. The first few days' hauling was back-breaking as we pulled, dragged, lifted and cursed our way uphill over a glacier that resembled an earthquake zone. There were 2m-tall ice mounds that we had to manoeuvre in, around and over in a crevasse-ridden zone. The crevasses were deep, sometimes scarily so, and it took us four days to get through this section.

By the afternoon of 8 August, the terrain had become more level and we were able to pick up our pace a bit. My sled got a 200mm gash when I was pulling through some rough ice and we made repairs to it using a plastic container and some Araldite. They didn't work too well, unfortunately, and the following day it took in water, soaking everything. In spite of that, the day went reasonably well and we all got safely across the snow bridges. That evening we spent three hours trying to repair my sled properly, drilling holes and bolting on bits of plastic using fairly basic tools. I felt more confident that it would hold as we were now out of the energy-zapping crevasse zone.

Five days after starting out on the ice, we finally reached the start of the plateau where the snow was better and we were able to put on our skis. There were still a few significant crevasses to get around and these slowed us as we had to haul along them until we found a suitable crossing point. We decided to make camp early and get up earlier the next day as the snow was better in the very early hours and we could make more progress. We covered 18km on 9 August and 21km the following day. That morning we said goodbye to the Paton team as we wanted to forge our own route and get practice on navigating as a team for our South Pole expedition.

Despite whiteout conditions on 10 August, we covered 28km. We got news via satellite that one of the Paton team had been helicoptered off the ice due to ligament problems. The next day, we heard that two more of the team had to be evacuated, leaving only Charlie and Jon to continue their expedition. Although the snow was sticky and adding drag to our sleds that day, we were hauling well and covered over 25km. The following nine days brought continuous snowfall which stuck to our skis and sleds, increasing the drag and slowing us down, sometimes literally to a crawl. The fact that my sled was damaged meant that its rigidity was compromised and it was warping, making it even harder to pull in powdery snow. I repacked it so that most of the weight was away from the site of damage and that helped a little.

The whiteout conditions also created another problem – the lack of sunlight meant we couldn't use our solar panels to charge our battery packs which kept our sat phone going. It was our only means of contacting the outside world and we didn't want it to go down, so we had to be very careful to protect our emergency supply of lithium batteries. To our relief, on 21 August the sun briefly broke through the overcast sky and the batteries could be charged.

We had a well-established pattern by this stage, hauling for eight hours daily. Each person took the lead for a leg when they navigated the team while cutting a trail in the snow to make the going a bit easier for the other two. We always used a combination of compass and GPS to navigate; the latter was particularly useful on a featureless landscape with no visible points of reference.

Seven days later, on 28 August and with 542km of man-hauling behind us, we finally reached DYE-2, a US Distant Early Warning Line site established to warn of Soviet air attacks against the USA during the Cold War. The structure appeared out of the mist like a long-forgotten alien craft. After making camp, we found the entrance and went into the building, which had been abandoned in October 1988. Everything inside was exactly as it had been left all those years earlier, with half-eaten meals and out-of-date beer bottles on the table, and workshops looking as if the workers had just stepped out shortly beforehand.

While we slept, Charlie Paton and Jon Bradshaw arrived and set up camp at DYE-2 also. Clare and I called to their tent the following morning to let them know that we were on the move again. I started chatting with Jon, an IT consultant who wanted a break from the corporate world and who was hugely interested in adventure. I told him about our upcoming South Pole expedition and he seemed really interested in our plans. 'If you make it across Greenland and feel strong enough, I'll consider you for our team,' I said. 'Are you serious?' he asked. 'Yeah,' I replied. I'd had my eye out for a fourth team member ever since Ger had bowed out and Jon, although a complete stranger, struck me as someone who had the strength, tenacity and endurance for the challenge. He was ambitious and outgoing and had great self-belief even though this was his first polar expedition. I felt that he had the mindset needed for the South Pole expedition. On a very practical level, having a fourth team member would mean that our overall costs would be less daunting.

Tested to our limits

There was now only 118km left before we reached the west coast and our finish line. Conditions were perfect as we set off and that day we covered an impressive 45km. The following day, however, we were faced with another whiteout, made worse by relentless rain. On top of that, a series of fast-flowing melt-water rivers forced us to make a 2km detour which meant our progress for the day was just under 28km.

Over the next four days we were tested to our very limits as we tried to negotiate a seemingly endless number of melt-water rivers. At times we were skiing under 600mm of water across what seemed like lakes, all caused by global warming. The fast-flowing water forced us to divert from our course, adding further kilometres to our journey. On one of the days, we covered only 9km when Shaun nearly lost his sled in a river and all his gear got soaked, adding to the weight he had to pull. The terrain was so tough that it was possible it would take us an extra week to finish if the weather didn't improve. We were running low on food and kept hoping for a lucky break, but what we got was another snowstorm that forced us to make camp early.

Time was now running out for us as we had flights booked for 31 August and we were still about 50km from the finish as that date approached. There was no way we could give up, however, so we had to bite the bullet and reschedule our flights for 6 September. We covered 9km on Saturday 1 September but the next day we were down to an abysmal 6km in total for the day and had to stop early because of a snowstorm. Still, we were getting there and by Monday night we had only 17km left to complete our crossing. There were more whiteout conditions over the next two days, by which time all three of us were tired, hungry and cranky from battling through hundreds of crevasses in almost zero visibility. Despite all that, our focus on getting over the finish line remained strong.

Miraculously, on 5 September, we came off the edge of the Greenland Ice Cap, exhausted beyond measure but thrilled to have completed the first-ever Irish crossing of Greenland on foot. It was a relief to stand on solid ground for the first time in thirty-one days. I quickly spotted Charlie and Jon skiing towards us; they had made it too. After catching up on our experiences, I spoke to Jon. 'You made it across, so my offer still stands. Do you want to join us in nine weeks' time on our expedition to the South Pole?' 'Are you honestly serious that I could go?' he said. 'It's something I've always wanted to do.' It was a big decision for him to make, but my instinct told me he was physically and mentally able for it; whether he had the time and money was another issue. He said he needed a week to think it over. I had discussed the proposal with Clare and Shaun and they agreed that if he made the crossing of Greenland they'd be happy to have him join our team.

We flew back to Ireland, delighted with our new national first and even more so with the experience we'd gained that would stand to us in Antarctica. Within a few days of arriving home, Jon got in touch and confirmed his position as the fourth member of the team.

IRISH SOUTH POLE EXPEDITION 2008

After our return home from Greenland, we had only two months to finalise everything for our South Pole expedition. Clare was instrumental in organising logistics with me, and Jon came over from England in October 2007 for a few weeks and stayed in the Mountain Lodge to help with the final preparations. My home in Kerry was filled to capacity with expedition gear, dehydrated food and communications equipment. It was amazing to see the vast amount of stuff needed to keep us alive and safe for the expedition. Thousands of minor details had to be attended to and there was no room for mistakes; there would be no possibility of replacing anything we hadn't thought of once out on the ice.

Never in any of my previous expeditions had we to be so meticulous about what the team would be carrying. Everything we needed, we had to haul on our sleds. Once our journey began, we would be totally isolated from other human beings except for contact via our satellite phone. The journey to the Pole, even in the best of weather conditions, was going to be brutal and relentless. All four of us knew that; what we had yet to find out was if we could meet those challenges head on and endure what Antarctica had to throw at us.

We packed each day-pack with ten 450-calorie, high-energy snacks that we would consume at hourly intervals while on the move. These consisted mainly of trail-mix, flapjacks, chocolate and sweets. These would be kept at the front of the sleds for ease of access. In temperatures as low as $-40°$, we had to avoid any delays or unnecessary rummaging in bags. We went to great lengths to ensure that our main meals, although dehydrated, would be varied and tasty, as these would be the only thing we had to break the monotony of our days. Breakfasts might consist of scrambled eggs, a muffin and hot chocolate, olive oil and butter, while soup would be a mainstay for lunch with more trail-mix. The evening meal – the highlight of the day – might be a powder chicken tikka or lamb mulligatawny with rice and a powered dessert of apple and custard. The icing on the cake would be coffee and special energy biscuits at the end of a hard day's hauling.

We also packed what we called 'degree treats'. These were only to be eaten when we crossed the next degree of latitude, which occurred approximately every 111km. Then we'd celebrate by rewarding ourselves with an extra bar of specially designed handmade chocolate that had 750 calories packed into a 100g bar injected with a probiotic to help our stomachs cope with all the fat we would have to consume. On this journey to the South Pole, we knew that food was not just for the body but also for the mind, and the thought of eating something that we liked would help keep us going when our bodies were screaming to stop.

Four people: 4,000 food items

When all the sorting and packing was done, we had 4,000 food items to be shipped to Punta Arenas in Chile, along with our tents, solar panels, sleds, skis, clothing and other equipment. We had encountered huge problems in Greenland when it came to charging our batteries in persistent whiteout conditions and minus temperature; to avoid the same happening in Antarctica, we sewed pockets into our thermal layers to keep the batteries warm next to our skin. We also customised equipment and added voltmeters to ensure we would know how much power we were getting from the sun for our electrical equipment.

I was planning on filming the expedition and Jon agreed to help, so we got ourselves up to par on how to use the equipment in polar conditions, while standing on skis, before we left Kerry. I had the expedition website upgraded so that we could blog daily to our supporters and followers. We couldn't receive email, but the fact of writing to people on a daily basis would help lessen our sense of isolation.

Another idea we came up with to give us a sense of being close to people while so far away was to name each camp after a friend, our family or our heroes. Naming our camps after people would lead to us talking about them – telling stories, remembering, laughing and sharing – something that was as important as ensuring we'd eaten our full complement of calories for the day. After all, we would be just four people, hauling sleds day in, day out for almost two months, and the last thing we wanted was to spend each evening talking about how hard the day had been.

We were very lucky to have an enthusiastic and dependable support team at the Mountain Lodge, including my close friends Gerry Walsh and Joe O'Leary, who were integral to ensuring that the vast amount of organising was finalised on time. It really was a massive undertaking to complete all the preparations to get four people onto Antarctica for this expedition.

Because of the isolated nature of the environment we were about to go into, we had to make sure our communications system was up to the standard. Niall Foley, who worked for me and had been involved on several previous expeditions as IT and communications manager, became a key person for us in the final weeks of preparation, testing our equipment and teaching all four of us how to become proficient in using it.

When everything had been shipped off from Cork, Jon and I went to Annascaul to have a pint in the South Pole Inn, the bar that Tom Crean bought when he finished his days as an explorer. I wanted to show Jon where this great hero had come from and I also wanted to take a bit of time to sit and remember Crean in his homeplace before we set off to that little-known landscape where he had spent so much of his life.

Landing on the white continent

On the last day of October, Clare, Shaun, Jon and I left Ireland to begin what is without question one of the toughest expeditions in the world: the Irish Beyond Endurance South Pole Expedition was under way. We arrived in Punta Arenas on 2 November and were incredibly busy over the next few days organising gear clearance and collection followed by sorting and repacking.

We were hoping to fly to Antarctica on Wednesday 7 November, but delays due to technical issues meant that all flights were cancelled. The Patriot Hills Base Camp staff finally got clearance to fly out on the following Friday. They were staying at Base Camp for the three-month visitor season and it was reassuring to know they would be in situ and on standby in case of a rescue situation and to accommodate a pick-up from the Pole. We couldn't fly out until the following Monday, 12 November, five days behind schedule.

Although we were all relieved to finally be on the Illyushin II-76 aircraft, my old fear of flying kicked in again. It always struck me as odd that this irrational fear had such a grip on someone like me, who spent his life dismantling risk and facing danger in the most extreme situations. But there was nothing I could do except grit my teeth and put my trust in the pilots during the four-and-a-half-hour flight to Antarctica.

Our route crossed the Drake Passage before reaching the west side of the Antarctic Peninsula and following the spine of the Ellsworth Mountains. The view from the bomb sighting windows, located on the underbelly of the plane, was stunning and I momentarily lost my fear as the beauty of Antarctica mesmerised me. Looking down at the white continent made me feel as if I was flying to heaven. Fear rose in me again, though, as we prepared to land and I looked out at the 4km blue-ice runway where the skill and expertise of the pilots – and my capacity to keep my fear in check – would be tested. The plane landed with a thud and the pilots immediately put the engines into reverse thrust as they couldn't apply the brakes because that action would flip the plane. This is truly one of the scariest landings on Earth, and I breathed a deep sigh of relief and gratitude when we finally came to a halt.

While our landing might have gone without a glitch, once the plane left we were hit by a storm with over 100kmph katabatic winds that grounded us at Patriot Hills and prevented us from flying to our start point at Hercules Inlet. After erecting our tents, we built snow walls around them for protection from the relentless, battering wind. The white continent wasn't going to go easy on us during our first night, but the conditions gave us the opportunity to see how quickly and efficiently we could put up our tents in severe wind and $-30°$ temperatures. The skill and speed with which we erected and dismantled them was hugely important. A minute less or more had not only an immediate but also a cumulative impact in relation to our use of energy and time. We would be putting up and taking down our tents every day for up to sixty days, and if we saved a minute each day that would amount to an hour saved from being exposed to brutal conditions over the entire expedition. We were aiming for military-style precision in all our actions and I was happy with how we handled ourselves during our first test on Antarctica.

The next morning we were told we would be the first team to be flown to Hercules Inlet at 11am in the ski-equipped Twin Otter. The twenty-minute flight to the edge of the continent where the land mass meets the frozen sea at our official starting point was exhilarating, but my fear of flying went into the red during the five attempts it took to land safely on the rough snow. Once all our gear was unloaded, the pilots didn't delay, leaving us in total isolation: four people on a vast white landscape. The only outside support we would have during the next sixty days was the food drop-offs the Twin Otter would make at 350km and 700km from our start point. We would be given the grid references and would have to navigate to them. It would be like finding a needle in a haystack and if we failed to find the exact points, it would mean the end of the expedition.

Using our harnesses, we attached our 2.1m-long by .6m-wide sleds to our bodies. Each sled had its own name; Clare's was 'Dudley Docker', Jon's was 'Stancomb-Wills' and mine was called 'James Caird'. All three were called after the lifeboats that Shackleton and his crew had used after the *Endurance* sank. Shaun called his 'Jack' after his young son. These sleds would soon become part of us. We loved them, hated them, cursed them and even talked to them, our silent partners and companions on our journey. We clipped into our skis and started to move from the edge of Antarctica in the direction of the South Pole. Hauling what looked like four large coffins, our journey had begun.

A long haul looms

We didn't go at it hell-for-leather straight away. I had learned from previous expeditions that success is all about pace, reserving your energy and getting used to the conditions. Our aim each day was to cover between 22km and 27km and my strategy was to establish a steady pace and maintain it throughout in order to prevent burnout. For the first few days, we concentrated on perfecting our skiing, man-hauling and camp craft, as well as getting our layering system right.

The hauling was exhausting, and we struggled to get used to the fact that every new day brought another eight to twelve hours of this excruciating work.

We also had to get used to the effect of the huge amount of food we had to consume each day. From the start, we were operating in whiteout conditions with zero visibility, and had to depend on our compass and GPS to ensure we were going in the right direction. We took it in turns to lead the team; this was backbreaking work as you could see nothing ahead and had the added pressure of not wanting to take the team off course and add to an already difficult journey.

On day six, having pulled our sleds up a 250m steep hill, the sun came through the overcast sky for the first time. Daytime temperatures plummeted to –25° and were made even more intolerable by windchill. It was tougher to move and we covered only 21.1km before stopping to set up camp. The wind was so strong that it took all four of us to put up each tent. Once inside, I realised that my left thumb had frostnip caused by exposure due to the way I was holding my ski pole. I felt very annoyed at myself for allowing this to happen. The frostnip was a warning sign that extreme vigilance was needed in the lethal windchill. If I had gotten frostbite, it could have spelled the end of the expedition. The following day, we crossed the 81st parallel south in similar conditions and had a celebration at reaching our first degree of latitude.

A day without wind was like a gift from heaven and on 22 November we covered 22.6km on a day when the wind was a mere twelve knots and the temperature was –12.7°. The next few days were similar in terms of both the weather and the distance covered. But the winds returned and we battled through them and low temperatures before crossing the 82nd parallel on 25 November. At this stage, nearly two weeks out on the ice, we were starting to feel the pressure and Antarctica was taking its toll on the team. Shaun wrote the list of ailments he was suffering from on his tent wall: *crotch rot and heat rash on testicles; swollen ankle; tweaked thigh muscle; allergic reaction, spots on chin, blisters on feet and frostnip on ear.*

Daily routines

Our days fell into a regular pattern. We'd finish man-hauling in the early evening and set up camp. Clare and I erected our stormproof Hilleberg tent in less than four minutes. Our nomadic home, measuring 3m long by 1.8m wide by 1.3m high, was our only protection from winds, storms, blizzards and katabatic winds. The tent comprised two compartments: the living area which was 1.8m by 1.8m and our tent vestibule which measured 1.8m by 1.2m. Once it was erected, we cut a 300mm by 600mm by 1.3m trough in the front porch area which we used for cooking and to create a makeshift toilet facility so we wouldn't have to exit the tent once we'd set up camp. Every evening we'd spend two to three hours cooking and boiling water from snow we gathered from the trough. After eating, we'd write up our blogs or listen to music on iPods. I tended to spend any free time looking at maps for the next day's journey.

We'd usually settle into our sleeping bags at 9pm and try and get some rest. I had a plastic pee bottle which I'd trained myself to use from the comfort of my sleeping bag. This meant I could avoid having to get up during the night and could also avoid getting cold in the morning. I'd also bring a litre bottle of boiling water to bed with me to drink during the night to remain hydrated. There were two important things to remember – to keep the bottles close to your body so they didn't freeze and not to drink out of the wrong one.

Every morning we'd wake up at 5.30am and without leaving our sleeping bags we'd start the stoves and melt snow for hot drinks and for the water we'd need during the day as well as for cooking breakfast. By 7.30am we'd be finished eating and would take ten minutes to get dressed. At 7.40am it was time for going to the toilet and the same platform where we had cooked was now used as a latrine, with only a zipped flysheet giving privacy from the main tent.

It was important that each person went to the toilet daily and we had trained to go at the same time every morning. It happened sometimes, however, that someone couldn't go at the appointed time and later in the day the entire team would have to stop mid-march and wait while that person went. This was dangerous for everyone as the person defecating was exposed to the elements and the other three got colder and colder as we stood around, waiting to get moving again. This issue proved contentious every time it happened, but it was virtually impossible to avoid.

From 7.50am to 8am, camp was broken. All our gear and tents were packed and carefully tied down on our sleds by 8.01am. Before setting off, all four of us would ensure any exposed skin was covered; we'd put on our mitts, pull down our face masks, clip into our skis, and begin another day of man-hauling on the ice. Every seventy minutes we'd stop to intake 450 calories of trail mix to fuel our bodies for the next hour's hauling. We'd packed our trail food in a special bag with a Velcro seal that we could open without taking our mitts off; we just

254

pulled it open and grazed from the bag like horses.

Lunch necessitated a longer break as we had more to eat. We'd unclip our skis and erect a lightweight kisu, or survival shelter, before dragging our sleds and ourselves under its cover to get some respite from the weather while eating. After ten minutes, we'd dismantle the shelter, put on our face masks and mitts, clip into our skis and start moving again. There was nothing convivial about our food consumption; even though we were close together, it was almost as if we were each inside our own individual bubble. We finished each day between 4pm and 6pm – if we'd lasted that long – and once we'd eaten, bedtime couldn't come quickly enough to rest our tired and sore bodies.

Before we ever started, we had to break this mammoth journey down into achievable parts, otherwise the mere thought of it would have overwhelmed us. From our start point to our end point, the landscape was mainly white. With so many days of whiteout and strong winds, not only was visibility down to zero but our heads were also down as we pulled and hauled our sleds, grateful if the terrain was smooth, and struggling with uphill terrain and sastrugi that put further drag on our loads. It was almost impossible to see any progress on the ground because the landscape was so undifferentiated, so having milestones was vital in helping us believe that we were making progress.

We never looked at the full map as the vastness of what was ahead was so great that seeing it could have undone our resolve. This elephant had to be taken out one bite at a time, so we broke the journey into eleven 100km segments. We knew exactly at what point we should reach the next degree of latitude, each one approximately 111km apart and bringing us closer to the magic 90° south. There were nine degrees in total that we had to cross, all of which we marked up on the inside of our tents. Those markers were often all that we had to hang on to at the end of the day.

The Thiels appear

I had an unusually good sleep on 28 November, which was noteworthy in a land of twenty-four-hour sunlight. It followed a day when katabatic winds had accompanied us ceaselessly and headwinds from the Pole seemed to be trying to push us backwards. The temperature dropped to $-34°$ so we were forced to stop early, just within 500m of achieving 83° south. The next day, I was tasked with taking first lead in the morning; each leading shift lasted for seventy minutes followed by a ten-minute break for food before the next person took the position. Leading was onerous, as every part of you had to remain alert so that you didn't take the team off course. In the followers' position, the hauling was still crushingly hard but at least you could go into a trance and let your mind wander wherever it wanted to go. Whenever I was at the back of the team, I used to become mesmerised by the movement of the sleds in front of me swaying from left to right, bouncing forward and then, suddenly, flipping over when the wind caught them or a particularly high sastrugi caused them to go off balance.

We welcomed the first day of December with a much-needed rest day. By now, we had been on the move for nearly twenty days and our bodies had taken a serious hammering from the Antarctic winds and cold. It was 10am before anyone stirred as we all took advantage of sleeping in, something we wouldn't be able to do for another 200km. There was a lot to do; sorting out gear, washing underwear, doing repairs and planning the next section of the route. We also took time to have a team meeting to discuss logistics and to check that everyone was doing okay and feeling positive about the challenge ahead. We had two great days after that, covering 27.9km and then 27.4km, all made possible by low winds. It didn't last, of course, and by 4 December we were plunged back into katabatic winds and sastrugi that looked like white horses on a rough sea.

Of the many tough challenges in this expedition, one of the toughest was not having visible markers en route to the Pole. But there was one coming up and we couldn't wait to see it. We knew we should soon see the Thiel Mountains and the highest peak standing 2,810m high. They were our halfway mark and a major milestone. We knew that, after the first sighting of them, we were still five days distant from them but, once seen, they were something tangible to latch onto and move towards. More importantly, seeing the Thiels was confirmation that we were on course. On 6 December, Jon, at the rear of the group, spotted them first and let out a roar. They were 125km away but they rose from the ground like a glorious point of reference; a sign that we were within touching distance of something significant. The thought of reaching the halfway point, along with the lure of a rest day, really buoyed our spirits.

Over the next few days conditions were horrible as we pushed our way towards the Thiels. Reaching our food pick-up point wasn't easy as Antarctica threw everything at us, including relentless whiteouts, katabatic winds and deep snow. Throughout 10 December, visibility was down to less than 50m and the snow from the previous night doubled the weight drag on our sleds. We had to operate blind-man leads, navigating all day with the person in front being directed by the second person so that we wouldn't drift off course.

It was an unbelievable relief to arrive at the pick-up point and set up camp, knowing now that we had travelled 590km and were over halfway to the South Pole. We'd survived twenty-nine days of everything Antarctica could throw at us and, using good navigation, GPS and compass, we'd managed to get here. The arrival of a full-blown blizzard that night was something we could have done without, but at least we weren't planning to move the next day. That was just as well, because our night's rest was hampered by the winds beating ceaselessly off the tents.

Next morning, we realised that it had snowed very heavily overnight. We knew this would make pulling our sleds much tougher but we put it to the back of our minds for one day while we repacked our sleds and sorted out our new cache of food. We needed to eat as much as possible while resting because we were all losing weight and needed to stock up on carbs and fatty foods. We ate happily despite knowing that the bad forecast meant that our bodies would soon be under severe pressure again.

Donkeys sinking in mire

Starting to move in these conditions after our rest day was so hard, but we knew we only had enough food left for thirty-one days and if we stayed put, we'd eat a day's supply of food without getting any nearer to the Pole. We were plunged back into blind-man leads and the drag on our sleds from the weight of the new food and the snow was pure torture. Despite our efforts, we only managed to cover 16.4km.

That night we had our worst fears confirmed from Patriot Hills: the bad weather was forecast to continue and to get even worse. The deep snow made the going tortoise-slow and the near-impossibility of making any real progress started to undermine our belief that we could make it. The next four days tested every member of the team to the limits of their endurance. With ceaseless winds, vengeful sastrugi, zero visibility and dense whiteouts, our journey became a hell on Earth. Day after day, we had to go through tremendous effort and pain with little to show for it at the end of another exhausting slog. In all my years on expedition, I'd never before been challenged so relentlessly.

Our hope of reaching the South Pole within the next twenty-five days started to disappear. Up to 200mm of snow was dumped on our route so that our backs felt as if they were actually breaking as we pulled our sleds through the soft snow. Half the usual annual snowfall had fallen in just three days, right on top of us. In addition, the temperature had risen to $-8°$ with the wind coming from the northeast and not the south as we had expected. We knew the weather could be inhospitable, but what was happening was totally unpredicted.

The going on 14 December was so hard that I knew we couldn't do another day. Physically we were all at the end of our endurance and, more importantly, I could see the team's spirit was being constantly undermined. Something was going to give, so we changed our strategy to ease the pressure on our bodies. Instead of each person navigating for seventy minutes, we reduced the leading time to thirty-five minutes. At this stage, our pace was like that of a funeral march and pulling our sleds was like pulling a 100kg dead weight for eight hours a day. The next forecast from Patriot Hills was also dismal; they were in full-blown blizzard conditions and there was a vast cloud sheet extending so far north it went all the way back to our starting point.

On Sunday 16 December, for the first time in days we woke to sunshine and visibility and our hearts lifted even though conditions were still incredibly tough underfoot. But by early afternoon the clouds had rolled in again from the northeast, plunging us back into zero visibility. We calculated that on total zero-contrast days with soft snow we were losing up to 6km per day and using extra energy to move forward. Nonetheless, we still reached $86°$ south, another milestone on our tortuous journey.

There was no sign of the sun the next morning and the team mood and energy were as close to zero as the visibility. It was going to be another bruiser of a day. However, the forecast was for better weather over the coming days and that, at least, was something. Our rest day was due two days later and I suggested to the team that we bring it forward to this dismal day where we would make very little progress. If we were lucky – and we were surely due a break at this stage – we could regain our strength and be prepared to strike out with the better weather, assuming it arrived. It was a risk, but I could see we were in a wretched state. Shaun was carrying a shoulder injury, Jon had torn his Achilles tendon and Clare was totally exhausted from pulling in the soft snow. I wasn't too badly off, but a piece of a tooth filling had fallen out while I was eating and I had to cover the nerve with glue to protect it.

The rest did us good but the next few days were exactly as the previous ones had been. It felt as if Antarctica was unleashing all its hostility on us. We were like four donkeys sinking into the mire but we continued to pull ahead, inch by inch. The morning of 19 December started bright and clear, though within two hours we were in whiteout again. Snow conditions had improved overnight, becoming firmer and making pulling a little easier, and we ended up traversing 25.9km, our longest ground covered in many days. Despite everything, we were making progress. But no one could definitively say how long this weather system would last and I could see we were all losing more weight than we should have been, which was a cause of concern.

Entering the torture chamber

Conditions on the ice were good on Thursday 20 December although we were again moving in whiteout and zero-contrast conditions. We were all hopeful that we could make up some of the time lost due to the bad weather. I decided to do a bit of filming for the documentary we were making and went ahead of the other three to shoot them pulling their sleds. As soon as they had all passed by me, I turned to put the camera away and a searing pain shot down through my back and into my buttocks. I fell to the ground in agony. The pain was so bad that I couldn't stand up. Over 100m ahead, I saw my three team-mates disappearing into the whiteout. I shouted at them but they couldn't hear me. They had no idea that anything was wrong and I knew there was little or no chance that anyone would stop and look back. Each one of them was in their own Antarctic trance, pulling, sweating and fully focused on taking the next step. None of us ever looked back when we were marching; there was no reason to, especially in the almost non-stop whiteout conditions we'd been in since the start of the expedition.

I knew I was in serious trouble. If I didn't get up, I would lose everyone in the whiteout. They were moving faster than we'd moved for several days due to the improved ground conditions. I struggled to a standing position and took a few steps before falling to my knees again. The pain was unbearable but the thought of losing the team filled me with terror so I kept trying to get up, no matter how often I fell. I could barely make out their shadows when they stopped suddenly. Clare was leading and had paused to check her bearings. While the others were waiting, they looked back and saw that I was on the ground and in trouble. When I caught up with them I explained that I'd pulled something in my back. Clare gave me an anti-inflammatory but I was still in agony so they all took turns hauling my sled. Within twenty minutes, I had to stop again. I lay on the snow and tried to stretch my body in the hope that this would help, but there was no improvement. We kept going for another half hour, but the pain was too severe and we had to call it a day.

I was now in nightmare territory: I was in the worst pain of life; I had no idea what damage was done to my back; we had only covered 3km on a day when we'd expected to cover up to 27km; there was no way I could move and if I kept trying it might cause further injury. To be grounded by such a simple thing as a back twist was hard to take but we all had to accept that this was a new challenge that had to be dealt with. We set up camp and used everything we had in the medication pack to try and bring down the inflammation and ease the pain.

As I lay in the tent, flinching each time I moved, my mind entered the darkest place it had been since we'd left Hercules Inlet, fearful that my injury was going to bring down the entire expedition. I stared at the roof of the tent and my attention was caught by some lines from *Don't Quit,* the poem my mother had given me years earlier and which I'd written on the inside wall at the start of the expedition:

> *... many a failure comes about*
> *When he might have won had he stuck it out;*
> *Don't give up though the pace seems slow—*
> *You may succeed with another blow ...*
>
> *And you never can tell just how close you are,*
> *It may be near when it seems so far;*

So stick to the fight when you're hardest hit—
It's when things seem worst that you must not quit.

I read the words again and again until their simple truth penetrated through the darkness of my thoughts and brought me back from the brink of hopelessness.

The atmosphere in the camp was sombre; we had another twenty days of man-hauling ahead of us and there was no way I could do it if my back didn't improve. Clare mentioned calling in a rescue; I couldn't bear to think that, having travelled 751km from the coast and with only 389km still to go to the Pole, this was the end of the expedition for us. I thought of the years of training and hardship I'd put my body and mind through to get to this point.

I thought of Shackleton and of Tom Crean. I didn't want this expedition to end in failure but I didn't want to jeopardise it for the others either, and had to seriously consider the prospect of a rescue. There were other considerations as well; we had a limited food and fuel supply and we simply had to keep moving, so either I got sufficiently better and moved or I had to get out, whatever the cost.

This was our biggest challenge to date and I was both grateful and humbled by the manner in which our small team came together in the middle of nowhere to formulate a strategy that would allow us all to keep moving towards our shared goal. We devised a plan whereby my gear would be shared between Clare, Shaun and Jon for the next few days, leaving me free to move without any extra drag on my body and so give my injury a chance to heal.

Despite all my years putting myself in situations of calculated risk and danger, I had never before been injured to the point where I was totally dependent on others. I hated the fact that I was slowing our progress and forcing my team to – essentially – carry me. But the alternative was to give up, and none of us wanted to do that. Instead, we focused on our goal and on the fact that we only had nineteen food packs left. We estimated that it would take us eighteen days to get to the Pole if we moved every day. That left only one day for rest and no day for injury or sheltering from bad weather. It was down to the wire now.

Running on empty

We agreed that we would push through to 88° south without rest. This meant marching through Christmas Day, when we'd planned to have a special dinner. The days ahead were going to be very tough for a multitude of reasons, but we kept our focus on our driving force: the South Pole. Clare, Shaun and Jon carried my gear and my empty sled while I moved slowly and in agony, trying my best to keep up but having to stop every few minutes. The only time I got relief was when I knelt on the ice. My morale was low but I locked onto the image of the team arriving at the South Pole and that kept me going.

Despite everything, we covered 20.2km on 22 December and the same distance the next day. We were lucky that the weather had improved; we now had sunshine and visibility though a drop in temperature exacerbated my back pain and there wasn't the improvement I'd hoped for. There was no way I could take any of my own gear and I felt guilty when I saw the others slowed sometimes to a snail's pace because of the extra drag on their sleds.

Antarctica's gift to us on Christmas Day was wind, severe cold and lots of sastrugi topped by several uphill climbs, but we reached another milestone when we arrived at 300km from the Pole. We were all exhausted but there were three more days to go until our next rest day. I had no doubt that the extra effort the others had to put in carrying my gear contributed to old injuries flaring up. Jon was finding it hard to breathe due to an aggravating injury he got the previous March when he cracked two ribs, while Shaun's shoulder was giving him trouble. Clare, thankfully, was injury free.

My pain was still very bad, but I had to start pulling my weight again. On 26 December, I pulled a half-empty sled for four hours. It was almost impossible, even for that short period of time, but I forced myself to keep going. The temperature that day was the coldest yet at –37°, and this, coupled with huge sastrugi, made the going really hard.

We had never looked forward to a rest day as much as that on 28 December. Our tanks were literally empty. We were all exhausted, hungry and at the end of our endurance after forty-six days on the ice. Everyone looked thin and spent. I was pulling my own sled again but my injury was still a danger zone, so Clare did all the back-bending work of setting up our tent, cutting out the ice blocks and making our meals.

262

Three days late, we were determined to celebrate Christmas in Antarctic style. Jon cooked a dinner of potato cakes, quiche and banoffee pie, all from dehydrated food but it still tasted good. Each of us had some small parcels in our sleds that family had given us as Christmas presents and we opened them with the anticipation of young children. Clare and I decorated our tent for the feast with a few small decorations we'd brought along and, when we'd finished eating, Shaun took out the tin whistle and played some tunes.

Daring to think of the end

By the last day of the year, we had hit two more milestones – we crossed 88° south and came below 200km to the Pole. On the first day of 2008, we reached a point whose distance from the Pole had both inspired and haunted me for years: the point at which Shackleton had turned and headed back to his ship. He was only 180km from his goal when many days of dehydration, hunger and near-hypothermia forced him and his team of Frank Wild, John Boyd Adams and Eric Marshall to turn. But they had established a new Farthest South which Shackleton named Beardmore Glacier in honour of the Scottish businessman who'd helped finance the Nimrod Expedition. They had extended Scott's record by six full degrees of latitude when they arrived at 88° and twenty-three minutes south. It was a special moment for us when we reached that point and thought of those men whose bravery took them to places no other human being had previously been.

Once we passed that point of latitude, I felt increasingly confident that we would reach the Pole. We'd had more than our fair share of challenges so far, between storms, soft snow, high sastrugi and injuries, but now we were within 140km of our destination. With the Shackleton family motto in mind, we knew that by endurance we would surely conquer. It was incredible to think that we were now only one week from the end. Up until this point, we hadn't allowed ourselves think about how much was ahead of us, but now, with so many kilometres behind us, our spirits rose, knowing the end was – finally – within reach.

But our energy was really low in these final days and we had to tap into our mental reserves to pull through each gruelling minute of slog. The pain in my back had eased considerably but never fully went away; it had become another weight I had to pull. Shaun was having terrible problems with one foot and we had to brace it every day just so he could ski.

On 4 January, we crossed into 89° south with under 100km to go. Now there was only one more degree to travel before reaching the magic 90° south. Although all four of us were hobbling, our pace was steady. Finally, it seemed, Antarctica had decided to be kind to us, although altitude was a new ingredient in the mix of challenges and we suffered from headaches and shortness of breath at 2,800m.

The weather for the next few days was clear, bright and very cold with little wind. With the smoother terrain and more consistent snow conditions, we managed to reach our daily target of around 24km. And then, on Monday 7 January, we saw in the distance the silhouette of the spaceship-like Amundsen-Scott South Pole Station, the US scientific research building sitting at an elevation of 2,835m on the Pole's high plateau. We were still a day away but now we had our final reference point within view. The moment we saw it, we smiled at each other before putting our heads down again and moving on.

There was no let-up as we pulled and pushed forward. We were all lost in our own worlds as we contemplated what was ahead of us and what we were within twenty-four hours of achieving. Antarctica was like nowhere else on the planet I'd ever been; its pristine, white beauty was heavenly but its tempests had catapulted us right into hell. On the bad days, it was hard to remember why we wanted to do this but, on the good days, the reasons were clear and compelling: we all wanted to stand in a place whose beauty was beyond description, where few people had travelled to and where some of the people we most admired had risked their lives to discover; a place of huge scientific, natural and emotional importance for humankind. The closer we got to the Pole, the more the brutal nature of what we had just come through faded. Success – so close now – shone so brightly it was all we could see.

A dream realised

In the mid-afternoon of 8 January 2008 we were skiing in whiteout conditions with almost zero visibility but it didn't matter; although we couldn't really see what was ahead, we could feel it – we knew we were nearly there. What we didn't know until some people – the first we'd see in almost sixty days – came running towards us shouting was that we were on a runway. They warned us to get off it as a Hercules plane was due to land.

Then, just before 4.30pm, we spotted the international ceremonial flags that surround the globe that marks the position of the South Pole. We formed a line, unclipped our skis for the last time and, united as a team, we walked together to the marker that signifies the South Pole. It was an incredible feeling to be at a point on the planet that I'd read so much about and planned on reaching for over two years. We took out the Irish flag and sang the national anthem as we celebrated the arrival of the first-ever Irish team and the first-ever Irish woman to this spot.

Some of the staff at the base gave us refreshments and took time to show us around inside. It felt like pure luxury when they allowed us to use their toilets. Their water was scarce so we couldn't take a shower, but that didn't bother us; all we wanted to do was sleep. We put in the call for our outbound flight, put up our tents and slept the sleep of the dead. The weather was starting to act up again, however, and it was fifty-six hours before the Twin Otter appeared. When it did, we quickly loaded our gear on the plane and began the six-hour flight back to Patriot Hills. It was strange to be leaving the South Pole with such ease when getting there had been such a challenge, but it was a place and a journey none of us would ever forget.

As we looked out at the vast expanse that we had just spent two months traversing it was fascinating, sitting in relative comfort and relishing the ham and cheese sandwiches that the Base Camp team had provided for us, to think of all the pain and joy we'd gone through on that white landscape, walking towards a tiny spot at the bottom of the world.

Just before 4am we touched down at Patriot Hills, exhausted and not relishing the thought of having to erect our tents on half-empty stomachs. But the staff at Base Camp had another very welcome surprise in store – a dinner of real steak, potatoes, vegetables, dessert and champagne. It was the best meal we'd ever eaten.

We set up camp and after a good sleep awakened to a familiar scenario: katabatic winds, whiteout and zero visibility. The one plus was that we didn't have to haul sleds anywhere. The forecast was bad for the next few days and we realised that we were stuck in Antarctica for another while after we heard that flight conditions had grounded our plane more than 3,000km away in Punta Arenas.

Over the next few days, Patriot Hills started to fill up with adventurers, explorers and researchers, all preparing to leave as the 'open season' was coming to an end. The bad weather meant, however, that it was going to be a while yet before any of us got home. The place that had gripped our imaginations for so long was now gripping our bodies, unwilling – it seemed – to let us go. On 14 January, six days after we'd arrived at the South Pole, we were finally able to leave Antarctica and make the journey back to civilisation.

I'd never been away from Ireland for so long – seventy-seven days – and relished seeing its lush greenness on my return. It was only then that I had time to really think about what we had accomplished and what it meant, not just to us, but to the history of Irish polar explorers and adventurers. Ireland had a connection with polar travel going back over a century, following on the expeditions of Shackleton, Crean, Ford, Keohane and the McCarthy brothers, and Irish people took pride in their Antarctic adventurers. I was both proud and humbled that Clare, Shaun, Jon and I had added to that history with our Beyond Endurance South Pole Expedition.

What's next?

Back at home, it was the final death knell for the Falvey Group of companies that I'd built up over thirty years when I sold off my Blarney Street property in Cork in 2008. I was doing a lot more corporate and personal development and training and also wanted to consolidate my adventure travel business, so I set up Pat Falvey Irish & Worldwide Adventures as a limited company. There was steady interest from Irish people in adventure holidays and I was also looking at adding the polar regions to my list of destinations for guided treks. Before we'd gone to the South Pole, Clare and I had already spoken about an expedition to the North Pole and I started investigating that area, not just for an expedition but also looking at its adventure holiday potential for my company.

Since 2001, when Freddy T. Bear had gone on his first expedition, I'd been very interested in bringing knowledge and information to kids about the most remote regions of the world. I was always happy to visit schools after expeditions and through those and via our website, my team and I opened up a world of adventure learning to younger people with Freddy T. Bear as the conduit. On our trips, Clare wrote up Freddy's blogs and when we came back we expanded the blogs into books. More than anything else, I wanted to use Freddy as a way of giving kids the message that it was good to have dreams and goals.

This relationship between younger people and the Beyond Endurance project gave rise to a new project for teenagers that we planned for our late 2008 Antarctic trip. Phil O'Flynn, a friend and secondary school teacher from the same part of Cork as me, got in touch with the idea of doing an adventure travel project with transition year students from socially disadvantaged areas, as well as working with students from more privileged schools. Together with a few other teachers and science lecturers, we devised a science project on global warming, climate change and wildlife in Antarctica.

Suitable schools were invited to submit applications for the eight places we had for teenagers. There was a fantastic response, and once the participants were confirmed they came to the Mountain Lodge to train during the year. A core belief of the project was that young people, no matter where they were from or what social class they inhabited, could excel if given the opportunity. Not only that, by going on an adventure like this, they would see that the world was much wider than they'd previously known. We wanted them to realise that they had a role to play in shaping that world.

I knew from my youth that your address and social background often determine people's expectations of you, and that these were very limited if you came from a socially deprived background. I had broken out of that box and very much wanted to give others the chance to do the same. Our project, we hoped, would let them know that their dreams shouldn't be curtailed by where they came from or by how much their parents earned. We wanted to show them that our life experiences should be limited only by our imaginations.

TRAGEDY ON K2

Golf is a sport I was never into but I was happy to watch when my sons invited me to join them at the golf course in Kenmare, Co Kerry, on the Friday of the August bank holiday weekend in 2008. We were having a drink in a bar in the town afterwards when my phone rang. It was Maarten van Eck, the webmaster and co-ordinator of the Norit Dutch K2 International Expedition. 'Just to let you know, Ger has reached the summit,' he said. I jumped out of my seat and punched the air. 'Yes! He's done it,' I shouted. Brian and Patrick looked at me as if I'd lost my mind. 'What's after happening?' Brian asked. 'Ger has reached the summit of K2,' I said. 'He has just become the first Irish climber to get there.'

I knew I was shouting, but I was so excited I couldn't contain myself. Ger McDonnell, one of the best people and finest mountaineers that I knew, had just written himself into the history books of Irish climbing. Maarten was still on the phone. 'Are they down?' I asked. 'No, not yet. They are starting to make their way down.' 'When are they expected at Camp 4?' I asked. Maarten wasn't sure; clear information wasn't coming through but he promised that he'd keep me informed.

We had a few drinks to celebrate Ger's achievement. The lads had met him a few times and, like everyone else, they had been captivated by Ger's warm personality. I'd been watching the progress of the Norit team – which Ger was a member of – on their website since they'd gone to Pakistan in May to climb

K2, the highest summit in the Karakoram mountain range at 8,611m. But this Friday I had been out for most of the day and hadn't checked for regular updates. After we'd toasted Ger's success, my sons could see I was distracted. I explained that I was concerned about the time Ger had reached the summit and was worried about him descending in the dark. Climbers descend in the dark all the time, but on K2 it wasn't the best option.

Back at home, I checked both the Norit website and ExplorersWeb, the go-to site for adventurers, but there were no updates other than a statement on ExplorersWeb that some climbers weren't back at camp yet. I wasn't too concerned; I guessed that Pemba Gyalje Sherpa had reached the top with Ger. Pemba was also a member of the Norit team and I'd been thrilled months earlier when I'd heard that he was joining them as a full climbing member. Pemba was one of the best mountaineers I knew and wherever he was, I felt people were safer. We had been working together for eight years by this point and I would have happily staked my life on him.

Rolf Bae, my Norwegian colleague from Fram who had done so much polar training with me for my Antarctic expeditions, was also on the mountain, though on a different team. That night, I found it hard to get to sleep, wondering where they were on the mountain. I had no worries about Ger and Pemba's climbing capabilities, but I was worried about K2's infamous objective dangers, especially the threat of avalanche and serac falls.

At 7am next morning, my phone rang. It was Damien O'Brien, Ger's brother-in-law. 'They're not down yet. I think we might be facing trouble,' he said. I felt a knot in my stomach as I went to the computer to check the websites. 'Trouble on K2' flashed on the screen. Up to ten people were still above the mountain's notorious Bottleneck and were, as yet, unaccounted for. Alarm bells started ringing in my head. *They're still in the Death Zone on one of the most dangerous mountains in the world.* My phone started ringing non-stop. Members of the Irish media, who, the night before, had reported the great news that Ger had reached the summit, were now calling me to find out what was happening. I was trying to get in touch with Maarten in the Netherlands and he, in turn, was trying to make contact with Wilco van Rooijen, the leader of the Norit team, who was also missing in K2's Death Zone. Damien and I spoke again; he was also trying to get through to Maarten for an update but wasn't having any luck.

Over the next hours, I was glued to the Norit website and ExlorersWeb as well as posts coming directly from climbers at various camps on K2. This mountain is in one of the most remote places in the world, but the world's media turned its attention to what was playing out in its Death Zone and were reporting back every word they heard, irrespective of the sources or their credibility. As the hours went by, terrible stories started coming through some of the more dependable sites. One climber posted outrageous comments from Camp 4 about bodies being pulled off the mountain. Very quickly, people around the world started responding to the information they were reading online. Within a short space of time, an unfolding tragedy turned to controversy even though we still didn't know what was actually happening on the upper reaches of K2.

The previous day, eighteen climbers had reached the summit; eleven people were now missing and some of those were already confirmed as dead. From Base Camp and at all the camps up the mountain, worried men and women had their eyes trained on the region above the Bottleneck, straining to see any sign of life. Climbers were spotted there during Saturday, coming into view and then disappearing. Sherpa teams were despatched to go back into the Death Zone to rescue those who were still alive. I saw Pemba's name on the Norit website; he was safely down at Camp 4. Relief flooded through me, but it was short-lived when I read on ExplorersWeb that Rolf Bae had died while descending the mountain with his wife Cecilie Skog. He had been swept to his death in front of her by an icefall. It was hard to accept that this highly accomplished young adventurer, whom I had spent so much time with in Norway and on the Beyond Endurance Expedition, was now lost forever on K2.

By midday on Saturday 2 August there was one word beside Ger's name on the Norit website: 'Unknown'. I had met the McDonnell family on several occasions since I'd gotten to know Ger, and they were as warm and welcoming as he was. I could hardly bear to think of the anxiety and pain they and Ger's partner, Annie, in Alaska were going through as they waited for news, hanging onto every word they read and heard.

On Saturday evening, word filtered through that the Italian climber Marco Confortola was alive and had been brought into Camp 4 by Pemba, who was risking his life co-ordinating the rescue mission in the Death Zone. Marco had a story to tell: he and Ger had spent the previous night not far below the summit and had started moving downwards in the morning. They were exhausted and disorientated as they tried to find the fixed ropes. As they descended, they came across three Korean climbers who were suspended from ropes, unable to move and more dead than alive. The two men spent up to three hours trying to untangle the ropes and save them. Eventually Marco said it was impossible and that he was going down.

The last time he saw Ger, Marco said, the Irishman was going back up the mountain, either to take photographs or because he had lost his mind and was trying to descend via the Chinese side of K2. It was insane talk, but the press ran with it. Later, Marco said that he'd seen Ger flying through the air after being hit by an avalanche. The press ran with that story too. I felt really angry at what was happening: climbers, who should have known better, were leaking information directly from the site of the tragedy. They didn't seem to care about the families of the injured and dead, or even about whether or not what they were stating was true. The press, in the rush to be first with the news, weren't interested in, or capable of, checking the veracity of the stories they were carrying.

Throughout Saturday, a person had been spotted high up on the mountain. *Please let it be Ger*, I thought. No one could identify the colour of the climber's down suit – which would help identify them – but this was the last person still moving on the upper reaches of K2. I knew Marco's story about Ger climbing back up the mountain was without foundation and utterly impossible so, if it wasn't him moving in the Death Zone, I didn't think he was still alive.

Early on Sunday 3 August, just before 5.30am, I got a call from the Netherlands. It was Marteen. He confirmed that the climber moving above the Bottleneck was Wilco, Ger's team leader. He was still alive, though not yet safely down. I knew then that Ger was dead.

Searching for the truth

I had said to Damien during the course of one of our phone conversations on Saturday that if the unidentified climber wasn't Ger, then the family would have to prepare to accept that he was gone. But I knew they were clinging to hope in the same way any family would. I phoned Damien straight after hearing from Marteen; I didn't want them to hear the news online or from some source that would put a tactless turn on it. Once I told him that it had been confirmed that the climber in the Death Zone was Wilco, Damien knew there was little point in holding out for a miracle. 'Do you want me to come to the house to talk to the family?' I asked. 'Yes,' he replied.

As I drove to his family home in rural Kilcornan in Co Limerick, I felt as if I was doing something that Ger would have wanted me to do. That didn't make my task any easier, but it did help me keep it together when I met his mother, whom he adored, and his sisters, brother, Damien and other family members. They all gathered to hear what I had to say, knowing that I held Ger in the highest esteem.

I wanted to be as honest as I could so that the family wouldn't harbour any false hope. I explained that, logistically, it was virtually impossible for Ger to have walked back up to the top of K2 to search for a route down the other side of the mountain. I said that I had it on the most reliable authority that there were no other survivors in the Death Zone. My opinion, based on my own experience and the information I had from Norit and ExplorersWeb, was that Ger was dead.

I knew what I was saying was true and, yet, I had my own moment of doubt. *What if Ger is still alive? What if he just turns up out of nowhere? Is it possible?* I said if they wanted to wait another twenty-four hours before giving up hope that was fine, but after that there would be no point. They asked me to explain what it was like in the Death Zone and why things happened up there that were hard to comprehend at sea level. I told Ger's family as much as I could and hoped that they could accept what now seemed to be the inevitable.

They needed time to digest what I'd told them, but the press was demanding information. It was agreed that, in the immediate term, I would act as the press contact person on behalf of the family so that they could have some space before making a statement later.

There was still endless confusion and contradiction coming from K2 about what had happened on the most terrible day in its climbing history. There were so many families left bereft and grieving, and the conflicting stories that continued to emanate from that distant corner of the world were adding to their pain. The truth, still unknown to all of us for another few weeks, was that Ger had been killed by a serac avalanche on his way down the mountain, having miraculously freed the three Koreans some time after Marco had left them. But on 3 August, the truth was still hidden behind the misinformation and lies being told.

The McDonnells would never get Ger's body back from K2, but the least they deserved was the truth. The only way they could get this, I believed, was to go to Pakistan and meet his surviving team-mates. Pemba, whom none of us had yet spoken to because he was still on the mountain in the final hours of his heroic rescue mission, needed to be spoken to. He was a man of integrity and deep kindness, and I believed he would help the family in any way that he could. Almost immediately, the McDonnells started to make plans to travel to Islamabad.

An incredible loss

Ger's death floored me and I found it very hard to accept that he was gone. He epitomised all that was good in life and brought happiness and joy with him wherever he went. From the first time we met, I had connected with him in a way I found hard to put words on. There was something about his enthusiasm and love of life that shone like a bright flame. I was never in any doubt that Ger was a great addition to every team he was on. He'd saved my life on the upper reaches of Everest in 2003 and I felt forever in his debt after that. Though he made light of what he did, Ger was always helping people. We'd kept in touch via phone or email when we weren't on expedition together and I loved hearing about new routes he was climbing in Alaska and other parts of the world.

When he died, I was struck not just by grief but also by a sense of guilt. Though I knew it was a ridiculous question, I kept asking myself if my encouragement of his passion for adventure had in some way contributed to his death. My logical brain told me that Ger was a man of his own volition and would have climbed Everest and K2 even if he'd never met me, but I couldn't get rid of the guilt that was consuming me for a long time. Maybe it was because I, at fifty-one, was still alive after so many expeditions and Ger's life had been cut short at the age of thirty-seven.

I had seen Ger and Clare as the next generation of Irish adventurers and had been looking forward to watching what both of them would do as I began to wind down my more extreme expeditions. Now Ger was gone and it felt that not only was he lost for the present, but also for the future with all he would have done, both personally and as a professional adventurer. His passing was a profound loss to all who had the honour of knowing him.

THE SUMMIT

In the spring of 2008, shortly before he went to climb K2, I'd met up with Ger in Dublin. One of the things we spoke about was his desire to make a documentary about the Sherpas and the work they did on the world's highest mountains. He believed that their contribution to high-altitude climbing was still unrecognised and undervalued. He had formed a strong bond with Pemba and the latter had agreed to being filmed while they were on expedition together later that year. The story was to focus on how Pemba, a Sherpa from Nepal, was climbing with the Norit team as a professional climber and not in his usual Sherpa role. Ger and I had a shared interest in, and respect for, the Sherpa community, and I was buzzed about the prospect of helping him with this project.

After he died and the story of what really happened on K2 over the first weekend of August 2008 gradually came to light, I saw that the Trojan rescue work carried out by Sherpas from Nepal and Pakistan was being ignored. They had, in fact, carried out almost all the rescue work but, yet again, their role was being overlooked. I started thinking about what Ger had wanted to do with Pemba's story; now, here was a new story, without Ger, but with Pemba, again as hero, along with his fellow Sherpas, including Chhiring Dorje, Pasang Lama and others. I spoke to the McDonnells about doing a documentary in Ger's memory and they gave it their blessing.

I knew I had to find the right team for this project as it was too big for me to do on my own. I had some contacts in the film world and got positive feedback when I made initial contact. Then cameraman Stephen O'Reilly, who had been on expedition with me and Ger and who had done filming work for me on the Beyond Endurance Expedition, suggested I contact Image Now Films, a Dublin-based production company. In September I met with producer Darrell Kavanagh and film director Nick Ryan. I told them about Ger and the documentary that he had wanted to do. I then spoke about the heroic work that the Sherpas had done during those terrible days near the top of the world's second highest mountain. Their interest in the project was immediate. That was what I wanted – a team whose passion for the subject matched mine – so we agreed to collaborate in the making of the film.

Pemba came to Ireland in October 2008 and had an emotional meeting with all the McDonnell family before returning to stay with me at the Mountain Lodge. I conducted the first official interview for the documentary with him in Kerry. Not concealing his anger at the tragedy he'd been caught up in, he told a story that led to more questions about what had happened during the 2008 K2 climbing season. It was as if a Pandora's box had been opened. The next interviews I did were with the Norit team in the Netherlands, and by December I was in Kathmandu with the film crew and director Nick Ryan interviewing the Sherpas who had been on K2 the previous summer.

Very quickly, we knew we had material for something much bigger than we'd initially thought. Various film boards and national television broadcasters were approached and came on board with the project. All the remaining interviews, which were carried out by Nick Ryan, and a re-enactment on the Eiger in Switzerland, were completed during the first six months of 2009. Then the long production process began.

Before it was publicly released, the McDonnells and some of Ger's friends were invited to view the film. It was a nervous time for me, waiting to see how his family would react. When Ger's voice filled the auditorium, we all cried and when we saw his face smiling out at us one more time, we smiled back through our tears. The McDonnells were happy with the end product and the film had its first public screening in 2012. It was very well received worldwide and went on to win eight national awards, including at Sundance, BANFF, Vancouver, Domzale, Boulder and the 2014 Irish Film & Television Awards, as well as being nominated for several other awards. The reaction worldwide was near unanimous: this was an amazing story. It had expanded out from the initial idea focusing on the Sherpas to encompassing the story of the 2008 K2 climbing season and how success turned to tragedy and then to controversy.

My time working on *The Summit* film was a steep learning curve in a business that I found to be quite challenging. I also learned a lot about the constraints in film, where the average length of a documentary is an hour and ten minutes. Even though it was a great film, I still felt that the full story of the role played by the Sherpas during that climbing season hadn't been told and I wanted to do this to honour both their work and Ger's memory. With that in mind, Pemba and I got together and produced a book based on his personal recollection of what had happened on K2, as well as using the transcripts from the other climbers and extended teams.

In addition to telling the story of the 2008 K2 tragedy in detail, the book opened a window on the psychology at work in high-altitude climbing and how summit fever, teamwork, leadership, self-leadership, communication, selfishness, honour, bravery and friendship played out at the top of the world's most feared mountain. I felt that we had much more scope in the book to cover the stories in fuller detail, especially the role played by the unsung heroes – the Sherpas. *The Summit: How Triumph Turned To Tragedy On K2's Deadliest Days* was completed in 2013 and with its publication, I felt I had finally completed the project that Ger and I had first spoken about six years earlier.

RETURN TO ANTARCTICA

In addition to working on *The Summit* project, I still had my normal work to do and had an expedition to Antarctica to organise. The value of having a good team was highlighted for me yet again when the people working with me kept all balls in the air through the later months of 2008. By November, everything was in place for our departure to Antarctica on the Beyond Endurance Educational Project and South Georgia Traverse Expedition.

The teachers and scientists travelling with us had a full hands-on programme prepared for the eight students over the twenty-six-day trip. The projects the students would be involved in covered history, scenery, wildlife, training, learning, filming, hospitality, leadership, team-building and – especially – friendship, safety and fun. The traverse team of sixteen had undergone the same rigorous training in Ireland and Norway as the 2006 team had done. We chartered the MV *Ushuaia* again, under the helm of Captain Jorge Aldegheri, and sold berths to people who wanted to do an Antarctic cruise and take part in the final day's trek from Fortuna Bay into Stromness.

After arriving in Ushuaia on Saturday 8 November we spent a few days in the city, giving the students a chance to explore the area and go horseback riding with local gauchos. Once on board the ship, a routine was quickly established, with the students' days starting at 8.30am with breakfast, followed by lectures, science classroom projects, surveys of wildlife from the deck, write-ups and presentations. We all settled in fairly quickly and, to the delight of the students in particular, all on board were treated to magnificent wildlife displays from our first days on the sea; wandering albatross flew alongside us while whale blows from fin whales were spotted 100m off our port side.

The traverse team disembarked from the *Ushuaia* on Friday 14 November in relatively good weather with little wind. However, just as the final Zodiac left the shore, the weather turned for the worse. Winds rose to 75kmph gale-force and there was a heavy snowfall; this was not the start we'd wished for. The second day of the traverse was very challenging as we tried to make progress across the Murray Snowfield and Trident Ridge in terrible winds and zero visibility. Just as we set out from camp, we encountered mist and snow cornices, which delayed us by at least six hours. We were pelted by snow and icy hail all day and had to operate a pulley system to get the sleds up the ascent to the ridge.

After a long and energy-sapping day, we set up camp near the western edge of the Crean Glacier. Conditions on Sunday were much better, with blue skies and few clouds. Just before 7pm, we heard four blasts from the ship's horn and knew our support team on the bridge had spotted us. A small group came to meet us on the beach and it was great to have their support. A few of the traverse team decided to return to the ship for a good night's sleep while the majority camped out on the beach at Fortuna Bay.

The next day, the entire group joined together for the final trek into Stromness whaling station. From there we boarded the ship and sailed to Grytviken to visit Shackleton's grave. The experience of visiting this great leader's final resting place held great meaning for me, but this visit was even more poignant as we remembered Ger McDonnell and Rolf Bae, both of whom had been on the Beyond Endurance Expedition in 2006. At Shackleton's graveside, I said a few words about these two adventurers and friends who had lost their lives on the same mountain within a day of each other only three months earlier.

The next few days were spent sailing around South Georgia, stopping off at various points and viewing the fantastic wildlife. By Friday we were crossing rough seas and heading towards Elephant Island. When we neared the forbidding rock, the Zodiacs were lowered into the water and we embarked in preparation for a shore landing but, due to safety concerns over the size of the swell, we were forced to abandon the landing.

On our last night before heading back for Ushuaia, many of the group took the opportunity to sleep on the Antarctic Peninsula. Almost fifty people, including all of the students, slept out on the ice, some in tents and some in snow holes they dug themselves. The weather was perfect – snowy mountains all around, calm waters, and mild temperatures. Then, at 3.30am, the weather turned. The mild temperatures of $8°$ dropped rapidly to approximately $-7°$ and winds increased to thirty knots with gusts of up to 60kmph. Then it started snowing heavily, making it very difficult for the group to get back to the ship. Once all were safely on board, it was time to head back to Argentina across the dangerous Drake Passage, sailing directly into the wind and swell for most of our two-day journey.

We were back on terra firma in Ushuaia early in the morning of 28 November and had a few days to chill out before flying to Buenos Aires, where we had an appointment with Ambassador Philomena Murnaghan, who represented Ireland in Argentina, Bolivia, Chile, Paraguay and Uruguay. She very kindly hosted a meeting with the eight transition year students, their teachers, the scientists and me. I looked at the pride on the faces of the young people as they lined up to meet the ambassador and felt a sense of joy at what had been achieved on the Beyond Endurance Education Project and the South Georgia Traverse Expedition.

PART SIX
THE NORTH POLE YEARS

THE POLE IN A SEA OF ICE

Clare O'Leary and I had been on expedition around the world for almost a decade when we were honoured as joint recipients of the Cork Person of the Year award in January 2009. I found Clare to be a brilliant adventure partner and over the years we had become a very efficient and self-sufficient team. We trusted each other totally and knew each other's strengths and weaknesses intimately. We had climbed the highest summits on all seven continents together and had travelled to the farthest point south when we'd reached the South Pole. But there was one other place we both wanted to stand at – the North Pole. Although I was very taken by the idea of standing at the farthest point north, I wasn't interested in doing a full expedition there because I wanted to spend more time with my family, as well as further developing my adventure, corporate and personal development business.

A full sixty-day expedition to the North Pole, starting at Ward Hunt Island in Canada, was a massive undertaking and I was starting to think that my days of hard-core adventure and pushing my body to its limit were coming to an end, so Clare and I decided instead to do the symbolic four-day 40km expedition to the North Pole. In February 2009, we travelled to Ottawa in Canada where we met Richard Weber, the renowned polar explorer who, by then, had completed more than thirty successful North Pole expeditions. My mission was twofold: I wanted to learn what extra skills we needed for the trek to the Pole and I wanted to find out about the wildlife and adventure tours available in that remote northerly region of Canada. Richard shared his vast knowledge about the movement of the ice, the winds and the conditions we would be facing on a sea of ice as opposed to a land of ice, which is what we were used to in Antarctica. I returned to the area later in the year, in July, for an Arctic safari to Somerset Island wildlife sanctuary where, for a week, we observed beluga whales, muskoxen, bison, eagles, polar bears and Arctic foxes in a stunningly beautiful region.

A little-known spot

Despite the fact that Santa Claus has his workshop at the North Pole, I'd often wondered why the region doesn't have the same resonance among the public as the South Pole. The Antarctic and its heroes are viewed in a kind of romantic light while few people even know the names of people who've stood at the farthest point north. That might be partly due to the fact that there is a degree of controversy about who the first person to reach the Pole was.

One of the earliest recorded expeditions to the North Pole region was in 1827 and, in the following decades, several claims were made to be the first person to reach the Pole. For years, an argument was ongoing as to which of two American explorers was the first person to stand at that point. Frederick Cook said he reached the North Pole on 21 April 1908 and Robert Peary said he reached the same spot almost a year later, on 6 April 1909. Both claimed to be the first. Each man, along with his supporters, maintained that the other's claim was fraudulent, whether intentionally or otherwise.

That debate continued over the decades and, despite many investigations into the claims, no clear consensus was arrived at regarding which of the two was first. What is beyond dispute, however, is that on 6 April 1969, accompanied by dogs and supported by air-drops, the British explorer Sir Wally Herbert was the first person to reach the North Pole on foot. Edmund Hillary, the first man to stand on Everest's summit, and Neil Armstrong, the first man to stand on the moon, landed at the North Pole in a small ski plane in 1985, making Hillary the first man ever to stand at both Poles and on the summit of Everest, often called the Third Pole.

The sun rises and sets only once a year in the North Pole region, where all lines of longitude converge. At 90° north, the North Pole lies diametrically opposite the South Pole in the middle of the Arctic Ocean in waters that historically have been almost permanently covered with constantly shifting ice. Unlike the South Pole, which is in an icy landmass surrounded by sea, the North Pole is situated in a sea covered by ice. The sea ice is generally up to 3m thick, though this can vary rapidly depending on weather and climate. Ice thickness has decreased in recent times and it has been predicted that within the next fifty years the Arctic Ocean will be entirely free of ice during the summertime.

Because of the constantly shifting ice, it isn't possible to build permanent structures at the Pole, but every year since 2002 the Russians build a manned drifting station called Barneo very close to the North Pole. It operates for a few weeks annually in early spring and acts as a base for scientists to carry out research and as a pick-up and drop-off airstrip for explorers and tourists to the Pole.

Standing at 90° north

In April 2009, Clare and I flew to Spitsbergen, the largest island in the Norwegian Svalbard archipelago, situated approximately midway between the North Pole and Norway. We spent a few days there training before taking a two-and-a-half-hour 1,700km flight on an Anatov 74 military aircraft to Barneo station, landing safely on its moving ice sheet. We estimated that it would take about four days to reach 90° north and brought all our gear packed on our sleds. From there, a Russian MI8 helicopter picked us up and dropped us on the ice about 40km from the North Pole. Very quickly, we were on a steep learning curve. The ice was a lot thinner than we'd expected and we could see immediately that global warming and climate change were having a huge effect.

At some points, the ice was only 150mm thick and we had to negotiate open leads – the water which appears when ice opens up due to the movement of the current – which presented the possibility of falling into freezing water. The ice under our feet was in constant motion due to the currents and the wind, and even though we were trying to move north we were at times being pushed south; one night the currents drifted the ice floe we were camping on 6km south while we slept. We also had to negotiate pressure ridges which were formed by colliding ice sheets crushing together, and had to push our way through massive ice blocks.

It was very hard to use GPS or a compass while we were pulling our sleds over pressure ridges, thin ice and open leads that we tried to skirt around so we didn't have to swim through them. We found that the sun was the best, fastest and most natural way for us to navigate and we used our shadows as our compass bearing, adjusting our direction by fifteen degrees every hour. We screwed protractors to our skis to help us adjust our direction and stay in a true north direction. The sun moves fifteen degrees every hour so, on the hour, we would stop, look at the position of the sun and check that our shadow was fifteen degrees west of the sun after midday or east of it before midday. Once we were fifteen degrees east or west of it, depending on the time, we were heading north. We would also turn on our GPS to check our location, compass bearing, distance to the Pole and the proper time on the longitude we were travelling.

After four days of immensely hard slog, just as we approached the North Pole, we met an open lead and had to wait for the ice to drift into position before we could ski to the exact spot where the Pole was. Then, on 17 April 2009, we were there, standing at 90° at the North Pole, delighted that we had succeeded in our dream of standing at both the top and the bottom of the world.

Hooked by the North Pole

I was ready to turn my full attention to developing my business and, at fifty-two, I was feeling the ravages of multiple expeditions on my body and was having doubts about my energy levels. My family and friends were advising me to take a step back, to focus on developing my business and planning for the future rather than spending so much money on further expeditions. I didn't have anything to prove to anybody, or even to myself, they said. They were right, but, for some reason, I couldn't stop thinking about the North Pole and what it would be like to do a full man-hauling expedition there; to actually walk from the edge of Canada on another sixty-day adventure and arrive at the most northerly point in the world. *Could I do it*, I wondered.

I knew Clare was up for it and, very quickly, my desire to do a full expedition outweighed all the reasons I had for not doing it. Once I stopped telling myself that I shouldn't do it, I knew that I really wanted to take on this final, big challenge. I believed that we could succeed but, at the same time, I knew that, because of the melting ice, this was the biggest risk that I'd ever taken in relation to possible failure on an expedition. However, we were very used to calculating risk, and once my adventure partner and I made the commitment to return to the North Pole, there was no turning back.

We had ten months to prepare for our trip to the Arctic region and were quickly immersed in training and sorting the logistics. Many of the skills needed for Arctic expeditions were similar to those we'd needed when travelling in Antarctica. We would be pulling sleds again, but the big difference was the terrain. In Antarctica we skied on a land mass whereas in the Arctic we would be travelling over constantly moving and erupting ice that was being pulled and pushed by the currents of the sea underneath it. Another difference from Antarctica, which is the driest snow and ice desert in the world, was the amount of moisture in the air, which would make it difficult for us to stay dry as we moved towards the North Pole. We also had to train in how to carry and use a pump-action twelve-gauge shotgun in the event of a polar bear attack.

Since we'd been to the South Pole, there had been huge advances regarding the food needed for physical endurance projects. In conjunction with our personal trainer John Kiely, Professor Phil Jakeman and his team at the University of Limerick, we devised a training programme and food plan that would help us be more efficient on the ice.

Our main food would be pemmican, a high-energy food made of a concentrated mix of fat and protein. This had been used by the early explorers, but our version of it was created by Richard Weber and made up of a mixture of olive oil, butter and high-calorie nuts. To help digest the fat and maintain our energy, we had a special chocolate bar that included a probiotic. We agreed to be subjects for scientific research by wearing monitors that would show the rigours on the body of being in extreme conditions and the effect of having to eat 9,600 calories a day and expend 25MJ of energy daily hauling our sleds.

We wanted another person to join the team. A talented County Kerry climber, John Dowd, had been on previous expeditions with Clare and me, including to Mount Vinson in Antarctica. He had reached the summit of Everest and was a long-time member of Kerry Mountain Rescue. John had a dream of going to the North Pole and jumped at the chance to join our team. Sharing the high expedition costs among three eased the financial burden, which was

286

fairly eye-watering. This was going to be a supported expedition, with two food drop-offs, after twenty and forty days, at a cost of $75,000 per drop. The charter flying us from Resolute, an Inuit hamlet on Cornwallis Island in Nunavut, to Ward Hunt Island was costing $35,000 to land us at the start of our 795km expedition.

From the North Pole, the flight back to Spitsbergen with the Russian scientists who were leaving Barneo for the season would cost $20,000 each. If we missed that flight because of any delay en route and had to charter a plane, the cost to be flown back to Canada would be $120,000. With increasing changes in the ice and more break-up of the floes, it was becoming more common for expedition teams to miss their scheduled date of arrival at the Pole only to find that Barneo was dismantled and the scientists gone by the time they reached 90° north. This outcome was one we wanted to avoid.

FIRST ATTEMPT 2010

By the start of 2009, only fifteen people had ever completed what had become known as the Three Poles Expedition – standing on top of Everest and at the South and North Poles. We were hopeful that our names would be added to that list by the end of April 2010 following what we called the Beyond Endurance Three Poles Expedition. In February, we flew from Ireland to Ottawa and travelled on to Yellowknife in the Northwest Territories, where we trained and acclimatised for over two weeks. From there, we boarded our Dornier 228 chartered flight to Resolute. During the five-hour journey, we flew over the Canadian wilderness where ice roads had been created to service the gold and diamond mines in the area. The remoteness of where the miners worked was mind-blowing, and from the plane I could see these roads that seemed to go on forever.

Conditions were calm in Resolute when we landed, with temperatures of –30°. However, bad weather soon followed, which caused a few days' delay before we could fly to Ward Hunt Island, one of the most remote inhabited regions in the world. On 2 March 2010, we finally began a six-hour flight north in clear weather. The scenery was unbelievable as we flew over glaciers, mountains and bays where there wasn't a single sign of human life in a land of snow and ice. The pilot pointed out Ward Hunt Island as the plane began its descent. He was looking for a landing site and finally spotted a flat space at the edge of the island. After two attempts, he made a successful landing and, as soon as the doors opened, we were greeted by temperatures of –40°. We lifted our sleds out on to the snow and checked the hold one last time to ensure that we'd left nothing behind.

As soon as the doors closed, the plane rose up into the sky. The Twin Otter did a low flyover while we were sorting our gear and the pilot saluted us before heading south; it was a great send-off. We were now at our starting point, in the middle of nowhere, 1,000km from the nearest human settlement and, according to our GPS, 795km from the North Pole. We put on our skis and started our journey northwards, hopeful of reaching our destination by 25 April in time for the final flight from Barneo.

Survival on melting ice

There was no easy lead-in, and the challenge of moving in this region began immediately as we skied to the edge of the landmass and erected our tent for the first night of our journey on the Arctic Ocean. The next morning the reality of the challenge ahead hit us hard as we faced navigating through heavy rubble ice fields and moving ice floes. For six relentless hours, we pulled, dragged, lifted and cursed our way through a maze of jumbled ice that was continuously moving under our feet. We had been told that we would face these conditions from the 83rd to the 84th parallel north, about 111km in total, and knew that it was going to be a ball-breaker getting through these initial pressure ridges before reaching flatter terrain where we hoped the conditions would be easier.

The following day was long and arduous. Constantly facing us were hundreds of massive blocks of ice rubble that we had to find our way over, with some of the pressure ridges up to 10m high. We pulled our 100kg sleds up and over ridges that were so high at times the sleds slammed against our bodies on the descent. The flatter ice between the pressure ridges also posed its own threats; because it varied in depth, we could find ourselves on thin ice that was only 25mm thick and in danger of falling into the freezing water – the liquid version of a crevasse. The difference was that, on top of freezing, we could also drown if we didn't get out quickly, or if our sleds got caught under the edge of the ice and we became trapped by the moving currents.

We had trained for ice water swimming and when we saw by its colour and texture that the ice looked thin, we knew it was time to put our dry suits on and to be ready to crawl on our bellies in order to distribute our weight more evenly over the fragile ground. These suits were like space suits, cumbersome to get into and to move in, so we only put them on if we knew there was an imminent danger of falling into the water. At night, before we set up camp, we had to make sure that the ice was sufficiently solid so we didn't fall through it while we slept.

In previous years, the ice was packed more solidly against the landmass of Canada but, with increasing melt and climate change, there was now more tidal movement, making travel infinitely more difficult, dangerous and unpredictable. When the water currents and wind gained speed, the ice floes moved faster, which was fine if we were heading in the right direction: if not, we had to make sure we kept adjusting our course. It was a total physical and mental challenge, especially trying to comprehend the fact that absolutely everything was moving all the time and nothing was ever static. Surviving in this region required complete focus and we barely spoke to each other, so immersed were we in the task of staying out of the water and on course for the Pole.

Expedition death knell

By the fourth day, I felt we were finally coming to terms with the multitude of challenges facing us and getting into a regular rhythm. Two days earlier, John had said he thought he had frostbite but, because he seemed okay, we had continued for another few days. However, by the morning of the fifth day, he said he had to get off the ice as he now had no feeling in his fingers or toes and was afraid of losing them.

My initial reaction was disbelief, followed by anger and, finally, concern. It surprised me that I was so angry, but there had been zero let-up in the harshness of what we'd been through over the previous days and we were all feeling the strain. I realised that John had to go back but, for several reasons – including the fact that we had only one tent – there was no way he could travel through the icy wilderness on his own.

The moment we turned and faced south again, I knew our expedition was over. Basically, there wasn't enough time for Clare and me to make another attempt to get to the North Pole in time for the final flight with the scientists from Barneo to Spitsbergen and we couldn't afford to charter a plane to come in for us at a later date. It was incredibly disappointing, but we knew that retreat was the only realistic option.

To move more quickly we had to dump some of our food; this action was the final death knell for the expedition. As soon as we decided to retreat, we called in a rescue and gave them our GPS co-ordinates. The pilot needed a flat area of ice, about 400m in length, in order to make a safe landing, but there was nothing only mountains of icy rubble around us.

It was two days of tortuous slog before we came across terrain that we thought might be suitable. We radioed in the co-ordinates and the pilot flew out to pick us up only to find that the runway wasn't long enough. After six attempts at landing he eventually departed, leaving us to continue our retreat on foot. About an hour later, we got a call saying that the flight team had identified a spot that looked suitable for landing. They gave us the co-ordinates and three hours later we were successfully picked up from the ice and flown back to Resolute.

On our long journey home, I had time to reflect on our aborted expedition. As a glass-half-full kind of person, I immediately looked for the positives: the North Pole would be there next year if we wanted to come back, we had gained a lot of experience and we hadn't spent all our money. I also realised that we had underestimated the hardships of travelling in the Arctic region. The first two days on the ice had been unbelievably gruelling; it was heartbreaking trying to pull the sleds over the ice blocks and searching endlessly for a way through the towers of ice that seemed to materialise out of nowhere. But it wasn't the end and, despite the hellishness of what we'd been through, I knew we weren't finished with the North Pole yet.

SECOND ATTEMPT 2011

By the beginning of February 2011, Clare and I were back in Canada having spent a lot of time and money on training to ensure we were well prepared for whatever the Arctic would throw at us. This time round, it was just the two of us, having decided that maybe we'd have a better chance with a smaller unit. We had been a tight team for a long time now and worked very efficiently together.

We spent three weeks at the training camp on Baffin Island in Nunavut, training, fine-tuning our navigational skills, testing our gear and sorting out our expedition food and equipment. Apex, the village where we stayed, was an old Inuit settlement and it was amazing to spend time among the people there and learn about their lives. Weather conditions were pretty brutal, with temperatures of $-50°$ accompanied by hard windchill. A severe weather warning was issued and it was advised to stay protected at all times because frostbite could occur within five minutes on exposed skin. Still, it gave us a good idea of what we'd be facing on the ice when we wouldn't have a warm house to return to at night.

By the end of the month we were back in Resolute, ready for our 25 February flight to Ward Hunt Island from where we were due to start our expedition, but the flight was postponed due to bad weather and landing conditions. There was a silver lining to the cloud, however, as Clare discovered two splits along the soles of her boots while we were doing a final gear check. We spent the day trying to repair the boots as it was impossible to source a new pair before setting off.

There was no flight the following day either and, on Sunday, when we brought all our gear to the hangar and met with the pilot and Base Camp manager, the news was not good. We studied the satellite weather maps and saw that there was no possibility of flying until the following Thursday at the earliest. Blizzards were predicted for each of the next four days, making it impossible for any flight to take off. The pressure started to mount.

No matter when we started the expedition, we absolutely had to be at the North Pole by 25 April for the final flight out of there. Including ourselves, there were three teams waiting to begin their expeditions – an RAF team of Matthew Stowers and Jules Weekes and a solo Italian adventurer, Michele Pontrandolfo. We were all sharing the same flight out, and all of us shared the same frustration as the first week of March slipped past in a storm of wind and snow. Each day, we went down to the runway to check the weather for the next day but it was always the same: there was no chance of a take-off.

Scuppered by the weather

By early March, we knew we were in trouble. With seven days already lost due to bad weather and no definite end in sight, the chances of a successful expedition became increasingly slim. We had allowed sixty days for the entire expedition and with seven now gone by, it meant we could very easily be caught for time if we experienced severe weather conditions on the ice. Not making the Pole by 25 April would automatically mean we would have to pay another $110,000 to be picked up by a flight from Canada. The final pick-up date for flights from Canada to the North Pole was 30 April and the expedition would be forced to end then, regardless of our proximity or otherwise to the Pole.

We were getting fairly desperate, and got an independent medium- to long-term forecast from a meteorologist who told us that near-blizzard conditions were expected at our start point that day, followed immediately by another low front. Wednesday or Thursday of the following week – 9 and 10 March – offered the best conditions. This was a full thirteen days later than we'd planned to start. The issue now became whether we would get going at all. If we started with a very low probability of making it to the North Pole by 25 April, we would end

293

up wasting a serious amount of money on flights – money that we could put towards a new expedition.

On Sunday 5 March, with very heavy hearts, we decided to abort the expedition. The other two teams followed suit, with the result that no team undertook a full expedition to the North Pole in 2011. It was the first time in almost seventy expeditions that I'd had to take this action, and Clare and I were both very disappointed. In spite of that, our desire to get to the Pole still burned bright and we made an immediate decision to make another attempt in 2012.

As we now had time on our hands and were intent on coming back for another attempt, we decided to do some further training and find out more about the culture and traditions of the Inuit, so we spent ten days doing a 130km traverse of Baffin Island on the northeast coast of Canada, starting from the Inuit hamlet of Pangnirtung and ending at the Inuit settlement of Qikiqtarjuaq.

THIRD ATTEMPT 2012

For the remainder of 2011, my main focus was on getting ready for our next expedition to the North Pole in February 2012. For me, this was going to be my final attempt: whatever the outcome, I wouldn't be going back. I had put a huge amount of time, energy and money over the past few years into North Pole expeditions without success, but I wanted to give it one last try. I was becoming more concerned about my financial situation; Ireland was emerging from the grip of another crippling recession and my adventure travel business hadn't been immune. I was almost fifty-five years old and had to get my financial house in order, and going on costly expeditions wasn't going to help me sort that one out.

On top of financial concerns, I was increasingly concerned about the objective dangers of Arctic travel. With global warming and climate change, it was getting harder every year to predict the state of the ice and I was worried that we could become stranded if we couldn't keep to schedule because of excessive ice break-up.

Having a bigger team was one way of reducing the per-person cost, so Clare and I made contact with people that we knew were interested in polar expeditions. Bill Hanlon, an Irish-born doctor living in Canada, had been following our earlier expeditions and expressed an interest as soon as we let him know there was a place on the team. He had been involved in adventure for several years and had completed the Seven Summits. Mike O'Shea, my former fellow rookie, expressed an interest and, even though he had no polar experience, I felt he could do it as he was an exceptionally strong climber with great technical skills. Shea quickly confirmed that he, too, was happy to join the team.

Having had experience of the unpredictability of ice break-up in 2010 and of the weather in 2011, I felt that not tying ourselves to getting that final flight from Barneo station by 15 April would give us a better chance of reaching our goal. We all agreed that, instead, we would charter a plane from Canada at a cost of $125,000 to fly us back from the Pole. It was a lot of money but, by chartering our own plane for pick-up, we would have more time to get to the Pole on what was increasingly unpredictable terrain. If we reached the Pole before Barneo was dismantled, we could fly out with the Russians and would be fully reimbursed for the cost of the charter flight. However, my strong belief was that we would have to use the chartered flight to get off the ice.

We had estimated the total per-person expedition cost at approximately $90,000 but, by December, oil prices started to go up and the value of the euro dropped. This drove up the cost of the flight out from the Pole and threw us another financial curveball. I suggested bringing in a fifth person to help with rising costs. An adventurer, Sarah Wilson, had made contact with us through the polar explorer Matty McNair, who was going to act as our Base Camp manager from Iqaluit, Nunavut, while we were on the ice. I arranged for Sarah to join us for training in Nunavut in December when a final decision on her suitability would be made.

Fractures appear

All five of us were in Canada by December, only nine months after Clare and I had last been there. Training went well and I was also busy finalising the logistics for our flights. I had to sign a contract for the plane we were chartering to fly us out and possibly pick us up from the Pole, which made me personally responsible for the full cost. Clare, Bill and I had already lodged what we owed, but Shea hadn't lodged his full contribution as yet. He'd had contact with a team from India that was also planning an expedition to the Pole and suggested that we share the charter costs with them, bringing the overall costs down substantially for all of us. In theory, this was a great idea. In reality, I was the one that had to sign the contract and the one who would be carrying all the costs if the Indians didn't show up or pay up.

Shea wanted us to go ahead without having our full costs already in situ in the bank on the assumption that the Indian team would pay up as soon as their financing issues were sorted, presumably sometime in the coming weeks. However, if I was going to go out onto the ice, I wanted to make sure that I could get off it at the Pole without being liable for everyone's costs, and that meant all the money had to be lodged in our expedition account beforehand. Arguments between Shea and me became heated and, eventually, I asked him to leave the team.

I was surprised that Clare agreed with his proposition. As far as I was concerned, it was way too much of a personal financial risk to go ahead without having all our finances sorted. It was also too dangerous not to have the pick-up at the Pole secured before leaving, and the only way we could secure it was by showing the flight company that we had the money in the bank. It quickly became obvious that there would be no agreement, so we decided to pull down the expedition. We had lost some money but not too much, and by January 2012 we had paid whatever was owed.

Clare and Shea decided to go back to Canada the following month and continue with an attempt to reach the North Pole as a two-person team. They went ahead with the informal arrangement to share flight costs with the Indian team, but that team wasn't able to leave Resolute due to bad weather and not having the funding in place. That left Clare and Shea liable for the full cost of the $150,000 food drops and $125,000 pick-up from the North Pole and meant they had no other alternative but to abandon their expedition. Yet again, the elusive North Pole proved itself to be a very hard challenge to surmount.

Reality check

I knew that the 2012 North Pole attempt was going to be my last major expedition, as both my body and my head were telling me that it was time to step back. I had a recurring back problem having pulled my L4 and L5 discs, and was suffering liver complications as a result of the weight gains and losses that my expedition life had demanded. I had also developed an enlarged muscle on the left ventricle of my heart from the constant pulling, dragging and carrying of heavy weights over a lifetime of adventuring. My doctors strongly

297

recommended easing back on big expeditions. I was feeling my mortality in a different way, and no longer wanted to take the kind of risks I'd taken without a second thought for years.

In our ten years together as adventure partners, Clare and I had achieved a lot but, by 2012, I was feeling the age gap between us more and more. She still had a lot of hard expeditions ahead of her and I didn't want to be an obstacle to that. I was very happy when she found a new expedition partner in Shea and believed they could go on to achieve a lot.

Although the North Pole felt like unfinished business, I was never going to undertake a sixty-day expedition there. At one level, it was hard to accept this fact, but the relief that I wouldn't be putting myself in that dangerous icy arena again was great. I had stood there, although not by getting there in the way that I would have wanted, but I knew now that it was time to stop. Failure, for me, would have been to persist in trying to achieve a goal when the odds were stacked so high against me.

PART SEVEN
NEW ADVENTURES

REASSESSING MY LIFE

'It's time for us to ease up, Pat,' my Polish friend said. 'We've done enough; now we can step back and share our stories.' I'd originally gotten to know Maciej Berbeka in 1993 on my first Everest attempt. He was one of the greatest mountaineers in the world and a longtime friend and mentor. We'd kept in touch over the years, and often met up on our way to or from some Base Camp around the world. 'I'm not going to do any more 8,000ers,' Maciej added as we chatted in late 2011. 'We're getting older and can't continue taking the same risks.' We spoke about the climbers we knew who had died on expedition, many of them much younger than us. Earlier that year, John Delaney, an Irish climber I had trained, died on 21 May, just 50m from the summit of Everest. He was in the Himalaya with a Russian company and I'd had to phone his wife to tell her the tragic news of her husband's death. A few days earlier, she had given birth to a baby daughter that John never got to meet. Maciej and I remembered Ger McDonnell and Rolf Bae, who had also died far too young.

I agreed with him. It was time to ease back and look at other, less risky, ways of being in the mountains or at the Poles and to set new goals for ourselves. But we each had one more big expedition to do: I was going to make a final attempt to reach the North Pole in 2012 and Maciej wanted to do a winter ascent of Broad Peak, the twelfth highest mountain in the world and one of the 8,000ers. He had a history of first winter ascents, including on Manaslu,

Cho Oyu and Rocky Summit.

He went on that final expedition and reached the summit of Broad Peak along with his team on 5 March 2013. The next day, he and his team-mate Tomasz Kowalski went missing while descending the mountain in the Karakoram range in Baltistan. They were declared dead two days later.

Maciej's death was a huge shock to me, especially in light of our final conversation. Over thirty people I knew, including close friends and colleagues, had now lost their lives on expeditions around the world. I had been very lucky, but I was starting to feel more vulnerable and knew that if I didn't listen to that inner voice – and to my body, which was getting creaky – my luck was going to run out. After the final North Pole attempt, I no longer wanted to put myself through what was necessary to beat the odds. Gradually, and then – it seemed – suddenly, the risks looked too great.

The bigger picture

Since I'd turned fifty, Gerry and Joe – two of my closest friends – had been constantly telling me that I needed to keep an eye on the bigger picture; that the years were passing by quickly; that the physical, mental and financial costs of big expeditions were going to catch up with me. I listened but didn't really hear them. It wasn't until another friend, Jim Leonard, spoke to me that the penny finally dropped. Jim, who was twenty years older than me, had been a climber and a very successful designer with an international mountaineering gear company. For some reason, he made me think about retirement and about securing some kind of financial security for my future. His warning brought home the reality that I was getting older and wouldn't always be able to do the things I had been doing. While I still had time, energy and my health, I needed to reassess my objectives and start making a new and viable plan for the future. I had put my neck on the line very often in the past, financially and otherwise, but this was no longer tenable.

My fifties were slipping by almost unnoticed and I had never given proper thought to how I was going to finance my life once I stopped big expeditions. The truth was, I didn't know how. I knew how to get to the top of Everest, I knew how to get to the South Pole, but I didn't know how I was going to finance the future that I wanted to have. I was still involved in a lot of projects that were absorbing a huge amount of my time, but the issue of a future after big expeditions wouldn't go away.

I finally made a conscious decision to focus on it; I stepped back, had a look at my life and formulated a new plan to consolidate and expand my adventure and guiding business. I also started doing much more motivational work with the corporate sector, as well as with ordinary people who wanted to achieve extraordinary things, including the Pat Falvey Forever Young Club, a new community of people aged over fifty who want to continue to undertake adventures with like-minded people.

Despite leaving school at fifteen, I've had a lifelong love of learning and an insatiable curiosity about what it is that makes people tick. One of the things I love most about travelling all over the world is hearing the stories of people from different cultures and traditions. I've learned that we are united by far more than that which divides us. I've seen that people everywhere – from the Sherpas on Everest to the Inuit living in the Arctic and the scientists working at the South Pole – want to live full, useful and joyful lives. We are all sources of inspiration for each other; if I had never heard of Shackleton, Amundsen and Hillary, I might never have been inspired to go to the highest and most remote parts of the planet.

But, ultimately, it's the unsung heroes that are closest to my heart; maybe because I feel these are the people I am most like – men who had no claim to being special yet who achieved the extraordinary by tapping into their own spirit of adventure and their drive to succeed. The more I've shared the stories of my own adventures and of those I've met, the more people have come to me and said that they, too, want to push back the boundaries of their lives, to explore their limits and to have an adventure. Each one of them has an Everest and in my motivational talks and workshops, I share with them the lessons and skills I've learned in a lifetime of pursuing my own 'Everests'.

There are many people who are frustrated and feel they will live their entire lives within the safety and complacency of their comfort zones because they are afraid to get beyond them. Lack of experience and a crashed economy pushed me out of my comfort zone and I was at a very low ebb when I climbed my first mountain. Getting to the summit of that mountain in Kerry was the start of a new life journey for me in which I set out to challenge the limits of what I could achieve and exceed the expectations that had been set down for me. I first became an explorer of the physical world and, later, of the inner world of the human mind and how it works. Now I work at helping people break out of old habits that limit who they can be. I guide them to explore their full potential and to become the hero in their own lives, just as my mentors guided me over the decades.

Looking in the mirror

Watching the story of my life unfold during the course of a three-part documentary on television was a surreal experience. *My Private Everest* was screened on Setanta Sports over three weeks in 2010. While being interviewed by programme maker, Helen Shaw, of Athena Media, I was asked to talk not just about my life, but also about my motivation and actions. This process forced me to dig deep and reflect on my life in a new way. Close family, friends and others were also interviewed, and when I saw and heard the people who knew me best talking about me, one thing was crystal clear: I had caused a lot of hurt and pain in the past and I needed to draw a line in the sand. I saw how selfish and obsessed I had been throughout my life. I'd talked in the past about changing and I had definitely made more time for my family, but there was so much more I needed to do.

I looked at my wife and sons, my parents, my siblings, my friends and colleagues on the screen and I listened to what they were saying. They had never lost sight of my good points but, for a lot of the time, my less acceptable traits had brought hurt and pain into their lives. They admired my work ethic, my self-belief and positivity but they didn't like my ruthlessness, my obsessive nature or my arrogance. 'He was always very driven, often to the detriment of a lot of those around him, including his wife and family,' one of my brothers said. My son talked about my absence during his early life. I was a workaholic and didn't have a work–life balance, he said. I hadn't taken into consideration the anguish they had gone through, caused by my absence and the danger I repeatedly put myself in.

It wasn't easy to witness, but what amazed me was that they were all speaking from a place of love. Even though I'd brought pain to them, they still wanted me to be part of their lives. None of them wanted me to stop being who I was; what they dearly wished was that I would see the value of having more balance in my life. All the time when I was on this non-stop roller-coaster, I was letting

303

so much slip through the net, but there was no escaping this wake-up call. I'd said this so often in the past, but when I saw old footage of my wife as a young woman and my sons as small children, full of joyful anticipation of our future together, sadness seeped into my soul.

My family and close friends hadn't given up on me and I needed to let them know that, without them, my life didn't have meaning. Ultimately, the joy and success I've had in my life have been due to these, the unsung heroes at home – Marie, Brian and Patrick, my parents, siblings and friends. Luck, yet again, was on my side because I still had the most valuable commodity of all – time – to make amends. Marie, in particular, had always been a hugely stabilising factor in my life, from the early days of my seemingly off-the-wall teenage dreams onwards, and her grounding influence facilitated my integration back into my family. Just in time, I underwent a sea-change in attitude and have never since lost focus on my number one priority: my family.

New dreams

Now in my early sixties, my goals, though still ambitious, are different and – I believe – more balanced. Being present in a mindful, loving way for my family is number one. As a grandfather, I don't want to miss out on those special moments that I now know are never repeated. Back at the Mountain Lodge, I look out at a beautiful green countryside and blue lake below me and give thanks for my life. I've been in more grey and white places over the years than most people, and I love to look out on the vivid green of Ireland and know that this is home.

I still enjoy travelling and leading adventure treks every year to the Himalaya, Africa, Russia, South America, Antarctica and the Arctic, but I also relish being in Cork and Kerry and going out on the mountains where my adventure life began. When I look at my photos, taken all over the world, and reflect on all that I have been able to do in my life, I am filled with gratitude for having had the chance to live such a full and exciting life.

I still love hearing people's stories, especially from those who come to the Mountain Lodge to share their goals and aspirations with me. These are ordinary men and women who have a dream to do something extraordinary. It is a joy to mentor and guide them to make their dreams a reality, and to share the skills I've learned over a lifetime as an adventurer and accidental rebel.

ACKNOWLEDGEMENTS

There are many people that I would like to acknowledge without whom my life as a son, brother, father, grandfather, friend, entrepreneur and adventurer would not have been possible and whose presence has made it all worthwhile.

A very special thanks to Marie and our sons, Brian and Patrick; I am eternally grateful for your love and support. To my grandmother, the late Mary B. O'Callaghan, who gave me the belief that I could do anything I set my mind to. To my father, Tim; you told me to dream big, to have a go-for-it attitude, not to procrastinate and, most importantly, to see failure as part of the road to success. To my mother, Bina; you taught me to never give up no matter how bad things get. The fighter mindset you gave me has seen me through many challenging days. To my siblings, Majella, Abina, Richard, Paul and Barry; thank you for your love and understanding of a maverick brother and for always being there for me.

To the mentors and trainers who taught me the skills of survival in business and extreme adventuring; you gave me the confidence to go for what many saw as impossible goals. Thanks to my early business advisors, Frank Sheahan, the late Joe Carey, the late Owen O'Callaghan, Tom Meade and Barry O'Driscoll; you helped me create the good times and were always there to help and advise when times got tough. To all the Falvey Group staff, directors and investors who worked with me over the years; thank you for your hard work, loyalty, advice and for staying the course, especially on some of my more hare-brained schemes!

To the late Val Dean, who encouraged me to go on my first hillwalk when I was at my lowest ebb after a very tough period in my life, and who opened the door for me to the world of climbing. To all the walkers and climbers in Cork Mountaineering who encouraged me to follow my dreams. To my friend and mentor, Con Moriarty; you opened up a world of adventure to me that I didn't know existed and which has since brought me to every corner of the planet. Thanks to Kerry Mountain Rescue and all the friends I made over my years as a team member. I am very grateful for the great training I got while serving with KMR. To my close friend, the late Eileen Cronin of Cronin's Yard, who, for over thirty years, made me welcome in her home with cups of tea, apple tarts and great company.

To the 150 plus teams that I have led and adventured with throughout the world over the last three decades; thank you for sharing your time, stories and adventures with me. Thanks to Dr Clare O'Leary who completed over twenty expeditions with me and who became the first Irish female to climb Mount Everest, to reach the South Pole, to cross the Greenland Ice Cap and to complete the Seven Summits; you are an inspiration to those who dare to dream. A special thanks to my Irish extreme expedition and support teams on Mount Everest, Cho Oyu, Ama Dablam, the South Pole, the North Pole, the Greenland and South Georgia crossings: Con Moriarty, Ciaran Corrigan, Mike O'Shea, Mick Murphy, Tony Farrell, Tim Hickey, Jim Leonard, Gene Tangney, the late Ger McDonnell, Mick Murphy, Hannah Shields, George Shorten, John Joyce, Shaun Menzies, Jonathon Bradshaw, Pat Duggan, Sheila Kavanagh, Adrian Rahill, Niall Foley, Gillian Roche, Lorraine Gordon, Con Collins, Eoin Sheehan, Gavin Bate, and the late Mick Hennessy. To my polar mentors, the late Rolf Bae, Richard and Josée Weber, Matty McNair and Børge Ousland, who taught me survival techniques for expeditions in the Antarctic, the Arctic and other cold regions of the world.

A very special thank-you to the unsung heroes of expeditions – the local teams that I have worked with throughout the world and without whom very few of my expeditions would have succeeded. Thanks in particular to Ang Rita, Sumba, Dawa, Mingma and Pemba Gyalje Sherpa in Nepal; to Freddy, Abel, Emmanuel and Godliving Tarimo in Kilimanjaro and Africa, for your loyalty, support and expertise over the last thirty years. A special thanks to my close friends Joe O'Leary and Gerry Walsh, who have been involved in all my expeditions and who have been the backbone on logistics and communications.

Thank you to Joe O'Leary, Jim Leonard, Niamh O'Donavan, Greg Butler, Mary Healy, Cliona McCarthy, Sharon Hutchison, John O'Shea, Tony Nation and Frank Greally for reading the early drafts of *Accidental Rebel*. Your honest feedback and constructive suggestions were much appreciated. I'd like to say a special thank-you to my editor, Bridget McAuliffe, for putting up with me throughout this project; thank you for your patience, skill, dedication and focus in working with me to complete this project; I know I drove you mad at times. Many thanks for your persistence.

To everyone who has been part of my life; I want to take this opportunity to thank you for your presence and for sharing your time with me.

GLOSSARY

ABC – Advance Base Camp

AMS – acute mountain sickness

Acclimatisation – the process by which organisms adjust and adapt to different climates, environments and altitudes

Alpine climbing – a self-sufficient approach to climbing in which climbers carry all of their equipment and supplies as they ascend a mountain, often without recourse to fixed ropes, porters or oxygen

Arête – a sharp mountain ridge

Belay – a method of securing a safety rope to an anchor point and feeding the rope through a crab to aid the safe progress of a climber

Bivouac/bivvy – an improvised temporary natural construction or shelter used for sleeping and often used to refer to sleeping in the open air

Carabiner/crab – a spring-loaded metal loop or catch for attaching ropes to fixed lines

Couloir – a gulley or narrow passage

Crampons – sharp spikes affixed to climbing boots to aid traction on ice and snow

Death Zone – the name given to altitudes in the troposphere above approximately 8,000m in which human existence is unsustainable for long periods because of a reduced capacity to process oxygen

Fixed ropes – ropes fixed to anchor points along dangerous surfaces or terrain and placed in advance of, or during, an ascent to provide safety for climbers

307

High Camp – the final camp before the summit

Hypoxia – a condition in which the body or parts of the body are deprived of an adequate supply of oxygen and which often occurs at high altitude

Ice axe – a tool used for climbing on icy surfaces which can also be used as an anchor or a walking aid

Katabatic winds – winds caused by localised downward motion of cool air

Lama – Tibetan cleric or head of a monastery

Moraine – rock and ice debris on a glacier

Objective danger – a naturally-occurring phenomenon, such as an avalanche, rockfall or icefall, which usually occurs without warning

Oedema –build-up of fluid in the body which causes the affected tissue to swell

Puja – a rite or ceremony involving worship of a deity through song, prayer and invocation

Sastrugi – small, parallel, wave-like ridges on the surface of hard snow, caused by wind and prevalent in polar regions

Serac – a large overhanging block or column of ice

Sherpa – member of, or referring to, an ethnic group in Nepal

Siege tactics – a style of mountaineering which involves the setting up of fixed lines and stocked camps in advance of a summit attempt

Sirdar – head of local logistics on an expedition

Note: all temperatures listed are in the Celsius scale

INDEX

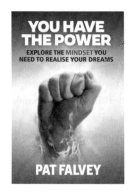

In *You Have The Power: Explore The Mindset You Need To Realise Your Dreams* (foreword by Dr John Demartini, international best-selling author of *The Values Factor - The Secret to Creating an Inspired and Fulfilling Life*), Pat Falvey shares the lessons he learned first-hand as an entrepreneur and adventurer about exploring the mindset you need to realise your dreams and become the person you are capable of becoming. He details how to explore and manage your mindset so that it is your friend and ally, enabling you to live your best life. *You Have The Power* will awaken you to the full possibility of your unique life. It will show you how to challenge yourself to explore your skills and abilities to go beyond what you thought you were capable of, always remembering that life is not a rehearsal, but a performance.

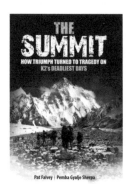

In *The Summit: How Triumph Turned To Tragedy On K2's Deadliest Days*, Pat Falvey and Pemba Gyalje Sherpa recount and explore the tragic 2008 climbing expedition to K2 during which eleven climbers from around the world lost their lives. Based on Pemba Gyalje's eyewitness account and drawing on a series of interviews with the survivors, which were conducted for the award-winning documentary, *The Summit* (Image Now Films and Pat Falvey Productions, 2012), *The Summit: How Triumph Turned to Tragedy on K2's Deadliest Days* is the most comprehensive interpretation of one of modern-day mountaineering's most controversial disasters.

While Pat was leading his team on Everest in the spring of 2003, more than 200,000 children logged on to the team's website to follow their story. Accompanying the team was Frederick T. Bear, Freddy for short. *Freddy's Everest Diary: The Dream of Fredrick T. Bear* chronicles in words and beautiful photographs the amazing adventures of Freddy as he attempts to climb Everest. Find out all about getting to Base Camp, living there, the food, the dangers of climbing through icefalls, coping with cold, thin air and working with Sherpas. Freddy's diary serves as an inspiration to all readers as he struggles to make his dream come true while never, ever giving up.

318

In *A Journey To Adventure: Stories I Never Thought I'd Tell*, Pat Falvey describes his climbs on the major peaks he has visited, revealing his motives, the dangers and joys at the limits of physical and mental challenges. Each chapter captures the highs and lows of a variety of expeditions to all the seven continents against a background of spectacular settings. The honest narrative and superb photographs recall the ordeals, terrible beauty and hardships of the mountains and give a unique insight into the mindset of this high-altitude mountaineer and Polar adventurer. Lavishly illustrated and inspiring, this book is for anyone who dares to dream the impossible.

Early in the summer of 2003, a team of four Irish men and two Irish women, led by expedition leader Pat Falvey, set out to climb the highest mountain in the world. *Against The Sky* tells their amazing story in which they fought against their own fears, against the mountain and, eventually, against the sky itself. This is a gripping film of their incredible battle to stay alive in one of the most inhospitable places on the planet.

The Summit documentary, on which Pat Falvey was executive producer, tells the story of the 2008 K2 disaster when eleven climbers lost their lives on the second highest mountain in the world over a period of twenty-eight hours. Using reconstructions, interviews from survivors and other climbers and footage from teams, *The Summit* tells a mesmerising and tragic story of what can happen in the Death Zone, even on a supposedly 'perfect day'. Winner of multiple awards (including at Sundance Film Festival, Boulder International Film Festival, BANFF, Vancouver and Domzale International Mountain Film Festivals and at the Irish Film and Television Academy awards), *The Summit* was directed and produced by Nick Ryan of Image Now Films.

Other books by Pat Falvey: *Reach For The Sky* and *Frederick T. Bear's South Pole Adventures* (with Clare O'Leary).

319

Pat Falvey Irish & Worldwide Adventures Ltd.

Ireland's leading adventure and team-training company for over 25 years

Life is an adventure. Explore it. Live it.

Adventure Travel

Guided treks to Kilimanjaro, Elbrus, Aconcagua, Mount Vinson, Denali
and Everest Base Camp (please go to our website
for a full list of destinations).

Expedition Training

Expert training for high-altitude and polar expeditions.

Skills Training

Comprehensive training to become a self-sufficient climber and adventurer.

Speak | Mentor | Coach

Pat Falvey is a world-renowned corporate and inspirational keynote
speaker on the challenge of change, risk management, team development
and achieving one's full potential. He has over twenty years' experience as
a personal mentor and coach. Join Pat on one of his personal development
and team-based courses, seminars, workshops or challenge-based adventures.

**E: info@patfalvey.com • T: +353 64 6644181
www.patfalvey.com**

320